THAILAND:
DEADLY DESTINATION

JOHN STAPLETON

D1616265

"The death of a tourist doesn't mean much to them at all."
Thailand Scribe.

"Thai people hate foreigners and love money."
"That's no secret."
Timothy Mo, from *Pure*.

"What is the appropriate behaviour for a man or woman in the midst of this world, where each person is clinging to his piece of debris? What's the proper salutation for people as they pass each other in this flood?"
Anon.

TABLE OF CONTENTS

Courtesy of Maps of Thailand

FRUIT FOR THE PICKING

The daily robbing, bashing, drugging, extortion and murder of foreign tourists on Thai soil, along with numerous scandals involving unsafe facilities and well established scams, has led to frequent predictions that Thailand's multi-billion dollar tourist industry will self-destruct. Instead tourist numbers more than doubled in the decade to 2014. Both the Thai Tourism Authority and the Thai Ministry of Tourism forecast an astonishing 30 million tourist arrivals per annum in 2015 and beyond. The world might not have come to the hometowns of the many visitors fascinated by Thailand, but it certainly came to the Land of Smiles.

While the Thai media is heavily censored, and bad news stories about tourists suppressed, nonetheless there is more than enough evidence to demonstrate that something has gone seriously awry with the nation's tourist industry.

In 2014, just as in the years preceding it, there were train, bus, ferry, speedboat, motorbike and car accidents, murders, knifings, unexplained deaths, numerous suicides, diving accidents, robberies gone wrong, anonymous bodies washing up on the shores and a string of alcohol and drug related incidents.

Thailand's carefully manufactured reputation for hospitality, as a land of palm trees and sun-drenched beaches, happy-hour bars, world class hotels and welcoming people, as paradise on Earth, is very different to the reality many tourists encounter. The rapid growth in Thai tourism has been a triumph of advertising and image creation; building the perception, firmly entrenched in the West, that Thais embrace strangers. In reality, the relations between ethnic Thais and foreigners are often difficult; and there has been growing friction and disengagement, a drift from curiosity to contempt, as visitor numbers have increased.

Tourists choose one destination over another for a number of reasons, most of which Thailand scores highly on: cultural uniqueness, climate, natural resources and environment, value for money, quality accommodation, modern transport infrastructure, a range of tourist activities and experiences, entertainment, and a hospitable reputation. But since the events of September 11, 2001 safety has been one of the factors underpinning a traveller's choice of one destination over another.[1]

And on the core issue of safety, Thailand scores very badly indeed.

While many foreigners leave the country happy, there are equally thousands of travellers from Europe, America, Australia, India and the Middle East, both short-time tourists and long-term residents, leaving the country impoverished, distressed, frightened and unlikely to ever return.

If, with the murder or accidental deaths of tourists a common event, they leave at all.

There is no doubt that Thailand, with its porous borders, massive influx of foreigners, well established local and foreign mafias, corrupt police forces and easily bribed officials, has become the 21st Century's crime capital of Asia.

The nation's strategic location, lax law enforcement and modern transport systems have assisted its role as safe haven to a number of international crime networks. Rackets include forged and stolen passports, drugs, wildlife and arms smuggling and people trafficking. Criminal milieus from around the world find The Land of Smiles a very congenial atmosphere in which to operate. Since the 1970s, when the influx of tourists first began, German, British, Irish, Russian, West African, and Filipino crime gangs have all proliferated in the Kingdom, as have Japanese Yakuza, Chinese Triads, South Korean and Taiwanese brotherhoods. The local police are also involved in everything from paedophile rings to drug smuggling. In Bangkok for example the police and the mafia work hand in hand to provide under-age victims to foreign sex tourists. Thailand is a signatory to the UN's Convention on the Rights of the Child. It does not comply.

A 2014 study by the Thailand Institute of Justice showed that more than 20 major transnational gangs were plaguing the country, including Russian and Romanian credit card skimming gangs.

---

[1] A model of destination competitiveness/sustainability: Brazilian perspectives, J.R. Brent Ritchie & Geoffrey I. Crouch,

A spokesman for the Institute Natee Jitsawang said their research showed foreign criminal gangs continued to develop and adapt their crime techniques while law-enforcement personnel were reshuffled regularly. As a result authorities could not keep pace with criminal operators using the country as a base.

Russian gangs had particular expertise in ATM and credit card forging, skimming and selling overseas bank customers' information. The gangs used modern technology that could skim the card information in 30 seconds and download it onto a computer so the card could be forged.

Fake cards were then used to withdraw cash from ATM machines at night to avoid police detection. Even when they were caught, they managed to destroy evidence quickly. The study found that a Romanian gang was also skilled in card skimming and had extensive operations in Thailand.

Natee said the gang imported an electronic card forgery machine from Spain to southern Thailand via post and then produced fake cards to buy goods at shopping malls and jewellery shops or withdraw cash. He said the gang installed card skimming devices onto ATM machines at various tourist attractions, especially Bangkok's Sukhumvit area.

German gangs stole personal bank details via the Internet by releasing viruses to hack information about bank account logins and passwords while the target accessed their online accounts. The stolen money was then wired to a bank account overseas. French and English gangs used cards containing stolen information from bank customers in France and Scandinavia to withdraw cash via ATM machines in Thailand, especially Phuket. These gangs installed small cameras or mobile card skimmer devices to steal information.

According to the Institute, there are four Latin American gangs - Colombians, Mexicans, Guatemalans and Peruvians - that commit crimes in Thailand, mostly thefts and robberies. The Colombians scouted rich housing estates to break in and steal valuables. Some of them also cracked bank safe boxes. Natee said the Mexicans, Guatemalans and Peruvians focused on car theft and stealing from houses, hotels and jewellery fairs.[2]

Western criminals love Thailand as a kind of tropical hideout full of cheap booze and accommodating women, well away from the cold climates and police surveillance of their own countries.

Asian expert Thomas Schmid writes that the foreign mafia operating in Thailand are not necessarily just branches of international organisations. The insalubrious band together in their adopted country to form their own syndicates: "This development has caused Thailand's foreign mafia scene to become extraordinarily complex. The authorities are unable (or perhaps unwilling) to disclose any reliable figures on the prevalence of foreign mafia presence in the country, but it is estimated that literally hundreds of mafia groups currently carry out their activities more or less openly. Prominent tourism centres such as Pattaya or Phuket are well known to harbour crime syndicates of every *couleur*. Thai gangs usually serve as facilitators or intermediaries to foreign mafia organisations, for example by procuring unsuspecting and naïve local girls and women to be sent abroad and be put to work as prostitutes."[3]

The arrival of other nation's mafias, in particular the Russian mafia, which has come to control a substantial slice of Thailand's "entertainment" industry, adds a new level of ruthlessness to the nation's already treacherous sex industry. And it is exactly in the nightly confluence of Russian, Thai and other criminal elements, operating arm in arm with the local authorities, in which many tourists, out for a good time in the bars and clubs, come dangerously unstuck. Within metres of their hotels and apartments foreigners enter a zone where their money, rather than protecting them, puts them at immediate risk.

This superficially alluring, adventure filled netherworld of go-go bars, massage parlours, nightclubs and brothels represents a kind of symbolic space between the respectable and the dissolute,

[2] Over 20 big foreign criminal gangs here, Piyanut Tamnukasetchai, *The Sunday Nation*, 14 September, 2014.

[3] The darker side of tropical bliss: Foreign Mafia in Thailand, Thomas Schmid, Thailand Law Forum, 25 February, 2010.

the legal and illegal, a fantasy escape from the conformist, over-regulated societies of the West. They lure the bold and the curious alike. Straight into some of the most dangerous tourist traps on Earth.

Traditionally the Thailand Tourist Authority and the Tourist Organisation of Thailand have touted ever increasing tourist numbers as the sole barometer of the industry's success. But the seemingly endless catalogue of dead and injured foreigners and the portrayal of Thailand as "Scam Land", along with all the daily mayhem of the tourist trade resulting from uncontrolled development and poor planning, have begun to impact badly on the nation's image. The ever changing caste of the wanted and the wanting within the expatriate community adds to the sense of a party which has run out of control.

Despite the industry's multi-million dollar advertising spend the sheer number of deaths and accidents befalling tourists and foreign residents alike creates a very different image to the one the marketeers want. Thailand has become known as the single most dangerous tourist destination on Earth.

The disaster cuts every which way. The Thais themselves, far from welcoming foreigners to their country, have grown immensely resentful at seeing their country overrun by disrespectful, drunken and uncaring hordes. The advent of mass tourism has desecrated many of the country's finest environmental treasures and turned entire districts into some kind of Rabelaisian distortion in the tropics. Tourism may have made a significant contribution to Thailand's prosperity and modernity. But the opening up of the country to the world had, by the early years of the new millennium, also led to entire stretches of coastline in the Andaman Sea and the Gulf of Thailand being transformed into gaudy collections of bars, nightclubs, massage parlours, hotels and restaurants.

Nor is the inland immune. Chiang Mai, 800 kilometres north of Bangkok and known as the "Rose of the North", is full of cheap guesthouses and upmarket hotels. The ancient capital of the Lanna Kingdom, from 1296 to 1768, Chiang Mai is surrounded by a moat and remnants of high defensive walls. Far from the fearsome mountain traders and warriors who once strode through the town, its narrow, medieval laneways are now jammed with casually dressed tourists, particularly during the peak season between October and February.

There is a kind of cultural revulsion against the aliens infesting their soil. The often enough offensive behaviour of Western tourists has also fuelled the Thais nationalistic and xenophobic instincts. Cries of "Thailand is for Thais" and "too many foreigners" can be heard across the Kingdom. "Pohm mai chop farang," I don't like foreigners, is a phrase often spoken, and often enough right in front of tourists; who the Thais assume cannot understand a word of their language.

The term "farang", or "falung" depending on proximity to the Laotian border, is a generic Thai word referring to an individual's European ancestry, and directly to their skin colour. It is the same word as used for guava, with its white flesh and can be used simply as an identifier. Or as an insult. The term "farang dam" refers to a person of African ancestry, a black foreigner.

Pool cleaners on Phuket, Picture by Peter Morgan.

Part of the resentment of Thais against foreigners is the same resentment the poor have for the rich everywhere: They are forced to work as everything from bar tenders and pool cleaners to prostitutes and hustlers for ungrateful people with an overblown sense of entitlement.

As journalist and author Elizabeth Becker observed in her landmark book *Overbooked: The Exploding Business of Travel and Tourism*: "On its own, travel is neither good nor bad. The travel and tourism industry, however, has good and bad impacts, and governments are central to determining what that outcome is. Tourists aren't neutral either. Individually they make profound choices and when travelling in hordes they can do tremendous damage. The flash points of tourism are the same around the world: local communities feeling powerless in the face of their governments and big industry; the industry feeling hamstrung by opaque regulations and corrupt government officials; civil societies feeling ignored when they try to protect their forests and beaches, neighbourhoods and children..."[4]

But despite the hostility of the Thais and the scandals plaguing the industry airbuses continue to unload tens of thousands of tourists every day. The Thai tourist industry, despite the many scandals plaguing it and the high death toll of visitors, had once seemed unstoppable and reform unlikely.

Until 2014, when the political convulsions which had seen violent demonstrations paralyse the country and close down major commercial districts peaked. Embassies worldwide issued heightened warnings. Many insurance companies stopped issuing policies for travel to Thailand.

At 3.30am on 20 May, 2014 Thailand's Army declared martial law.[5] Twenty eight people had died and hundreds been injured in the preceding seven months of unrest.

At 4.30pm on 22 May, 2014, Thailand's Army chief General Prayuth Chan-ochaa announced the takeover of the government and the suspension of the Constitution. It was the country's 19th

---

[4] *Overbooked: The Exploding Business of Travel and Tourism*, Elizabeth Becker, Simon & Schuster, 2013.

[5] Thailand's army declares martial law, troops take over TV stations, acting PM still in office, Australian Broadcasting Commission, 20 May, 2014.

coup since 1932; more than any other country. Twelve of the coups had been successful.[6]

A curfew from 10pm to 5am was imposed across Thailand, including the holiday areas of Chiang Mai, Pattaya and Phuket, impacting on tens of thousands of tourists.[7] For once the country's nightspots went quiet.

Soldiers were given the authority to detain people without charge, and political demonstrations were banned. Media organisations were occupied and local television stations began broadcasting military declarations and songs. The BBC, CNN and other international news agencies were taken off the air. Internet forums catering to the expatriate community were locked. Facebook was blocked and thousands of radio stations closed. Journalists were ordered not to interview anyone who did not hold an official position.

Travellers encountered numerous check-points manned by armed soldiers. There was chaos at Thailand's transport hubs. The military announced people could travel to and from airports during the curfew hours as long as they could show they had a valid ticket. If stopped, they were asked to show their passport.

Many countries updated their travel advisories for citizens to exercise a high degree of caution. The US State Department warned its citizens: "Martial law remains in effect throughout Thailand. Be aware that under martial law the governing National Council for Peace and Order (NCPO) has considerable security powers. These powers grant the NCPO the authority to prevent public gatherings, restrict media, set up checkpoints, and search for weapons. Individuals have been detained for publicly criticising Thailand's military takeover, the NCPO, and the Thai monarchy. Security operations against possible demonstrations have led to traffic disruptions as well as temporary closures of some public transport services, and restriction of access to some areas around major shopping and hotel districts in central Bangkok."

---

[6] Image of *Bangkok Post* headline Charter Suspended: Jon in Thailand. Flickr Commons.

[7] Australian tourists caught in Thailand coup, *Sydney Morning Herald*, 22 May, 2014.

While governments everywhere encourage their citizens to acquire travel insurance, most plans exempt military coups. The travel plans of the hundreds of thousands of tourists were thrown into disarray, without any financial compensation.

Thailand had a dying king and serious succession problems, weak democratic institutions, an economy slipping into recession, faced issues of corruption across many of its key services and was host to international crime syndicates, awash with despised foreigners and drifting perilously towards civil war.

Most of the thousands of travellers, from backpackers to businessmen, caught up in the coup had little knowledge of or interest in the politics of the country in which they found themselves. For some it was little more than a picture opportunity.[8]

But the coup was to have both immediate and lasting impacts on the experiences of short-stay tourists, long-term residents and Thailand's relationship with other countries.

The West, which universally condemned the coup, did not anticipate the military junta's popularity with the Thai people. In large part this was due to announcements that there would be a moral cleansing of the country; including clamping down on crime, reforming the police, and a crackdown on taxi mafias operating at the nation's airports. Much of the criminality of Thailand was directed at foreigners. Coup leader General Prayuth Chan-ocha said he did not like the way the country was portrayed in the movies as a haven for drugs, thugs, lawlessness and ladies of the night. He believed the country should be ashamed of its image.

Prayuth repeatedly said he wanted to return the country to its Buddhist roots, to a place of moral standing where people respected the law. He did not want Thailand to be a place where politicians, police and other authorities readily took payments to ignore crime. Ending corruption was one of the major justifications for the coup.

"Foreign tourists should not have a perception that they can come to Thailand to commit illegal activities as often portrayed in the movies," he said in one of his weekly broadcasts. "I am

---

[8] Lord Tongy at Suvarnabhumi Airport. Picture taken 6 June 2014. Courtesy Freelifer.

ashamed. Do you not feel the same when this is portrayed in foreign movies? We have to change this perception."⁹

Countries issuing strong statements against the coup included America, the UK, France, Germany, Canada, Australia and New Zealand. Japan's Foreign Minister called the situation "regrettable" and Singapore urged all sides to avoid violence. Australia downgraded military cooperation and called for a return to democracy.

"There is no justification for this military coup," US Secretary of State John Kerry declared, urging immediate return to civilian government and the lifting of curbs on the media. "This act will have negative implications for the US-Thai relationship, especially for our relationship with the Thai military."¹⁰

United Nations Secretary General Ban Ki-moon appealed "for a prompt return to constitutional, civilian, democratic rule and an all-inclusive dialogue that will pave the way for long-term peace and prosperity".

The Council of the European Union also issued a joint statement urging the military leadership to urgently restore democratic processes and reinstate the Constitution, remove censorship and to respect human rights: "Fully functioning democratic institutions must be brought back to ensure the protection and welfare of all citizens. Against this background, the EU is forced to reconsider its engagement. Official visits to and from Thailand have been suspended; the EU and its Member States will not sign the Partnership and Cooperation Agreement with Thailand, until a democratically elected government is in place. Other agreements will, as appropriate, be affected. EU Member States have already begun to review their military cooperation with Thailand.

"Only an early and credible roadmap for a return to constitutional rule and the holding of credible and inclusive elections will allow for the EU's continued support. The Council

---

⁹ General Prayuth Chan-ocha Say's Thai's (sic) Should Be Ashamed of Country's Image, *Chiang Rai Times*, 20 June, 2014.

¹⁰ Thai coup draws swift condemnation; US says reviewing aid, David Brunnstrom and Arshad Mohammed, Reuters, 22 May, 2014.

decided that the EU will keep its relations with Thailand under review and will consider further possible measures, depending on circumstances."[11]

Accustomed to coups, and tired of the rampant corruption which had characterised former administrations, local reaction was quick, and highly offended. On the internet messages telling foreigners to mind their own business proliferated.

Editor of the influential newspaper *The Nation* Thanong Khanthong said the international pressure on Thailand was unjustified and could lead to a realignment of the country's international relations.

"Without the coup, political polarisation would have got worse and threatened to tear apart the fabric of the social order. The authorities continue to discover caches of war weapons and ammunition around the country, stockpiled by hard-core supporters of the previous government. By pressuring Thailand to hold an election without first forging political reforms, the US and the EU are effectively asking that Thailand remain a divided nation. A weak and polarised Thailand could, indeed, benefit the US and EU. It would fit world powers' traditional divide-and-rule formula.

"The blatant interference in our internal affairs by superpowers in the Western world is unacceptable. As a sovereign and independent nation, Thailand has every right to put its house in order in its own way. Public opinion is mostly in favour of the coup, which has effectively restored order and ended the bloodshed. Now, the Thai people are looking forward to a reform process that hopefully will lay the foundation for political, economic and social stability. All now depends on the commitment and the capability of the military regime to guide Thailand through this transition."[12]

An editorial in the equally strategically important *Bangkok Post* declared: "The anti-foreigner response, coming mainly from coup supporters, is not a surprise considering how entrenched the

---

[11] Council Conclusions on Thailand, Foreign Affairs Council Meeting, Luxembourg, Council of the European Union Press Release, 23 June, 2014.

[12] The West might regret forcing Thailand into a corner, Thanon Khanthong, *The Nation*, 27 June, 2014.

country's political problems have been. It's still by no means a healthy development. If left to fester, the anti-foreigner sentiment will quickly grow into xenophobia. Such an inward and backward attitude is not befitting the present time when connectedness and globalisation are the rules of the game. What the junta will have to do is to address the international concerns seriously. These include a return to civilian rule and democracy as soon as possible, a release of political detainees plus avoidance of arbitrary detention and respect for human rights and media freedom."[13]

Western journalists tended to simplify Thailand's often bewildering politics into a simple coding of rich against poor, with, despite their personal wealth, the Shinawatra family aligning themselves with an impoverished rural constituency. In the crudest of divides, Red Shirts equalled the rural poor, while the Yellow Shirts equalled the traditional elites.

Veteran CBC News reporter Patrick Brown summed it up thus: "Strip away the colour coding, the personalities and the ever-changing alphabet soup of organisations and parties, and you find a familiar political divide. Rice farmers, peasants and workers on the red side, the moneyed class and aristocracy on the yellow."[14]

Brown went on to describe the "red machine" as the creation of telecom billionaire Thaksin Shinawatra, who had won a succession of elections with a program of subsidies, loans and cheap health care wildly popular with rural Thais.

"The yellow alliance brings together royalists, who think Thaksin was too big for his boots, and the urban elite, who are often frank in their bewilderment that the votes of peasants, drivers and maids have a value equal to their own," Brown wrote. "When the red majority has prevailed, the yellows have taken to the streets to shut the capital down. When the yellows have managed to use institutions such as the courts and the electoral commission to get the reds removed, then the reds in their turn, resort to the politics of the street."

---

[13] Xenophobia no solution, Editorial, *Bangkok Post*, 7 June, 2014.

[14] ANALYSIS: Thailand's 19th Coup underscores the country's fatal flaw, Patrick Brown, CBC News, 30 May, 2014.

But Thai commentators were critical of the Western media's tendency to paint Thailand's polity as a two-sided battle. Instead, leading newspaper *The Nation* declared, Thais had been faced with wrongheaded economic policy and widespread corruption in the corridors of power. The paper condemned as a dangerous myth the representation of the coup as the elites acting to overthrow a democratically elected government: "Those seeking to portray the protests as a battle between rich and poor are missing the truth: most Thais are united by frustration with corrupt government. Bangkok's elite and middle classes have been cast in the same role by overseas press ever since Thaksin Shinawatra was first targeted for street protests. This view of events ignored the corruption scandals.... The current protest is not about a class struggle or a power struggle. This is tens of thousands of citizens furious over misrule."

In his official announcement that civil rule was suspended, General Prayuth asked the international community for understanding of the reasons behind the coup.

"In order for the situation to return to normal quickly and for society to love and be at peace again ... and to reform the structure of the political, economic and social structure, the military needs to take control of power."[15]

Until elections were held, the country would be run by a collection of senior military figures known as the National Council of Peace and Order. The Council subsequently appointed Prayuth as Prime Minister.

The previous two years of unfolding drama had seen numerous scandals and a string of deadly accidents and episodes involving foreigners. The junta moved quickly to reform the police. It also began a crackdown on the nation's dizzying array of scams; from the country's beaches, which had become little more than open market places with pedlars of all kinds selling their wares to tourists, to the mafia run bars and gangs brazenly preying on tourists in the nation's infamous red light districts.

---

[15] Thailand Army Chief announces Coup, *Sydney Morning Herald*, 23 May, 2014.

The former government had announced a couple of ultimately futile inquiries into the mafia involvement in the Thai "entertainment" industry, read sex industry, and into tourist resorts on the famous holiday island of Phuket. There had been no result from the inquiries and no genuine official action. Apart, that is, from renewed attempts by Thai authorities to downplay the many stories of tourists in trouble and shift the focus of blame onto their delinquent behaviour. It was true enough that foreigners often conducted themselves in ways they would not do in their countries of origin. But this was a consequence Thailand had invited on itself, with deliberate marketing of Thailand as Party Central, a notorious limit-free zone.

That as a result the country had attracted some truly unsavoury characters, along with millions of normally well behaved travellers out to have a good time away from the watching eyes of their own communities, was predictable.

Also predictable was that the failure to maintain even rudimentary safety standards would lead to a high number of accidental deaths amongst tourists; and with so many holidays turning into tragedies, damage the country's reputation. So dire is the record of the tourist industry that all major governments have expressed concern over the welfare of their citizens. As time has passed and the death toll risen, diplomatic warnings to the Thai government have became blunter.

China, Thailand's principal source of tourists, along with members of the European Union and many other nations, have all made strong representations as a result of the string of deaths, accidents and litanies of complaint about dangerous scams and unsafe facilities.

Tourism Minister Somsak Pureesrisak said protection from harm was the top priority in regaining traveller confidence following a spate of high-profile cases of violent crime: "Tourist safety is now on the national agenda, in particular a crackdown on mafia gangs in Phuket and Pattaya. Gangsters are now involved in enterprises that directly affect tourists, such as jet-skis and taxis."

Tourist revenue was the country's leading source of foreign exchange, but many operators of tourist related businesses ignored the most basic of safety precautions. Despite the rhetoric nothing at the coalface, or more precisely the beachfront, changed. No internationally acceptable safety standards applied. Tourists could hire snorkel-equipment and boats without having to show any competence at all, while vehicles and boats were loaded beyond their capacity. Buses and trains were poorly maintained and boat drivers untrained.

Leading newspaper *The Nation* editorialised: "Tourist safety has become a big concern for the governments of countries whose nationals form a sizeable share of the visitors to Thailand, including China and member-nations of the European Union. There has been a string of recent cases of theft and violence against tourists, in addition to drowning deaths off beaches and deaths in road and boat accidents.

"Lack of security and safety measures have been blamed for numerous tragic deaths of foreign tourists. Many of these incidents and accidents could have been avoided through the simple enforcement of existing rules and regulations.

"A lot of the problems in tourist safety boil down to the Thai authorities' lax law enforcement—or none at all in some cases."[16]

Whether the locals like it or not, and attitudes range from prurience to pride, the name of Thailand has become synonymous with the sleaze of sex tourism. The country boasts thousands of bars, nightclubs and massage parlours catering exclusively to foreigners. Prostitution has a long history and high level of acceptance within Thai culture; on some estimates only about 20 percent of the prostitution in Thailand involves foreigners. The influx of tourists has simply, sometimes grotesquely, expanded a pre-existing condition. The red light districts catering to Thai men and, in an often startlingly liberated culture, to women, are entirely different to those which most foreigners encounter. But it is on the garish clusters of bars and strip joints catering to Westerners that the nation's international reputation has floundered.

---

[16] PROTECT the goose that lays the golden egg, Editorial, 19 September, 2013, *The Nation*.

The comparatively naive sex industry of the 1960s and 70s, the Vietnam War era, is naive no longer. The women who once called out to American soldiers from dilapidated bars, "Hey mister, you number one, you velly handsome, I like you velly much," have been replaced by a new generation of sex workers who, like the bars from which they work, are now far more sophisticated.

Bangkok itself has several red light districts operating exclusively for foreigners, including a strip in the city's oldest red light district of Patpong which services only the Japanese. For the gay market, adjacent to Patpong is Soi Twilight, while near the main thoroughfare of Sukhumvit are the world famous sex centres of Soi Cowboy and Nana Plaza.

Two hours south of Bangkok lies Pattaya, one of the largest centres for sex tourism in the world. A small fishing village until the 1960s, the area has been transformed, with up to 100,000 sex workers estimated to be working on any one night. The stretch along its foreshore is often described as the largest open-air brothel in the world.

Walking Street, Pattaya. Picture by Brendan Brain.

Critics condemn sex tourists as exploiters of the underprivileged. Human rights journalist Deena Guzder, for instance, wrote for the Pulitzer Centre on Crisis Reporting: "Imagine standing naked under flashing lava-red disco lights and gyrating to blaring techno music before dropping to the ground, splaying your legs like a starfish, and using your pelvic muscles to pop a dozen ping-pong balls out of your vagina for the amusement of giddy, affluent, and intoxicated foreigners. Now imagine shoving live turtles into your vagina and dancing around a pole before ejecting the turtles into an aquarium ("Wow, the turtles can still swim!") Imagine repeating the same act with, say, a large frog or bagful of goldfish. Welcome to Bangkok, Thailand's Red Light District."

Guzder claims Thailand's infamous Ping Pong Shows do not lure clients through promises of sexual arousal, but promises of sexual perversion — if not sexual torture. They offer freak shows where women's bodies are reduced to grotesque objects exploited for tourists' entertainment. Thai women travel from their villages to cities such as Bangkok for work and are hired not as sex entertainers, but circus animals: "These shows are inherently misogynistic; after all, there is no equivalent of a 'ping pong show' for men, in which they use their anal muscles to pop out frogs and pull out razors. The vast economic disparities between Thai locals and Thailand's tourists have long enabled affluent foreigners to request massages with 'happy ending specials' or 'rent a girlfriend/boyfriend' for a holiday. Now, the global economic crisis has spawned new, dangerous ways of objectifying, commoditising, and demeaning women. Thailand's sex tourism industry is more risqué, less regulated, and more dangerous than ever before. This is a story of destitute Asian women subjecting themselves to extreme degradation for the guffaws of affluent Western benefactors. This is a story where the messy intersection of class, race and sexuality are taken to their disturbing logical extremes."[17]

---

[17] Thailand: The World's Sex Tourism Capital, Deena Guzder, the Pulitzer Center, 14 August, 2009.

John Stapleton

Siriporn Skrobaneh from the Foundation for Women in Bangkok is of like mind, describing the sex industry in Thailand as a human tragedy: "Thailand is like a stage where men from around the world come to perform their role of male supremacy over Thai women and their role (of) white supremacy over Thai people…The solution to international sexual exploitation lies, not only in changing the commercialised pattern of relationships in Thailand, but also those between the people of the West itself; for the sake of liberation, both for the exploited of Thailand, and for the whole of humanity."

That is all as may be. Reality is rarely as straight forward as theory would allow.

There are many grounds for misunderstandings between the Thai and Western cultures; sex and relationships being one of the unhappiest of all the many hunting grounds.

There is often little sympathy for Western men who fall for the "I love you I miss you I stay with you forever" patter of Thai sex workers. Hundreds of thousands of elderly tourists, mostly men, with dreams in their hearts and twinkles in their eyes, regularly fail to understand the difference in cultural emphasis or understanding of romantic love, the hierarchical and village based nature of Thai society and the way many sex workers have been co-opted into the industry through financial necessity; sacrificing themselves for the larger good of their families. The misunderstandings between workers and clients mean these men fall prey to their own late-life delusions on the allures of the East and ignore or fail to comprehend the ill intent of those with whom they wish to party. They are routinely robbed and the fleeting relationships they establish frequently end in tragedy.

With their complex social and sexual lives, multiple partners, the physical beauty of the Thais themselves and widespread revulsion towards foreigners, the life of a sex worker is not always easy. But in an environment where elderly and not so elderly foreigners are encouraged to think all their dreams have come true, exactly who is exploiting who can be a moot point. Out of their own environments, often without any long-time friends around them to reference reality, with family and support groups far away,

18

they find themselves in a place where, rightly or wrongly, they have not a clue what they are dealing with. They have no facility with the local language, no understanding of the place prostitution plays in Thai culture, no comprehension of the real feelings of the sex worker in their bed, and are dealing in intimate and sometimes embarrassing ways with prostitutes invariably in cahoots with the local police and backed by some of the world's most dangerous mafias. Western men can find themselves dangerously alone in a dangerous place.

Often enough, they will find themselves being shoved off balconies by people they once thought were lovers; and their deaths, if recorded at all, will be attributed to suicide.

The improbably high number of deaths of foreigners labelled as suicide, often blamed by the authorities on the breakup of a short term relationship with a Thai prostitute, is simply a device to excuse a Thai policeman from investigating and charging a fellow Thai.

The harshness of the industry, the intensity of competition for clients and money transforms Thai sex workers into superb actors. Out of their home environments Western men, lonely, vulnerable and desperately deluded as they try to relive their youths, rarely understand enough of the local languages to comprehend that they are being openly ridiculed in Thai by those around them, including their sleeping partner. Most Thais think that foreigners cannot understand a word they say. To the sometimes uproarious amusement of the gaggle of people the Western man assumes are friends, or at least grateful for the drinks he is buying, he is in fact being described as old, ugly, smelly, stupid, without sexual power and mean with money. As a tonal language Thai is uniquely complex and difficult for Westerners to understand or learn. Its syntax bears no resemblance to European languages and its vivid imagery is patterned in a way difficult for novices to comprehend. And that is before the listener gets to the major regional languages, particularly Issaan, a group of Lao dialects which is widely spoken in the north of the country, as well as by the droves of rural poor working in Bangkok. There are also a number of tribal languages.

Broken hearts aside, the river of cash flowing from the trade has far broader implications, empowering and emboldening local and international criminal networks and the interlinking mafias, police and corrupt officials making up Thailand's criminal milieu.

At more than 10 per cent of Gross Domestic Product, tourism has been the principal source of foreign exchange since 1992.

The daily headlines of catastrophe and misadventures involving foreigners is now a very long way from the optimism that greeted the creation of the modern industry.

It all began, humbly by present standards, half a century before with enthusiastic hopes that tourism would become a way of showcasing the nation's spectacular landscapes and unique culture.

Then Prime Minister Field Marshal Sarit Thanarat founded the Thailand Tourist Organisation in 1960, thereby beginning the country's dramatic transformation from a predominantly agrarian society. Thailand, with its hyper-development, sky trains, ribboned expressways and rapidly multiplying, masterfully designed shopping precincts, often resembles a science fiction movie director's vision of the future. In contrast to the latter-day plethora of high quality hotels and resorts, studies of the time showed a shortage of appropriate accommodation for tourists.

Thanarat gave many speeches on the benefits of establishing a tourist industry in Thailand. He believed it would prove an important mechanism in enhancing economic development and through the international promotion of its physical beauty and the hospitality of the Thai people, foster national pride.[18]

The inauguration ceremony of the Tourist Organisation of Thailand, subsequently renamed the Tourism Authority of Thailand was a gala affair attended by foreign ambassadors and numerous dignitaries. The Prime Minister declared:"The revenue generated by the tourism industry will not be solely directed to the Government but will be distributed among people of all walks of life. This revenue will be something which is indiscernible. However, what is most important is the role the tourism industry

---

[18] An oratory made by Field Marshal Sarit Thanarat, the Prime Minister who founded an agency for tourism, Tourism Authority of Thailand.

will play in spreading to the whole world the culture, virtue and moral principles of the Thai people. As a consequence, the world will come to appreciate Thailand for what it is. This, I believe, is more important than any monetary benefit...

"I would like every individual, whether he or she is directly or indirectly in the tourism business, such as hoteliers, restaurant operators, tour offices, gift shops, taxi drivers, students and even the general public to consider your own important role in the success of the tourism industry. I would like to request every individual's co-operation in order to bring benefits to our beloved country. The achievement of those engaged in tourism will bring you self-esteem and honour."

While the industry's founders may have dreamt of more upmarket fans, much of the early tourist tracks were pioneered by budget conscious backpackers, a group enthralled by the country's cheap drugs, relaxed lifestyles, beautiful women and pristine beaches. At the less idealistic end of the spectrum, the nation's red light districts catering to foreigners received their initial boost from American soldiers on "rest and recreation" leave from the Vietnam War. The backpackers made way for glampackers, and the soldiers made way for sex tourists.

As *Time* observed in a piece celebrating the work of photographer Jorg Bruggemann, something happened along the way: "Through the 20th Century, writers, poets and artists have all wrestled with the troubling reality of modernity, that we live, as one famous German theorist put it, in a disenchanted world, sapped of mystery by our own modern, secular, technological society. The search for wonder has animated a host of new age faddish trends in the West. It sent hippies to ashrams in India, made Tibetan Buddhism hip in Hollywood and launched travellers down paths of wanderlust and serendipity across the globe."

Bruggemann documented South and South East Asia, "a stretch of turf that has been densely charted already by Lonely Planet, that is lined with tours and scams ready to swallow up the unsuspecting, and that is trod over by millions each year. Many of these young people are on gap years or study abroad, journeying ostensibly on latter-day quests of self-discovery, financed on a shoestring. But what were once whimsical, individual explorations have turned into banal spectacles of packaged mass tourism."

Just as untrammelled development in Spain saw its once picturesque Costa del Sol transformed into what critics call the Costa del Concrete and the Greeks have watched their beautiful islands become trashy resorts dotted with nightclubs and garish hotels, so for Thailand.

In a few short decades the once seemingly sacred, magically beautiful Kingdom of Siam became the victim of industrial-scale mass tourism. "Thailand is already like Mallorca," Bruggemann said.[19]

The influx of tourists and the build-up of problems that foreigners experience in Thailand, generated in part by the dislike locals hold towards them, predates the 2014 military coup by many years. However forecasts that holiday makers and retirees would choose the safer destinations of its neighbours, Cambodia, Laos, Myanmar and Malaysia all proved false. While surrounding countries have seen substantial rises in foreign visitors, Thailand retains a unique allure despite its political turmoil and the daily record of poorly policed assaults and routine scamming.

In 2013 Bangkok outflanked London and Paris to be rated the most visited city in the world, according to the MasterCard Global Destinations Cities Index, the first time an Asian city had topped the list.

Bangkok had also been ranked the world's best city by the hugely influential magazine *Travel & Leisure* for four years in a row. Readers rated destinations on their landmarks, culture, arts, restaurants, food, people and value for money.

The next year was a different story. In 2014, with international attention focussing on Thailand's political turmoil, dangerous tensions on the street, the moral dilemmas of pro-democracy travellers supporting a military junta and the mishaps and misadventures bedevilling so many travellers, Bangkok not only lost its top spot, it slipped out of the Top Ten list altogether. Kyoto,

---

[19] Same Same But Different: Tourism in Southeast Asia, *TIME*, 24 August, 2011.

which recorded 51.6 million tourists in 2013, replaced Bangkok as the world's top city.

There are many reasons why foreigners are drawn to Thailand, both as short-term tourists and long-time residents: the world class service in its high-end hotels, a well established tourist infrastructure, intoxicating landscapes, an internationally renowned cuisine, beautiful temples, the cultural uniqueness of its peoples, a relaxed attitude towards prostitution and, of course, a seemingly inexhaustible nightlife. Foreigners often display an almost obsessional love for the country and its peoples, and a great admiration for its many beauties. Newcomers find easy friends in almost any bar. As long as the foreigner is paying, there is always a party to be had. In a sense, there is an eternal present. Problems are for another day. "Mai kit mahk", don't think too much, is one of the most common of all Thai sayings.

Another of Thailand's major appeals is the favourable exchange rates to Thai Baht. Tourists can stay in a far higher standards of accommodations at a far cheaper price than in their own countries. Long term stayers can expect to pay a quarter of the rent they would pay in their countries of origin. Houses and apartments are cheap by Western standards. A perfectly good meal of chicken and rice can be had at street stalls for $2, and for the dwindling number of people who still smoke tobacco, a packet of cigarettes cost one tenth of what smokers pay in the West.

The country is without a well developed social welfare system, one of the factors propelling its low unemployment, minimal regulation on owner-operated businesses and preparedness of the rural poor to engage in prostitution with foreigners. The flickering maze of street stalls, bars, restaurants, shops and spruikers which characterise Thai towns and cities provide great appeal to Westerners accustomed to the claustrophobic, sanitised, over-regulated atmospheres of their own countries.

As thriller writer Timothy Hallinan observed in *The Fear Artist*, one of a series of novels including *The Queen of Patpong* set in Thailand, "Bangkok is many things, but it is never empty".

Nowhere are the pitfalls of mass tourism more evident than in Thailand. France is held up as a contrary example, a country with a similar sized population and more than double the number of tourists but which manages to integrate tourism into all levels of governance, and avoid the profound dislocations Thailand has experienced. People don't travel to France to avail themselves of its prostitutes. Whole strips of coastline are not dedicated to garish go-go bars. The French don't hate the tourists that come to their country. And the world's mafias have not made France their home.

At one end of the spectrum of tourism models lies the mountain kingdom of Bhutan, which has deliberately worked to prevent the destruction of local cultures and customs, and the adoption of consumerism inherent in globalisation and mass tourism. Backpackers and budget travellers are not encouraged. There is no such thing as sex tourism. The world's disenchanted and disenfranchised do not stay for months or even years. Instead visitors are expected to spend a minimum of $250 a day and their movements are closely proscribed.

The approach has led to Bhutan being labelled "The Last Shangri-La".[20]

In 2011 Bhutan had 37,482 visitor arrivals, a quarter of which were for corporate-style purposes including conferences and exhibitions.

In contrast Thailand had 19,230,000 arrivals in the same year.[21] The numbers jumped another three million in 2012. Despite political turmoil and cautionary travel advisories from embassies, the tourist industry boomed. Official figures recorded 26.7 million international visitors for 2013, in a population of 69.52 million.[22] This was a 19.6 per cent increase on 2012, a 4.4 million rise in the number of visitors in a single year.

Not only were there more international visitors to Thailand year upon year, they were staying longer. In 1960 the 81,340

[20] *The Living Edens, Bhutan: The Last Shangri-La,* Public Broadcasting Service. Taktshang cropped" by Douglas J. McLaughlin - Own work. Licensed under Creative Commons Attribution 2.5 via Wikimedia Commons. http://commons.wikimedia.org/wiki/File:Taktshang.jpg

[21] International tourism, number of arrivals, Data, The World Bank.

[22] World Population Statistics, Thailand Population 2013.

visitors had an average stay of two days and one night.[23] By 2013 the average stay had risen to more than 10 days.

The flood of money, black or otherwise, accompanying the arrival of short and long-stay foreigners, fuelled the coffers of the country's criminal networks by way of their control of the sex industry, bars, clubs, hotels and multiple property interests.

When it came to the military takeover, Westerner commentators and Western travellers, imbued with democratic principles, leant towards the basic dichotomy of democracy good, military bad, but nothing was ever quite so simple in modern-day Siam. A fortnight before the coup, if visitors had been noticing anything beyond a few extra soldiers in the environs of their resort or local nest of bars, clubs, restaurants and massage parlours, they would have seen on the television screens of their briefly adopted country a well groomed, elegant looking woman surrounded by besuited advisers.

Yingluck Shinawatra, Thailand's first woman Prime Minister, had a Bachelor of Arts degree from Chiangmai University and a Masters of Public Administration from Kentucky State University. A senior executive in her family's telecom company AIS, Thailand's largest mobile phone operator, Yingluk was investigated by Thailand's Security and Exchange Commission for insider trading after selling stock in AIS, but no charges were laid. A military appointed Assets Examination Committee argued that she had made up false transactions, but no case was pursued against her.

Yingluck was a descendent of the ruling monarch of Chiang Mai through her grandmother, Princess Jantip Na Chiang Mai.

The wealthy and as far as their critics were concerned infamously corrupt Shinawatra family had their power base in the north of the country. To their opponents the Shinawatras illustrated all the frailties of modern democracies, that power, protection and privilege can be bought; just as can the voting public.

---

[23] Reminiscence of the Thailand Organisation of Tourism, Lt General Chalermchai Charuvastr, Director of TOT, 1960-1976, Thailand Authority of Tourism.

Yingluck came to power after a populist "red shirt" uprising which closed down the centre of Bangkok during 2010, ridding its normally crowded landmarks, upmarket shopping precincts and entertainment districts of tourists. Demonstrators, many from impoverished rural villages, shut down Hermes and Gucci stores. The wealthy Thais and cashed up foreigners who frequented the world's largest interlinking network of malls were forced to shop elsewhere. Almost 100 people were killed in the violent denouement of the demonstrations and several major buildings in central Bangkok were torched, but in the end the demonstrators went home and the Hermes stores reopened.

In 2011 Yingluck won the the second largest electoral majority in Thai history, following that of her brother's success in 2005. Despite the turmoil surrounding her, Yingluck cut a composed figure as the country's 28th Prime Minister. But as the youngest sister of former policeman and Prime Minister Thaksin her term in power was never going to be an easy one.

Described as ruthless and untrustworthy by his critics, Thaksin is one of the world's richest men. He chose to live in exile in Dubai rather than face a term in jail in his native Thailand on corruption charges. It was Thaksin's thuggish influence that the military were keen to expunge from Thai politics.

If an election had been held, Yingluck would very likely have won. Instead, in the days following the coup she was taken to an army camp in central Thailand and temporarily detained.

Foreign Ministers around the world warned of a volatile situation on the ground. The UK, Canadian, Singaporean and some 50 other governments issued travel alerts. With five million of its citizens travelling to Bangkok every year, the Indian Embassy warned citizens to be cautious. The Australian Department of Foreign Affairs cautioned that firearms and hand-grenades had been used in attacks against protesters in the preceding months, often at night-time but also during the day in busy public areas around protest sites in central Bangkok. There had also been attacks on protestors and other violent incidents in other provinces across Thailand. Further indiscriminate attacks were considered likely.

Mirroring the advice, the Canadian government warned visitors to exercise a "high degree of caution due to ongoing large-scale political demonstrations in Bangkok and elsewhere in the country. There have been multiple incidents of violence associated with these protests, which have resulted in injuries and fatalities, including in areas adjacent to popular tourist sites and commercial centres in Bangkok. The risk of further violence remains high. There is a risk of civil unrest, sporadic violence, and attacks throughout the country. Political instability in Thailand has created a volatile and unpredictable security environment, which has persisted throughout the country, particularly in the capital, Bangkok, since November 2013. Large-scale political demonstrations and associated events such as rallies, processions and political gatherings have been taking place regularly in several Bangkok neighbourhoods, as well as in other parts of the country, including Phuket, Chiang Mai, and Surat Thani. Several incidents have resulted in deaths and injuries. Indiscriminate attacks using explosive devices and firearms have taken place in busy public areas during the day and at night. Clashes have also occurred between pro- and anti-government demonstrators. On occasion, police have responded with tear gas, water cannons and rubber bullets in their attempts to deter protesters.

"Attacks do not specifically target tourists or foreigners, but the danger of being in the wrong place at the wrong time is always present. Avoid all protest sites and movements, political events and rallies, as well as large gatherings due to the high risk that they turn violent without warning. In 2010, similar demonstrations led to violent clashes, occasionally involving the use of explosive devices, and resulted in more than 90 deaths and several injuries. Demonstrations, civil unrest, sporadic violence and attacks remain an important risk anywhere in the country at any time."

At the same time as countries issued heightened travel alerts there had also been official notices of increased terrorist threats. There are concerns that Thailand, through its trade in stolen, forged and doctored passports and other international identification papers, along with a badly managed Muslim insurgency in the south of the country which has already killed more than 6,000 people, has incubated a threat to the broader travelling public.

Most embassies advised against all but essential travel to the Muslim dominated southern provinces of Pattani, Yala, Narathiwat and parts of Songkhla, where martial law has been in place for years.

Thailand is linked to many of the world's largest terrorist attacks, including the Bali nightclub bombings in 2002 in which 102 people died, the Madrid train bombings in 2004 in which 191 people died and the Mumbai hotel bombings in 2008 in which 166 people were killed. At least two of the 298 people on board missing flight MH370 were travelling on passports which had been stolen in Phuket but never checked against INTERPOL's database of dodgy passports. A number of prominent terrorists, including personnel from jihadist groups Jemaah Islamiah and Hezbollah, have been arrested on Thai soil.

The British Foreign Office warned: "There is a high threat from terrorism. Bomb and grenade attacks have been indiscriminate, including in places visited by expatriates and foreign travellers. There have been attacks in the past in the main cities of Thailand, including in Chiang Mai in 2010 and in Bangkok in February 2012. You should remain vigilant and keep abreast of local security advice and media reports.

"Since 2004, there have been almost daily attacks in the far south of the country, including arson, bombings and shootings. Targets have included civilians and members of the security forces, government offices, tourist hotels, discos, bars, shops, marketplaces, supermarkets, schools, transport infrastructure and trains. Some foreigners have been killed and injured. The security authorities can detain suspects without charge, censor the media, conduct searches and seize documents."

The Australian government joined the international community in warning of potential terrorist attacks. "Reporting indicates that extremists may be planning to target westerners in the southern border provinces."

Despite the interruptions to their travel plans, most foreigners, sunning themselves in emptying resorts but barely cognisant of Thailand's internecine political complexities, the country's turmoil was all a somewhat distant circus.

For others it had immediate and life changing impacts, including for celebrated crime writer Jake Needham, who ended up leaving the country.

While insisting his thriller *A World of Trouble* was a work of fiction, Needham wrote of being spooked by the accuracy of his predictions of political breakdown being played out on the streets of Bangkok: "There is sometimes in fiction ... a truth that rises above the specific elements of its narrative, and I do think in that sense that *A World of Trouble* conveyed a good deal of truth. The flavour of the passions and corruption and confusion and downright stupidity that have led Thailand to where it is today are all on full display."

The endearingly flawed protagonist Jack Shepherd finds himself with only one client, Charlie Kitnarok aka Thaksin Shinawatra, the world's 98th richest man, who controls billions in personal assets. But he is also a former Prime Minister of Thailand living in exile in Dubai while plotting his return to political power; a mirror of Thaksin's own ambitions.

The book[24] begins with a high speed assassination attempt in Dubai, all filmed by CNN and broadcast worldwide, along with a plan to shift hundreds of millions of dollars out of Thailand, set amidst pithy observations such as: "There are few things that make the average Thai happier than seeing foreigners humiliated, even when that humiliation is just a figment of their imagination". The *Bangkok Post* suggested that "a society simultaneously brutal and graceful is wonderfully illustrated".

Of the 2014 coup Jake Needham wrote that the military was increasingly vilifying foreigners — claiming it was protecting Thailand from being plundered by a conspiracy involving foreign governments, principally the United States, and the international press.

In the days immediately following the coup Needham wrote: "Thailand is not now and had never been a democratic state. Too many people writing about Thailand start from the assumption the government here works like government anywhere else, that it has

---

[24] *A World of Trouble*, Jake Needham, Half Penny Ltd (Hong Kong), 16 January, 2014.

the powers the government of any other democratic state has. It doesn't. It never has. There are powerful forces in the military, the bureaucracy, and the palace that can pull down the government any time they wish. And they have done it over and over again when the people have affronted them by electing a government they don't like. The civil government elected by the people of Thailand is the least powerful institution in the country. The military takeover, its apparent endorsement by the palace, and the arrest of most of Thailand's political leaders is just the latest manifestation of that central truth."

Needham said on the whole Bangkok's middle classes were not very interested in having a democratic state and could afford the bribes they must pay for their children's education: "They are accustomed to the instant fines at police checkpoints that help the police put their children into the same schools; and they have learned constant obsequiousness requires less effort than the hard work needed to survive in a meritocratic system.

"If a determined and well-led movement to restore democratic government in Thailand arises to challenge the army, and I think it most likely will, almost certainly the country will slide into an ever-deepening spiral of violence.

"It is that simple, and that sad.

"Poor, benighted little Thailand and its people deserve better than that. But they are not likely to get it."

A month later Needham announced to his fans he was safely out of the country and was unlikely to ever write another book set there: "The military takeover of Thailand has resulted in the absolute suppression of all dissent. Hardly a day passes without yet another Orwellian pronouncement from the junta about what Thais are allowed to say and what they cannot say without risking arrest. Any comment at all about the army, the military takeover, the generals of the junta, or the palace and its acolytes is strictly forbidden, unless of course the comment amounts to unrestrained praise."

The junta moved aggressively to give themselves absolute control over who can access the internet and what they are permitted to read and to say when they do. The generals also showed their willingness to cut Thais off from international news sources any time those sources reported something about Thailand they didn't like, and the local cable and satellite television operators seem anxious to cooperate.

"By far the saddest part of the whole upheaval for me has been watching how many Thais appear desperate to be seen bowing down to their new and entirely self-appointed masters and heaping praise on the army for putting an end to democratic government and limiting their personal freedom."

By the time of the 2014 coup, which quickly gained royal assent, King Bhumibol was the world's longest reigning monarch, having ascended the throne in 1946. At 86 years of age and in poor health, the end of his long reign and uncertainty over the succession was fuelling unease throughout the kingdom.

This coup around the tone of academic and journalistic commentary owed much to journalist Paul Handley, whose book *The King Never Smiles: A Biography of Thailand's Bhumibol Adulyadej*[25] was published by Yale University Press in 2006. It was banned in Thailand prior to publication but continues to be admired around the world as the first work on the Thai king to transcend hagiography. With strict laws suppressing even the slightest criticism of the king, its publication would have seen Handley arrested if he had stayed in Thailand.

There is no secret as to why *The King Never Smiles* was banned and why Handley was unlikely to ever return. The belief in a dhammarajic or enlightened king owes more to the ancient Hindu-Brahmin belief systems of India than to Buddhism itself. On the surface this reverence is universal and unquestioned. The book argues that the Thai people's belief in the God-like nature of their king as a living Buddha has inhibited the country's development of democratic institutions and a European-style constitution, and therefore contributed to Thailand's on-going political instability and acceptance of a coup culture.

One of the very first things any tourist notices about Thailand is the king's all-pervasive influence, with his image flying from

[25] *The King Never Smiles*, Paul Handley, Yale University Press, 2006.

flag poles or encased in statuary and his portrait adorning restaurants and hotels. The country stops twice a day for the playing of the national anthem. Statues of the king and the royal family adorn villages and towns. Numerous institutions, including the Royal Thai Police and the Royal Thai Tourist Police, are named in his honour. That these institutions are dysfunctional and corrupt seems not to matter. The belief in the enlightened nature of their king, reinforced throughout his long reign, has transmogrified into a unifying belief in the superiority of Thai culture and of the Thais themselves, and fed into their worst xenophobic instincts. The unquestioning reverence for the King, sustained throughout his reign by an extensive devotion to public ritual, is the most visible aspect of a belief system which fits poorly with the multi-cultural, multi-lingual, multi-perspective and largely secular internet world of the 21st Century and has fuelled the Thais intense dislike of the millions of foreigners flooding their sacred land.

Most Western tourists come from countries where royal privilege is regarded as anachronistic and members of royalty good for little more than celebrity gossip. As a result they often failed to comprehend the profound nature of the Thais devotion to their royal family. The King is seen not just representing the nation's highest ideals, but in a sense of being them. King, country, religion and the people are indivisible. To insult one Thai is to insult them all.

Prior to the publication of *The King Never Smiles* most of the Western coverage of the Thai Royal family had been uncritical, noting his magnificent wealth, the people's devotion and the ornate beauty of royal ceremonies. But by 2014 a number of international commentators were making the observation that the people of Thailand might now be paying a high price for their beliefs.

Professor Andrew Walker of the Australian National University and co-founder of *New Mandala*, a news-centred academic website focussing on Asia, wrote: "The key problem in Thailand is that they don't have a culture of strong and stable political institutions that can manage political conflict. This is essentially due to the pre-eminent role of the monarch in Thai political life. The king has regularly been held up as a virtuous example in order to undermine the credibility of elected politicians. And over the years, the king has consistently allowed anti-democratic acts such as military coups to be performed in his name."[26]

Before Bhumibol came to power Thailand had been well on the way to developing a modern democratic system. In 1932 a mix of civil servants and soldiers overthrew the absolute monarchy of King Rama VII and replaced it with a constitutional monarchy loosely based on British institutions. The royal culture and the court's once immense wealth was largely dismantled.

But the nature of the country itself, with most of the poorly educated population living on farms and their lives centred around village life and temple ritual, made them susceptible to the idea of a virtuous and inviolate Buddhist king: "From him came all good, from seasonal rainfall to disaster relief to scientific innovation and above all justice, rather than from the bureaucratic government's elected representatives or constitutional laws. These were only sources of misery. Through disciplined training, astute image and news management, and above all dedication to an incessant regime of ritual, Bhumibol assumed this exalted role."

The King, despite his Western education, came to believe that European-style democracy, constitutionalism and capitalism only divided the people and partnered the palace with a series of army generals who pockmarked his reign with military coups and brutally corrupt administrations which exacerbated the country's social problems. An uncrossable chasm was established between the virtuous throne and virtueless politicians. Bhumibol associated with bureaucrats and soldiers, but steadfastly avoided being seen with politicians, even those in high leadership positions, unless they wore the uniforms of army generals.

Handley wrote: "Starting from the end of World War II, the remnant princes shrewdly and subtly recomposed the state and culture around the throne, just as in absolutist times. With Bhumibol as their tool, they made the throne's interests paramount over the state. Attacking not communism but the rise of liberal democracy, they entered alliances with anyone who would advance

---

[26] Video: Andrew Walker on latest Thai coup, New Mandala, 4 June 2014.

the palace's power, from brutal army bosses, drug dealers, and exploitative bankers and business monopolists to the US government and the CIA."

King Bhumibol came to power in 1946. In the same year the first United Nations narcotics conference criticised Thailand for being the only country in Southeast Asia still operating a legal government monopoly, the Royal Thai Opium Monopoly. Opium production by hill tribes in the north of the country expanded dramatically in the years following Bhumibol's ascension to the throne, and would continue in the following decades. The King sat atop a system which centralised power and made Thailand's heroin trade more efficient than its divided neighbours. Graft, patronage and power operated behind a thin veneer of Western-style bureaucracies and courts. Historically, a Hindu world view had spread eastward from India into Thailand, carrying its sensuous vision of a despotic god-king who squandered vast amounts of the national wealth on palaces, harems, and personal monuments. His oppressively conspicuous consumption was but further proof of his divine right to power. In the early years of his reign the deep involvement in the narcotics trade of two of the king's most loyal lieutenants, Generals Phao Sriyanond, former Chief of Police and Sarit Thanarat, former head of the Army, has been well documented. Both had close relationships with the Royal Household; and the trade was one of the early sources of the crown's wealth. Thailand has been a principal player in the world's heroin markets since the 1960s. The King is listed as the world's richest monarch by *Forbes Magazine*, with assets worth more than $35 billion.

Fast forward through the much exalted reign of Bhumibol to Thailand's political dramas of the 21st Century, and it was becoming clearer that the belief in a divine king may not have served the country as well as many had first believed. "His political activeness has often fomented conflict and cleaved deep fissures among his people," Handley wrote. "Although promoted as leading the way for pluralistic, liberal democracy, the palace instead became a boundary limiting it."

In an interview Handley said he accepted when he wrote the book that he would never be returning to Thailand: "Of course I would want to. It's a lovely place, I have friends there, it was a big part of my life, altogether 13 years or so. Can you really get good Thai food outside the country? But I understood in writing this book that I would not be welcomed back. I have received no warning or threat, I haven't checked whether they have me on any blacklist. I know of no charges filed in absentia. Remember, the official view of my book is, it doesn't exist. So filing charges against me would just recognise it."[27]

For the Thais, the tourist industry had once seemed like the goose that laid the golden egg, a gift which kept on giving. The number of foreigners attracted by their country's multiple appeals continued to escalate year on year no matter what scandals plagued the industry, how many deaths of foreigners there were or how much political turmoil wracked the country.

According to the UN World Tourist Organisation Thailand ranked 7th in global tourism destinations for 2012 and 2013, with revenue of $US38.3 and $42 billion respectively.

The World Travel and Tourism Council calculated that in 2013 travel and tourism generated 17 percent of the country's GDP, an estimated $US66billion.

But as the *Bangkok Post* chose to put it, the face of Thai tourism, a once blossoming, beautiful young lady, was now a middle-aged matron undergoing a midlife crisis. With continuing political unrest, months of protest, a coup and martial law, rising competition from Laos, Cambodia and Myanmar, plus a string of tourist murders, how long the lucrative industry could continue to seduce visitors was a moot point.

Deputy Governor of the Tourism Authority of Thailand Sugree Sithivanich told the newspaper that Thais and Thainess had changed for the worse in recent decades, with a litany of troubles, frauds and crimes growing as a result of the increasing greed of the people, business operators and government officials. Rising numbers of international tourists were being cheated, harassed,

---

[27] Interview with Paul Handley by Nicholas Farrelly, New Mandala, 19 September, 2007.

abused or murdered: "Thailand's tourism trade will remain a leader in the region for now but the future is quite doubtful. The key reason is that the quality and morality of Thais these days are terrible. Thai tourism won't be able to move forward if Thais don't improve their mindset. A number of tourism operators take advantage of tourists, noticeable from the increase in tourism frauds."[28]

The greatest beneficiary of Thailand' untrammelled rush into tourism and the associated property and building booms has been the King himself. His assets are managed through the Crown Property Group, which holds significant land holdings, including one third of central Bangkok, as well as substantial banking and hotel interests. He also holds a major interest in Siam Cement, which benefited enormously from the country's hyper-development.

Censorship and media control remained tight in the months following the coup. No criticism of the King was tolerated. And since the military junta had received royal assent, any criticism of the National Council for Peace and Order was a criticism of the King.

In July of 2014 General Prayuth, in his weekly televised address "Return Happiness to the People", told editors and news chiefs that if any media ran groundless reports that damaged the country, they would have to take responsibility for their actions.

"Our country is not in a normal situation," he said. "I have to call your attention to limit reports which stir or widen conflicts, including those of which the facts are not verified."

Within the country some 20 ultra-royalist groups helped to stifle dissent on the internet, including one, calling itself "The Garbage Collection Organisation", which dismissed people holding contrary views as "trash".

The king maintains his power in part through recourse to draconian lèse-majesté laws. Hundreds of people languish in Thailand's medieval prison system, many for the most minor or

---

[28] Calls for return to Thai values, Chadamas Chinmaneevong and Sriwipa Siripunyawit, Bangkok Post, 6 October, 2014.

tangential of criticisms. A crackdown on perceived slurs against the royals, and therefore against itself, was at the heart of the military junta's online surveillance operations.[29]

Since its introduction in 1932 the Constitution had contained the clause: "The king shall be enthroned in a position of revered worship and shall not be violated. No person shall expose the King to any sort of accusation or action." Over time the definition had expanded to include any criticism against any historical Thai king, any royal development project or the institution of the monarchy itself. Following the coup additional public servants were assigned to so-called "cyber patrols" with the task of crawling the internet for alleged insults to the King. Lèse majesté suspects were tried in military courts with no recourse to appeal.

Meanwhile, outside of Thailand dissident material, including lists of some of the tens of thousands of banned and blocked websites, were readily available on the internet, freely accessible to any educated Thai travelling abroad.

"Lèse majesté is our priority," said Police Major General Phisit Pao-in, head of the Technology Crime Suppression Division. "Since the coup, we were asked to intensify our surveillance and to focus on threats to national security."

The lèse majesté laws led to many absurdities and injustices, including pitting family members against one another and political opponents making the claims simply to destroy each other. One of the most absurd of all the cases was that of Australian author and university lecturer Harry Nicolaides, who was sentenced to three years imprisonment.

He went to jail for the following passage in his 2005 novel *Verisimilitude*: "From King Rama to the Crown Prince, the nobility was renowned for their romantic entanglements and intrigues. The Crown Prince had many wives 'major and minor' with a coterie of concubines for entertainment. One of his recent wives was exiled with her entire family, including a son they conceived together, for an undisclosed indiscretion. He subsequently remarried with another woman and fathered another child. It was rumoured that if

---

[29] Thai military crack down on slurs against royal family, SBS Australia, 15 June, 2014.

the prince fell in love with one of his minor wives and she betrayed him, she and her family would disappear with their name, familial lineage and all vestiges of their existence expunged forever."[30]

What made the charges even more absurd than the innocuous nature of the offending text was that *Verisimilitude* was a self-published book which had sold all of seven copies. Nicolaides, described by former Australian Democrats leader Natasha Stott Despoja as a "creative, clever soul", had, to no avail, taken the trouble prior to publication of sending a copy to the Thai Ministries of Culture and Foreign Affairs and the Bureau of the Royal Household for them to check that the contents were acceptable.

Dr David Streckfuss, an historian from the University of Wisconsin who lived in Thailand and specialised in the country's lèse majesté laws, described the Nicolaides case as more unusual than most: "It's not clear that any Thai ever read the book in the first place—and there has never before been a charge made on a novel."[31]

The dissident website Political Prisoners in Thailand records that people accused, charged and sentenced under lèse majesté laws include journalists, bloggers, academics, authors, political and social activists and average Thais. A number of foreigners have also been charged and jailed.

Their commentary became more virulent: "Just about every right-wing and military regime since 1957 has been about bolstering, enriching and protecting the symbol of dictatorship and authoritarian rule that is the monarchy. In return, the monarchy has lent its support to these regimes and become very, very wealthy. Various Thai governments have made the point that the monarchy should be untouchable and that it is universally admired and revered by all Thais. The massive expansion of censorship and

[30] Imprisoned Australian author Harry Nicolaides censored novel: Verisimilitude, *Wikileaks*, 2005.

[31] The trouble with Harry, Thornton McCamish, *The Age*, 22 November, 2008.

state vigilance showed this claim of universal reverence as patently false."

While moving quickly to re-establish order within the country, the junta also made a number of immediate moves to clean up the tourist industry; including arresting ladyboy gangs, cleaning up the haphazard development encroaching on many of the nation's most popular beaches and tightening visa controls.

The inflow of foreign capital into Thailand had been ably assisted by an open-slather approach to visas; with 30-day tourist visas provided at the airport for most nationalities and a multitude of business, retirement and other visas for those who wished to stay longer.

For years, those who found life in Thailand all too much fun could extend their stays almost indefinitely through what had become a normal part of expatriate life, "the visa run".

A land border crossing into Burma, Malaysia, Laos or Cambodia got the traveller an extra 15 days. There were seven land crossings into Malaysia, Burma three, with only day trips permitted, Laos six, including by river, and Cambodia also had six crossings.

Little more was involved than walking through Immigration one way; and then turning around and coming back. The procedure may have been inconvenient, and often enough the subject of complaint, but it was a damn sight better than going home.

A cheap return plane trip to neighbouring Malaysia, Cambodia or Laos and an application to the Thai Embassy in the respective capitals fetched an extra 60 days, no questions asked.

In any case, the Thai Immigration Department was notoriously corrupt. It was relatively easy for foreigners, even those with criminal records, to come to some sort of arrangement for, by Western standards, a perfectly reasonable fee. There were also a number of visa services prepared to help any foreigner having difficulties. And if all else failed, it didn't really matter. The maximum fine for an over stay of any length of time was 20,000 baht, about $US625, which could be paid at the airport with no difficulty. The fine was not enough to discourage the many foreigners who wanted to make Thailand their home without bothering with the tedium of forms and legal niceties.

Tightening up visa regulations was not always popular with the foreigners making Thailand their home. One senior member of the expat discussion board Thai Visa Forum, before it was shut down in the wake of the coup, speculated: "I think this country intends to keep squeezing and squeezing and squeezing until they force out most Westerners of whatever visa status. Both sides of the political debate want Westerners out. And most Thais would probably celebrate."

In the immediate aftermath of the coup there was a bewildering and inconsistent crackdown by Thai Immigration at the nation's multiple border crossings. But by July of 2014 it was clear the "visa run" was headed for extinction. The government announced tough new measures, including the blacklisting and barring from the country of those who overstayed. For the first time, an over stay of 90 days attracted a ban of one year. In cases where the foreigner did not come forward voluntarily and had overstayed for more than a year, they would be barred from the country for a decade.[32]

For the Thais themselves, finally putting restrictions on an apparently uncontrolled mob was a populist move. The locals had grown tired of the sometimes sad often colourful flotsam and jetsam of the expatriate community cluttering up the centres of their major cities and living dissolute lives in tourist locations. Farang khi nok, "bird shit foreigner", is a Thai expression referring to unkempt foreigners with little money, many of them retirees with late onset alcohol or addiction problems. Determined to drink themselves to death with a woman on their knees and surrounded by easy company, to have one last party before surrendering to the cemetery, they became a parody of themselves. And an insult to the elaborate courtesies of Thai culture.

One of the first widely publicised vows of the new junta was to banish the so-called "taxi mafias" which controlled the taxis at

---

[32] Blacklisting proposed for foreigners who overstay in Thailand, *Phuket News*, 7 July, 2014.

Suvarnabhumi Airport, Bangkok's renowned international gateway. Military spokesman Major General Nirundorn Samutsakorn said the first priority in taxi management should be at the airport for the sake of the country's image and to prevent problems such as passengers left stranded on the side of the road, over-charging and drivers acting improperly.

The most common racket involved extortion gangs screening passengers to select those who wanted to travel longer distances, such as to the beachside resorts of Pattaya or Hua Hin, both a couple of hours drive from Bangkok and substantially more profitable than a trip into the city.

Nirundorn said men in uniform were implicated and computerisation of the system was a priority to end the frequent problems experienced by passengers. "It is expected that the mafia system will disappear, as there will be no need for someone to screen passengers for taxis. I would say that we will be seeking their cooperation, but if they do not cooperate some soldiers may be stationed at the taxi queue counter."[33]

On Phuket, where scandals over the island's "taxi mafia" dated back years, a task force was consigned to the airport. Some 1,150 army, police and volunteers fanned out across the island and arrested drivers and officials.

One of the first impacts of the coup that the average holiday maker noticed was the removal of umbrellas and loungers along some of the country's best known tourist beaches. As well, restaurants and bars encroaching onto the beaches were cleared, provoking a backlash from those whose livelihood depended on them.

The moves, less dramatic than some of the other initiatives of the National Council for Peace and Order, was a heavily symbolic attempt to repair decades of environmental vandalism. The once world famous, pristine beaches of Thailand had become, with the advent of mass tourism, little more than sand based marketplaces fronting on to polluted seas. In July of 2014 clearances took place at some of Phuket's most famous beaches, including Patong, Surin,

---

[33] Taxi mafia clean out at Suvarnabhumi airport, *Bangkok Post*, 18 June, 2014.

Kamala, Kata-Karon, Nai Harn and Laem Sing. Vice Governor Jamleran Tipayapongtada said when visitors returned for the high season later in the year they would find a holiday island transformed, returned to its natural state, free of the commercial free-for-all. Similar moves took place at other tourist destinations.[34]

In one of those "only in Thailand" moments the junta also announced a crackdown on the ladyboy gangs of Pattaya. On one day alone police rounded up 50 kateoys, as they were known.[35]

Lieutenant Colonel Phairot Petchploy of the Pattaya Police said the ladyboys offered sexual services to foreigners and promptly robbed them: "They pretend to be embracing or touching the foreign tourists and then steal their phones or wallets."[36]

The transformations and tensions within Thailand had their origins in a modern day revolution in travel. For the first time, in 2012 the United Nations World Tourism Organisation recorded more than one billion international trips in a single year. Numbers grew again in 2013 to 1.087 billion, generating $US1.4 trillion worldwide. The industry was forecast to grow another five per cent in 2014.[37]

Travel was once the domain of the rich, adventurous and eccentric.

No longer.

With the growth of mass tourism, the world is on the move. Naive young and not so young travellers are more likely to be factory workers than travellers protected by wealth or experience.

Hordes of this new breed of traveller now disembark daily from giant air buses at Bangkok's Suvarnabhumi airport, often transferring straight to flights for Chiang Mai, Pattaya and Phuket.

---

[34] Army Begins Patong Beach Clearance: Umbrella Loungers To Be Banned Across Phuket, Chutima Sidasathian and Alan Morison, *Phuket Wan*, 8 July, 2014.

[35] Pattaya—'Police crack-down;--40 Ladyboys arrested! Pattaya One, 30 July, 2013.

[36] Thailand's Underworld: Drugs, Thugs and Ladyboys, *News*, 23 June, 2014.

[37] International tourism generates $US1.4 trillion in export earnings, Press Release, UN World Tourism Organisation, 14 May, 2014.

All these individuals know about Thailand is what they had read in tourist brochures or heard from friends. Far from acting as if they've just flown half way across the world to one of Earth's most exotic and dangerous destinations, they act, and dress, as if they were just heading down to their local strip of sand for a surf. Or to their local bar.

Life in Thailand is cheap. And the deaths of foreigners often go unlamented; even unrecorded. Only a smattering of the murders or accidental deaths of tourists and expatriates make it into the newspapers. Tourists are still given few warnings of the reality of the situation they are entering.

Despite the window dressing of a dedicated Tourist Police, and the recent establishment of Tourist Courts, in reality aggrieved foreigners have little or no recourse to justice. Soon enough they are gone, their personal losses swept away in the tides of their personal histories.

Just as tens of thousands of tourists depart the Kingdom's international airports each day, at the same time airbuses disgorge thousands more holiday makers with only one thing on their minds, to have as good a time as they possibly can.

Only a taxi ride away from the triumphs of functionality and style that are Bangkok, Phuket, Chiang Mai and Pattaya airports lie the nation's infamous bars, clubs and massage parlours, waiting for the next crop.

"Fruit for the picking," as the locals describe tourists.

A view beloved by foreigners, Bangkok's Chao Phraya River at night.
Picture by Weerakarn Satitnuramai

PASSPORTS

Visitors to Thailand are not warned by travel agents, airlines or their own governments that their passports are highly prized in Thailand, and stand a very good chance of being stolen.

Depending on the nationality, a passport can fetch thousands of dollars on the black market, several months pay for many Thais. There are gangs stealing passports to order. European, American, Australian and Canadian passports are particularly prized.

Foreign embassies, fearful the documents are ending up in the hands of Islamist militants and international criminal networks, have made repeated representations to the Thai government without affect.

INTERPOL Chief, Secretary General Ronald Noble describes passport fraud as the "biggest threat facing the world".[38]

But for decades the Thai authorities have done little to stop their country's blatant trade in stolen, doctored and forged documents. By inaction and complicity, Thailand has become an epicentre for the trade, a key link in international terrorist networks and a danger to the travelling public worldwide.

Forged passports from Thailand are regarded as the highest quality of any in the world.

There is an established practice across the country of bike, car, jet-ski and other rental services requiring passports as collateral. When punters return to claim their documents, they have disappeared.

With jihadist networks one of the main purchasers of fake documents, a perfectly innocent peace-loving tourist can be associated with a terrorist act, simply by leaving their passport as collateral in a hire shop while they are on holiday in Thailand. By their choice of destination, by choosing a country notorious for its lax law enforcement they can find themselves inadvertently contributing to the deaths of others.

---

[38] Preventing use of stolen passports by terrorists and criminals key to global security, says INTERPOL Chief, INTERPOL News, 24 February 2014.

No travel association explains this moral dilemma—for exactly the same reason that motivates the criminals on the other side of the ledger, the river of easy money tourists represent.

Not only is the trade in passports and fake documents fuelling terrorism and international crime gangs, it is also facilitating false job applications through counterfeit academic qualifications, bank fraud through the establishment of false identities, and illegal access to restricted areas in various companies, not just at airports.

There are few official warnings to tourists that they can expect zero help from the hire company involved in the theft of their passports, from their hotel, from the local police or from the Thai Tourist police.

Their money might be welcome, but they are not. No amount of protest will bring their documents back. The black money from the stolen passports makes the complaints or distress of a foreigner very easy to dismiss.

There has been no action taken by the police against the hire companies routinely stealing from tourists for one simple reason. The police benefit financially from the practice. Nor have Thailand's dysfunctional series of governments done anything to stop businesses demanding passports as collateral, or initiated a crackdown on the police and criminal networks involved. The trade in forged documents is not seen as impacting on the welfare of the ultra-nationalistic Thais; and therefore not an issue worthy of action.

Foreigners are forced to go through considerable inconvenience as they get their passports reissued.

Partly a result of the Thai authorities complicity in or failure to act against the trade, international embassies have seen a drain on resources as they assist their distressed and confused citizenry replace stolen passports and readjust travel schedules.

In other words, it is the tax payers in the tourist's country of origin who are ultimately paying for the well established racket of thieving passports from holidaymakers in Thailand.

The Thai Ministry of Foreign Affairs reported more than 60,000 lost or stolen passports in the period from January, 2012 to

June, 2013. According to the British Foreign Office, some 600 of their citizen's passports were stolen in Thailand in 2012-13.

Theft by hire companies is not the only way Thai criminals are procuring foreign passports.

Every sex worker in Thailand knows the exact value of a foreigner's passport. On the street, in hotel rooms, bars, clubs, massage parlours and shops, passports are lifted from travellers at any opportunity. Tourists should never make the mistake of thinking they are amongst friends.

Thai craftsmen are known as master copiers. There is, for instance, a healthy trade in fake war medals, the product being so close to the original that most collectors cannot tell the difference.

For decades any foreigner in the know who wanted to masquerade as anything from a journalist to a policeman to an airline employee has simply taken themselves to the backpacker centre of Khao San Road in Bangkok. There fake IDs, despite an international outcry, are brazenly peddled as if they were tourist trinkets rather than threats to international security.[39]

The false documents are almost impossible to differentiate from the genuine article. Their production is fast, cheap, and of remarkably high quality. And nobody has to look very far to find the pedlars.

Credible identification cards for the international police agency INTERPOL, along with America's Federal Bureau of Investigation and Drug Enforcement Agency, are readily available. Staff identification passes from multiple airlines, citizenship and driving licenses for numerous different countries, as well as diplomas and certificates from a number of prestigious universities in Australia, the UK and the US, are all on sale.

The United Nation's International Civil Aviation Authority estimates that 3.1 billion people travelled by plane in 2013. INTERPOL's record of lost or stolen passports exceeds 40 million on their database. That is 40 million possibilities of someone using

[39] Khao San Road fake Ids look like the real thing, Nirmal Ghosh, *The Nation,* 15 March 2014.

a fake identity to board a plane with the sole intention of causing as much damage and loss of life as they possibly can.

And those documents are easily purchased on the streets of Bangkok.

By 2014, with the advent of the age of terror and airline security paramount, Thailand was one of the only countries in the world where counterfeit documents were openly displayed for sale in the street for anyone who wanted to buy.

Malaysian Airways flight MH370 disappeared on a flight from Kuala Lumpur to Beijing on 8 March, 2014. There were 227 passengers and 12 crew onboard.

Malaysian officials failed to detect that a number of people boarded the plane with false documentation.

Two passports were traced to Thailand, to the island resort of Phuket where there is a thriving trade in fake passports.

In the wake of the disappearance of MH370 the world, if it had not been paying attention before, quickly learnt that Thailand was one of the world's key sources of stolen and forged passports.

Aviation expert Sylvia Wrigley, in her book *The Mystery of Malaysia Airlines Flight MH370*, suggests that a stray bullet from hijackers may have caused the plane to decompress.

Whether or not terrorism was involved in the flight's disappearance remained unclear for many months. But the revelation that some of the passengers were travelling on false passports set security organisations scrambling to the Thai resort of Phuket.

A once quiet and particularly picturesque island with an economy based around fishing boats and small farms, by 2014 Phuket was swamped with more than a million tourists a month and its landscapes utterly transformed.

Italian Luigi Maraldi and Austrian Christian Kozel were both surprised to find themselves listed on the passenger manifest of the missing flight.[40]

---

[40] Missing plane highlights Phuket's stolen passport trade, Lindsay Murdoch, *The Age*, 3 September 2014.

On a trip to Phuket in 2013 the Italian had his passport stolen from a car rental agency. At the time he was being caught up in the greatest aviation mystery of modern times Maraldi, 37, was once again holidaying in Thailand. [41]

The Italian said he lost his passport on a vacation the previous year, in a motorcycle rent shop deal gone wrong. He said the woman at the shop had told him she gave his passport to another man. Having returned home to Italy on temporary travel documents, he said he learnt of the Malaysian flight going missing when his family rang to check whether he was the same Luigi Maraldi on the flight's manifest.[42]

Austrian Christian Kozel, a 61-year-old retired massage therapist from Salzburg in Germany was informed of the missing flight when the police came knocking on the door of his apartment. He said his passport was stolen at Phuket airport two years earlier during a moment of inattention. Kozel said he had been through considerable difficulty to procure an emergency passport and get back to his native Austria, but had since almost forgotten about the incident.

The two passengers travelling on passports stolen on Phuket were both Iranians, Pouri Nourmohammadi, 18, and Delavar Syed Mohammad Reza, 29.[43]

The two men were believed to have travelled from their home countries to Phuket, where they had purchased the stolen passports for around $US10,000.

Both INTERPOL and the Malaysian government claimed the men did not appear to be involved in terrorist activity, but simply wanted to live in Europe, one to join his mother.

The pair, who were friends, entered Malaysia using valid Iranian passports.

---

[41] Missing plane highlights Phuket's stolen passport trade, Lindsay Murdoch, *The Age*, 3 September 2014.

[42] Italian Man Luigi Maraldi reveals how his passport used on flight MH370 was stolen in bizarre circumstances in Thailand, 10 March, 2014, *News*.

[43] Picture supplied by INTERPOL

Dr Carl Ungerer of Queensland's Bond University said: "To buy a stolen passport in Thailand in order to go to Europe is not something you do accidentally. You want to be able to make sure the person sitting next to you on a plane is travelling on a legitimate travel document. MH370 has thrown into sharp relief the flourishing black market in false passports in Southeast Asia."[44]

INTERPOL declared that while the passports had been entered into their Stolen and Lost Travel Documents (SLTD) database there were no checks by any country, and INTERPOL was therefore unable to determine how many times the passports had been used to board flights or cross borders.[45]

The SLTD database was created in 2002 following the September 11, 2001 terrorist attacks. It was aimed at helping countries secure their borders and protect citizens from terrorists and other criminals known to use fraudulent travel documents. By 2014 the database had grown from a few thousand passports to more than 40 million entries from 167 countries and had more than 800 million searches per year.

But a number of countries, including Thailand and Malaysia, do not systematically search INTERPOL's databases.[46] In an official statement INTERPOL's Secretary General Ronald Noble said it was clearly of great concern that any passenger was able to board an international flight using a stolen passport. The failure of countries to systematically use the SLTD database had left a major gap in the global security apparatus which was then vulnerable to exploitation by criminals and terrorists.

"This is a situation we had hoped never to see," Noble said.

"For years INTERPOL has asked why should countries wait for a tragedy to put prudent security measures in place at borders and boarding gates. Now, we have a real case where the world is

---

[44] Missing Malaysia Airline flight: How MH370 will change travel, Anthony Dennis, *Sydney Morning Herald*, 18 April, 2014.

[45] INTERPOL confirms at least two stolen passports used by passengers on missing Malaysian Airlines flight 370 were registered in its databases, INTERPOL, 9 March 2014.

[46] Thailand exposed as crime hub over MH370 passports, Amelie Bottollier-Depois, Agence France Presse, 11 March 2013.

speculating whether the stolen passport holders were terrorists, while INTERPOL is asking why only a handful of countries worldwide are taking care to make sure that persons possessing stolen passports are not boarding international flights."

He pointed out that in 2013 passengers were able to board planes more than a billion times without having their passports screened against INTERPOL'S database. There was a predicted increase in international travel to 1.5 billion passengers a year by 2017.

"If Malaysia Airlines and all airlines worldwide were able to check the passport details of prospective passengers against INTERPOL's database, then we would not have to speculate whether stolen passports were used by terrorists to board MH370," Noble said. "We would know that stolen passports were not used by any of the passengers to board that flight.

"For the sake of innocent passengers who go through invasive security measures prior to boarding flights in order to get to their destination safely, I sincerely hope that governments and airlines worldwide will learn from the tragedy of missing flight MH370 and begin to screen all passengers' passports prior to allowing them to board flights. Doing so will indeed take us a step closer to ensuring safer travel."

In a pointed reference to Thailand he said countries which placed an emphasis on protecting their borders from terrorists, money launderers and other criminals provided a safer and more stable environment and were therefore in a stronger position to ensure the sustainable development of their economies and societies.

Former commander of the Royal Hong Kong Police Criminal Intelligence Bureau and an expert on terrorist financing Steve Vickers said Thailand had become the epicentre for the worldwide trade in false documents because under Thai law it was difficult to prosecute. A complainant under trademark legislation was required. Vickers said stolen and counterfeit passports were providing a very lucrative revenue source for criminal organisations and called on the Thai government to take action.

"I must say that I am quite surprised at the blatant manner in which these fake documents are sold on the streets," he said. "I see many instances of identical documents being used in fraudulent bank loan applications or in attempts to obtain credit through false pretences or in support of other fraudulent activity.

"The airline staff identification papers and US driving licenses which I saw are scarier, however. This is because in many US states all you need to buy a firearm is a current driving license. They may do a quick check, but in practice they often don't, and the holder of the fake card walks away with a semi-automatic firearm in his hands. Likewise, fake airline passes used in a third-world environment may facilitate access to restricted areas." [47]

In an effort to boost tourism 2014 was named "Visit Malaysia" year. To no avail. The publicity could hardly have been worse.

Malaysian Home Minister Datuk Seri Ahmad Zahid Hamidi said they skipped checks against INTERPOL's database because it would have slowed down the clearance of passengers.[48] He claimed Malaysian Immigration computers could not handle the global data base of 40.2 million entries but immigration officers guarding the country's entry points were trained by other countries, including the US, Canada, Australia and the UK and had met "world standards".

INTERPOL hit back at Home Minister Zahid's claims of competence, saying Malaysia's decision not to consult INTERPOL's database before allowing travellers to enter the country or board planes could not be defended by falsely blaming technology.[49] In an official statement, INTERPOL declared: "If there is any responsibility or blame for this failure, it rests solely with Malaysia's Immigration Department.

---

[47] Thailand a Hotbed for Fake and Stolen Passports, *Wall Street Journal*, 9 March 2014.

[48] Minister: Using INTERPOL database may have slowed down immigration checks, *The Daily Mail*, 27 March 2014.

[49] INTERPOL rejects claim attributed to Malaysia that checking INTERPOL's databases may have slowed immigration checks, INTERPOL News, 28 March 2014.

"INTERPOL's SLTD database takes just seconds to reveal whether a passport is listed, with recent tests providing results in 0.2 seconds.

"The fact is that the US consults this database more than 230 million times per year; the UK more than 140 million times; the UAE more than 100 million times and Singapore more than 29 million times. Not one of these countries, or indeed any INTERPOL member country, has ever stated that the response time is too slow.

"The truth is that in 2014 prior to the tragic disappearance of Malaysia Airlines Flight MH370, Malaysia's Immigration Department did not conduct a single check of passengers' passports against INTERPOL's databases.

"Malaysia's Immigration Department owes it to all passengers boarding flights originating in, or passing through, Malaysia to make sure that passports registered as stolen or lost in INTERPOL's databases cannot be used to board any flight.

"In this regard, despite this unjustified attack on INTERPOL, we remain ready, willing and able to help Malaysia better safeguard its citizens and visitors from those seeking to use stolen or fraudulently altered passports to board planes."

Back in Phuket, where the stolen passports originated, veteran journalist Lindsay Murdoch recorded that the "curious" thefts of the passports were a focus for a team of FBI investigators flying from the United States to assist Malaysian and other international investigators. "Hundreds of passports are lost or stolen on Phuket each year, raising fears they could fall into the hands of criminal or terrorist networks," Murdoch wrote. "Honorary consuls representing countries there often deal with tourists who report their passports missing."

One of the most publicly outspoken of all the diplomats, Australian Honorary Consul Larry Cunningham, said: "Some passports were certainly lost, falling out of pockets or being genuinely misplaced. But there were also substantial incidents of passports being stolen."

The *Phuket Gazette* reported that senior police claimed they were powerless to stem the trade but were trying to "stymie the fallout" from the stories.

"Something needs to be done, especially after learning that these ... passports were used to board the plane," Phuket Provincial Police Deputy Commander Arayapan Pukbuakao said. "We are looking into what measures we can take, but as far as I know, there is no law in Thailand prohibiting foreigners from handing his or her own passport to another person to hold as per their own agreement."

The Colonel said he would initiate a campaign to stop vehicle rental operators from holding passports. But as the newspaper observed, "Such campaigns have been held time and again in Phuket, usually resulting from a collective, concerted push by ambassadors and honorary consuls."[50]

Thailand's trade in forged, stolen and doctored passports was ringing alarm bells among international security experts, airlines and immigration authorities long before the disappearance of MH370.[51]

International news outlets including CNN had repeatedly highlighted the issue in the preceding years, but far from the media coverage shaming Thai authorities into action, instead each news story acted as an advertisement, boosting the trade. The number of places selling forged documents increased, the displays got bigger and the range of products on offer broader. No action was taken by the police or other authorities. The international publicity simply attracted yet more customers from abroad.

The trade had started in Thailand decades before with student cards sold by travel agencies near the Malaysia Hotel in Bangkok. The cheap hotel, 10 minutes walk from the major business thoroughfare of Sathon, was a backpacker haven in the 1960s and 70s in a sprawling low rise city which had barely begun to discover the tourist dollar.

---

[50] Raging Phuket black market passport trade, *Phuket Gazette*, 16 March, 2014.

[51] The global passport security loophole: how serious is it? David Beirman. *The Conversation*. 14 March 2014.

While upmarket condominiums, hotels and the internationally famous gay sauna, Babylon, have all sprung up around it since then, the Malaysia Hotel itself remains almost identical in appearance to 40 years ago.[52] Except that its corridors are no longer filled with long haired travellers exchanging stories about the wiles of Afghanistan while comparing the quality of marijuana and hashish. Instead a mix of elderly Americans and British on retirement incomes, a smattering of gay massage workers and customers, and random travellers looking for cheap accommodation now grace its time-worn foyer.

Originally the budget travellers at the Malaysia Hotel, with the full cooperation of nearby travel agents, used the fake student cards to buy discounted airline tickets. To the adventurous but money conscious travellers of the day, it all seemed innocent enough.

Then the trade took off.

By the 1980s the easily faked student cards made way for the far more lucrative product of forged passports. At the time most businesses required supporting identification before converting then widely used and easily stolen traveller's cheques into cash, and false passports were therefore in demand.

Because many tourists kept their valuables in their luggage or left them in hotel rooms, where they mistakenly believed their belongings would be safer, several gangs employed prostitutes, hotel staff, tour bus attendants and others to steal them.

The forgeries were less sophisticated than those of later years, but they were usually good enough.

In the month prior to the disappearance of MH370 there was a spate of stories around the world on the ready availability of high quality faked documents in Thailand following an expose in the leading Bangkok based expatriate news and lifestyle magazine *Big Chilli*.

Just as journalists everywhere build on the work of each other, so the magazine's research provided background information for

---

[52] Malaysia Hotel. Courtesy TravelPod

other news outlets alerted to the issue by MH370, including *The Guardian* in Britain.

When traveller's cheques became almost obsolete in the late 1990s the Thai gangs began to focus on passport fraud, which with the rise of militant Islam and a flood of foreign criminals wanting to make Thailand their home, showed great money-making potential.

The gangs got in touch with foreigners who were looking for stolen passports. And thus began a long and profitable relationship.

"Some of these foreigners are still here and running the passport fraud gangs," *Big Chilli* reported. "Today the way the business works is that thieves steal passports from tourists and sell them to Thai or foreign criminals. Some lost and stolen passports are sent from abroad to the foreign gangs. The worldwide demand for fraudulent passports means that these gangs will continue to operate in Thailand as long as they can evade international and local law enforcement agencies."[53]

Feature writer with *The Guardian* Jon Henley wrote that Thailand's trade in forged and doctored travel documents was propping up criminal activity around the world, supporting enterprises from human trafficking to terrorism: "The gangs have targeted Thailand mainly because of the very large numbers of European, US and Australian holidaymakers who travel there every year."[54]

The sheer volume of tourists made for easy pickings.

Other experts agree. Dr Peter Chalk, Senior Political Institute at the RAND Institute, said: "Thailand is one of the world's main hubs for fake ID papers though there are others such as Russia, India, Dubai, South Africa and Nigeria. Corruption, a free-wheeling capitalist market, an internationally-linked transportation infrastructure, weak law enforcement and very high through flows of tourists/travellers are the major factors that have stimulated the

---

[53] Thailand's crime-busters set sights on passport fraud gangs, Maxmilian Wechsler, *Big Chilli*, 15 August, 2012.

[54] How Thailand's trade in fake passports fuels crime gangs around the world, Jon Henley, *The Guardian*, 11 March 2014.

trade. I believe a good quality western passport can be bought for around $10,000."[55]

*Man advertising false documents on the
backpacker mecca of Khao San Road in Bangkok.
Picture courtesy of Big Chilli Magazine.*

Big Chilli's article, "Khao San's fake document industry", noted that while the trade was the subject of international condemnation and more clandestine aspects of the operation occurred behind closed doors, the streets of one of Bangkok's oldest tourist areas remained its' most visible portal: "The stalls offering counterfeit documents blend effortlessly into the pandemonium of Khao San Road, best known as a haven for backpackers in Southeast Asia, with its cheap hotels, guesthouses, internet cafes, restaurants, travel agencies and tattoo parlours. It is nothing new to find these stalls among the other vendors selling a tremendous variety of merchandise..."

In the 1970s Khao San Road was part of the so-called Coca Cola trail, where heroin and marijuana, the famous China White and Thai Sticks respectively, could be "scored" within minutes, if not seconds. Ragged backpackers and hippies sat eating banana

---

[55] Interview with author, 6 May, 2014.

pancakes in makeshift restaurants and surrounding hostels catered for the "under-five dollar a day" crowd.

Five dollars doesn't buy you much on Khao San Road anymore.

Still a tourist mecca, it now caters more for the so-called "glampackers", backpackers with money, offspring of the West's middle classes on their almost obligatory world tours prior to settling into a life of study, work and children. They cluster in the crowded streets of places like Khao San Road as if to repel the vast foreignness of the Asia beyond. The only Thais they ever meet are hotel staff, shop keepers, street vendors, touts and taxi drivers.

Drugs are no longer readily available, no bars remain where heroin can be bought as easily as a beer, and the only aging hippies in sight stand out from the thronging crowds of Westerners like relics from a medieval age.

Khao San Road, Bangkok.
Picture courtesy of the blogsite American Expat Chiangmai.

Foreign police and security experts have repeatedly warned that the fake identity documents originating in Thailand, coupled with stolen and altered or forged passports were being used by terrorists to gain access to the European Union and other countries.

"We are really concerned about this matter," a foreign police liaison officer told *Big Chilli.* "We have evidence, and so do the Thai authorities. Criminals and terrorists know they can go to Khao San Road and get a good quality counterfeit document quickly. The quality of the fakes is getting better and the activity represents a serious threat to the security of many countries."

The officer, acting as a spokesman for the intelligence community, said the number of passports reported stolen from foreigners living around the Khao San Road area had been high for years. This applied particularly to passports from EU countries.

"Stolen or bought passports obtained in Thailand – with a corroborating counterfeit ID, like a driving license – make it possible to enter an EU country," he said. "The holder of the altered passport must make sure they don't enter the country the passport was issued in because its theft would have been reported to that country's authorities.

"Anyone who steals a passport in Bangkok can then freely travel through all the other 25 Schengen countries. No visa between these countries is required and it's not necessary to show a passport while crossing to a different Schengen country, only a form of ID is enough. Again, the EU country where the stolen passport originated must be avoided."

Some countries, such as Italy, take as little as five seconds on average to check the travel documents of those crossing their borders from neighbouring countries.

The term "Schengen" originates from a 1985 agreement signed near the town of Schengen in Luxembourg and proposed the abolition of border checks at the borders of signatory countries.[56]

The borderless Schengen area consists of 26 countries with a population of more than 400 million and covers more than four million square kilometres.[57]

---

[56] Fortress Europe, BBC World Service.

[57] The Schengen Area, European Commission, 12 December 2008.

The countries with free movement across their borders are: Austria, Belgium, Czech Republic, Denmark, Estonia, Finland, France, Germany, Greece, Hungary, Iceland, Italy, Latvia, Liechtenstein, Lithuania, Luxembourg, Malta, Netherlands, Norway, Poland, Portugal, Slovakia, Slovenia, Sweden, Spain and Switzerland.

Illegal immigration into these countries is big business, and the forgers find a ready market, including from the Arab states.

With the initial flurry of news stories linking the disappearance of Flight MH370 to Thailand's trade, Indochina Bureau Chief for *The Straits Times* Nirmal Ghosh decided to take himself off to Khao San Road to see for himself. A nervousness had overtaken the normally brazen business. While the vendors peddling false IDs were normally clearly visible on the main street, touts now led potential customers up to the vendors positioned in nearby streets. Masquerading as a buyer, Ghosh was quickly shown a large album.[58]

"In it there were well over 100 samples of identity cards, from driving licenses to student passes to airline crew passes and many others. There was even an INTERPOL ID card and a Singapore identity card. When I expressed surprise he stared and said: 'Are you INTERPOL? Are you INTERPOL?' But I laughed it off. I chose a Singapore driving licence and a Qatar Airways crew card. They cost 800 baht each."

Eight hundred baht is around $US25, not much to pay for a change of identity.

After an hour and a half's wait Ghosh had in his hands a spanking new Singapore driving licence and a Qatar Airways crew card. The only difference from the real Singapore licence was the absence of holograms. "Yet, on the face of it, the cards were startlingly realistic."

The complicity of the Thai authorities in the trade in false papers was never in doubt. Fake identification cards have normally been sold directly in front of the local Chanasongkram Police

---

[58] Fake Singapore driver's licence just like the real deal except no hologram, *The Straits Times*, 13 March 2013.

Station, which fronts directly onto Khao San Road. A giant screen shows two police patrolmen and the words "24-Hour Protection and Services".

There was ample warning of the dangers of the passport trade even prior to the disappearance of Flight MH370.

The Bali bombings of 2002, executed by jihadist group Jemaah Islamiyah in or near popular nightclubs in the tourist district of Kuta, killed 202 people and injured 240.

There was a Thai connection.

The death toll by nationality was: 88 Australians, 38 Indonesians, 27 Britons, 7 Americans, 6 Swedish citizens and 3 Danish citizens.[59]

Military head of jihadist group Jemaah Islamiyah and alleged mastermind of the Bali bombings Riduan Isamuddin, better known as Hambali, was an Afghan war veteran often described as the Osama bin Laden of South East Asia.[60] Trusted by Al Quaida itself, he was close to the planners of the Twin Towers terrorist attacks.

According to Western intelligence sources Hambali had an ongoing association with Muslim cleric Abu Bakar Bashir, fellow mastermind of the Bali bombings.[61] Hambali was captured in a joint CIA and Thai police operation on 11 August 2003.

Ayutthaya, the old capital located in the Chao Phraya river valley where Hambali was apprehended, has a stronger Muslim presence than any other Thai city. It was originally settled in the 17th Century by Muslim traders from India, Malaysia and the Middle East. Many Thai Muslims send their children to university in Egypt or Saudi Arabia, where the fundamentalist sect of Islam known as Wahhabism originated; and there are fears they may become radicalised before returning to Thailand, and to centres such as Ayutthaya. Once one of the largest cities in the world, it fell into decline after being destroyed by the Burmese in 1767. Beginning in the early 1970s, in less than 50 years Ayutthaya, much like the rest

---

[59] Remembering Bali Ten Years On, Shandon Harris-Hogan, *The Conversation*, 12 October 2012.

[60] Hambali. Source: CIA.

[61] We will fight until we run out of blood, Tony Parkinson, *The Age*, 15 October, 2002.

of the country, went from being a sleepy backwater where foreigners were conspicuous by their rarity, to a bustling centre and tourist destination. The Islamic population has been bolstered in the 21st Century by people fleeing the Islamist violence of Thailand's southern provinces. It is an easy place for foreigners to hide.

When arrested Hambali was reported to be wearing jeans, a t-shirt, sunglasses and a baseball cap, and to be in the company of his common law wife. He envisioned creating a Muslim super-state, or caliphate, across South East Asia, including Thailand, with a population of more than 400 million.[62] He was carrying a fake Spanish passport he had purchased in Bangkok.

The Bali bombings exposed the fact that radical Islamists were using safe houses across Southeast Asia, particularly in Thailand and Cambodia. Hambali had made full use of the system. The country's open borders, chaotic politics, loose government structures and dysfunctional municipal systems, combined with widespread corruption within the military and the police force, made the country the perfect place for terrorist groups to operate. The ready availability of forged and doctored documents turned it into paradise.

Hambali's associate Mohammed Nazir Bin Lep, also known as Lillie or Suicide Ali, was arrested in Bangkok only hours before Hambali was taken into custody.[63] The American government accused him of helping Hambali to plan operations, case targets and transfer money.

Both Hambali and Lillie are reported to have been tortured in a Thai detention facility during the days following their arrest. They were then flown out of the country to Afghanistan via Sri Lanka on a privately owned Gulfstream jet N85VM contracted from DynCorp by the CIA, where the torture is believed to have continued.

---

[62] The quest for SE Asia's Islamic 'super' state, CNN, 29 August, 2002.

[63] The Rendition Project, Mohammed Nazir Bin Lep.

There are few reliable reports of the two men's whereabouts until their transferral from the CIA secret prison system to Guantanamo Bay in 2006, where they remain. [64]

Hambali's arrest was heralded as a significant victory in the war on terror. [65]

At the time of his arrest Hambali was alleged to be planning a series of attacks centred around the October, 2003 Asia-Pacific Economic Co-operation meeting in Bangkok; including hotels and embassies. Leaders who attended the conference included: Russian President Vladimir Putin, American President George Bush, Australian Prime Minister John Howard, Vietnamese Prime Minister Phan Van Khai, Chinese President Hu Jintao, South Korean President Roh Moo-hyun, Indonesian President Megawati Sukarnoputri, Japanese Prime Minister Junichiro Koizumi, Mexican President Vicente Fox and Thai Prime Minister Thaksin Shinawatra.

In a joint statement the leaders committed themselves to ensuring the security of their peoples and agreed that transnational terrorism posed a direct threat to APEC's vision of free, open and prosperous economies: "Dismantle, fully and without delay, transnational terrorist groups that threaten the APEC economies... Strengthen our joint efforts to curb terrorist threats against mass transportation. Increase and better coordinate our counter-terrorism activities, where appropriate, through effective collaboration, technical assistance."[66]

Two months prior to Hambali's arrest then Thai Prime Minister Thaksin Shinawatra announced the detention of several senior Jemaah Islamiah operatives planning a bombing spree around the Summit. Plans included hitting the Australian, Israeli, United States, British and Singaporean embassies and tourist spots such as

---

[64] The Rendition Project, Riduan Isamuddin (Hambali).

[65] The capture of Hambali, *Sydney Morning Herald*, 16 August, 2003.

[66] 2003 Leader's Declaration, Bangkok Declaration – A World of Differences: Partnership for the Future, Bangkok, Thailand, Asia-Pacific Economic Cooperation, 21 October, 2003.

Khao San Road, Bangkok's red light district of Nana, and the holiday destinations of Phuket and Pattaya.

In the wake of Hambali's detention then Thai Prime Minister Thaksin Shinawatra declared that all JI leaders had been rounded up. He promised to toughen immigration procedures and curb the widespread availability of fake passports.

Thai police had previously viewed forgery as a petty crime. But under pressure from Western governments after the September 11 attacks and the clear evidence of the black market that had aided Hambali, the authorities began to act. The most commonly seized fakes were Belgian, French, Portuguese and Spanish passports, which Thai police said were easily copied. Up to 90 percent of fake passports leaving Thailand were bound for London, where the growth of terrorist networks and home grown Islamic radicalisation were already of massive concern to national security.[67]

In 2004 Mohammad Ali Hossein, the counterfeiter who supplied Hambali with a forged passport, was arrested. The Thai Immigration Police Bureau, which oversaw the investigation, declared: "The people who use these fake passports are terrorists, fugitives and people illegally transferring or laundering money or opening bank accounts."

But Hossein's arrest did not stop the trade.

Authorities reported that a number of highly sophisticated counterfeit rings continued to operate in Thailand, run by Thais, Iranians, Burmese and Bangladeshis utilising stolen passports, visas and immigration stamps, as well as passports that the counterfeiters had bought off tourists. Travellers down on their luck and looking for a quick buck could sell their passports, American and European passports fetching the best price. The practice was one of the reasons behind embassies worldwide raising the price for replacement passports.[68]

---

[67] Thailand Now Fake Passport Capital for Criminal Underworld, Terrorists, Alisa Tang, AP Writer, 8 September, 2005.

[68] Fugitives in Thailand, Jason Armbrecht, 10 November, 2008, Thailand Law Forum.

Thai police seized 353 such passports from a Greek courier en route to London in March 2004.

A further 100 passports were confiscated in February of 2005 from a Spaniard and Dutchman trying to sell them to an undercover policeman in Bangkok.

Another 452 were taken from Algerian-born Briton Mahieddine Daikh, who was going to deliver them to London in early August.

That year both Thai and foreign police forces attempted to bring attention to the issue by making public statements that Thailand had emerged as one of the world's main sources of passports for fraudsters, fugitives and terrorists, including al-Qaida.

In 2007 almost 250 fake passports were discovered at Suvarnabhumi Airport.

Immigration officials received help from a $10 million passport verifying machine. But with airport workers granted an average of 45 seconds to determine the validity of a passport, a measure designed to facilitate the passage of tourists, and no cross checking against INTERPOL databases, Thailand remained an easy place to enter and exit using a false identity.

In 2008 there were several sweeps on passport counterfeit rings. An April raid netted 1300 passports.

In May authorities netted 20,904 fake passports, along with 200 genuine US passports, in the nation's biggest raid on false documents.

Twelve people were arrested, including the leader, a Myanmar national. All were charged with falsifying documents and trafficking in drugs and weapons.

The gang's clients were believed to be from South Africa and South Asia. Commander of the Thai Immigration Police Lieutenant General Chatchawal Suksomjit said most of the fake passports were at various stages of manufacture. But 2,300 of them were completed passports from France, Suriname, Norway, Belgium, Italy and Myanmar.[69]

Also by 2008 police officials from eight different countries were meeting monthly in Bangkok with the Thai police to discuss passport forgery and other identity fraud issues.

---

[69] Thai police seize nearly 21,000 fake passports, AFP, 9 May, 2008.

In December 2010 three Pakistani nationals were arrested, suspected of running a forged passport gang and believed to be linked to terrorist groups.[70]

The forgery gang operated with impunity in Thailand for 10 years under the protection of powerful individuals, according to the Thai Department of Special Investigations. The arrests created headlines around the world after the forgery gang, which had connections in Europe, was linked to terrorist groups in Spain responsible for the 2004 Madrid train bombings and several other bombing and arson attacks."

The gang of master forger, Pakistani Muhammed Ather Butt, was believed to number at least 10 associates and have close relationships with Spanish racketeers. After his detention seven men, six Pakistanis and one Nigerian, were arrested in Barcelona and accused of providing fake identification documents to groups linked to al-Qaeda.

In a major investigation, the *Bangkok Post* reported: "The gang also allegedly provided forged passports for the Pakistan-based Lashkar-e-Taiba group, which has been accused of plotting the November, 2008, Mumbai attacks, in which 10 militants killed at least 166 people. They also allegedly supplied passports to the defeated Liberation Tigers of Tamil Eelam separatist group in Sri Lanka."

Head of the DSI investigation, using the codename Agent Suerte, told the newspaper Pakistani, Iranian and gangs from other countries would look for a Thai lady to support their criminal activities by opening bank accounts and renting a post box or apartment in their name. He said the operation's leader "found a Thai girlfriend, learned the Thai language and other culture and also established good relations with certain Thai authorities to give him protection. He learned how to survive in Thailand while doing this type of business. You can't usually do such business in Thailand unless you know some officials."

---

[70] Operation Alpha: The inside story of how DSI investigators helped shut down an international forgery ring that faked documents to terrorists and other criminal elements for a decade, *Bangkok Post*, 12 December, 2010.

Butt's business grew until he became the most famous passport forger in Thailand.

"Everyone in the business admired him," the Head of the DSI Investigation said. "He was well connected to the authorities; had a lot more money, more than anyone else in this business, and his network reportedly involved Iran, India and other countries. He has been doing this business for 10 years, so you can imagine how big his network and how many customers he had."

Butt was reported to have never opened a shop but would drive a car to meet his customers and often sit with people inside the car and talk. He went to the post office to send the passports. Sometimes he went to Soi 3 off Sukhumvit Road, an area of Bangkok where Arabic is widely spoken and Middle Eastern restaurants dominate.[71]

Investigators described Butt's room as like a small factory, with computers, a high-definition scanner and printer. There were almost 1,000 pieces of evidence, including photos, passports, counterfeit data pages for EU, Canadian, Chinese and Israeli passports and visa stickers for the US and Schengen countries. Among the seizures were more than 100 passport-sized photographs of people of Middle Eastern appearance.

The Head of the DSI Investigation said Butt chose Thailand as a base because "you can negotiate with some law enforcement people. It is easy to enter and leave the country, and, importantly some people don't regard passport forgery as a serious offence. They counterfeit only foreign passports but not Thai, so why should we worry, is their attitude."

Thai Department of Special Investigation's agent Tinawut Slilapat said there were around 20 groups operating in 2010, often headed by criminals from south Asia or the Middle East, which were engaged in various forms of passport fraud in Thailand.

They used passports stolen in Thailand but also in countries such as Spain, France and Belgium, added new photographs, data

---

[71] Soi 3, Bangkok. Picture by Aimaimyi. Courtesy Wikimedia Commons.

pages and signatures, and sold them to customers who either travelled to Thailand to buy the documents or sent couriers.[72]

Almost all the passports were used to commit crimes outside Thailand.

The gangs were dealing in such high volumes that they could afford simply to wait until a potential client showed up of approximately the right age and appearance for their preference, an undoctored, stolen passport.

While estimates ranged up to $US10,000 for fake passports, depending on circumstance, nationality, condition and the number of years left to run, Tinawut said they typically sold for between $1,500 and $3,000. Italian, British, Spanish and other European passports fetch about $1,000, Tinawut said, while Israeli passports cost $1,500-$2,000 and Canadian could go for up to $3,000.

"There is still huge demand for passports, and identity fraud is a tool to support other criminal activities," Tinawut said.

Thailand's Department of Special Investigations cracked another counterfeiting ring in June of 2012. The gang was accused of issuing some 3,000 falsified passports and visas over the five years of its existence. Two of the passports were used by Iranians convicted of carrying out a series of botched bomb attacks in Bangkok in February of 2012. One of the men lost his limbs as he hurled an explosive device at police. The pair were among five Iranians suspected of involvement in bomb attacks in India and Georgia targeting Israeli diplomats. They were ultimately sentenced to between 15 years and life.

The counterfeiting gang's alleged ringleader, Iranian-born Seyed Paknejad, 45, was arrested but jumped bail and fled, on a fake Turkish passport, to Malaysia where he was re-arrested in 2013 carrying 17 stolen New Zealand passports. Thailand subsequently asked for his extradition.

The Global Terrorism Index, a project run by the privately funded think tank Institute for Economics & Peace, ranked

---

[72] Thailand's crime busters set sights on passport fraud gangs, Maxmilian Welscher, *Big Chilli*, 15 August, 2012.

Thailand as the most dangerous country in Southeast Asia for terrorism, and the eighth most dangerous in the world.

The Index, claimed as the best dataset on terrorism available, was based on information collected by the USA's National Consortium for the Study of Terrorism and Responses to Terrorism (START) and relates to the period 2002 to 2011. It showed that nations severely affected by terrorism share high levels of corruption.

The Index took in a basket of 158 countries and measured the impact of terrorism through the number of incidents, deaths, injuries and the level of property damage.

Thailand accounted for five per cent of the world's terrorist incidents.

Much of Thailand's poor ranking was due to Southeast Asia's longest running and most dangerous insurgency, in the Muslim southern provinces adjacent to the Malaysian border. More than 6,000 people had been killed since 2004, including school teachers and Buddhist monks. Explosive devices had been found in tourist areas and feared to be linked to the southern insurgency. The provinces are separated from the rest of the country by ethnic, cultural and religious differences. Administratively and socially there is little connection to the rest of the country. In a predominantly Buddhist country there is little sympathy for or understanding of the Muslim minority in the south. Ethnically the population is closer to the Malaysians than to the dominant Thai population.

There is a difference of emphases between various writers on the links between Thailand's fake passport trade, the southern insurgency and the international terrorist threat.

Professor Rohan Gunaratna, head of the International Centre for Political Violence and Terrorism Research in Singapore, is the author and editor of 12 books including *Inside Al Qaeda: Global Network of Terror*, an international bestseller. He co-authored *The Terrorist Threat from Southern Thailand: Jihad or Quest for*

Justice?[73] The book argued there was strong potential for the localised insurgency in southern Thailand to be sucked into the global jihad and to spread to neighbouring countries, including Malaysia, the Philippines, Singapore and Indonesia.

Gunaratna said the trade was centred in Thailand because the scale of human trafficking in Thailand "was huge" and "law enforcement weak".[74] While Africa and Latin America also had trades in forged passports, Thailand's quality of printing was the best in the world. He argued that Thailand lacked the capacity to address the issue, and rather than criticise the international community needed to work with and support Thailand in dealing with the problem.

"There is an infrastructure of agents who provide passage for people who travel to North America, Europe, Australia and New Zealand," Gunaratna said. "Terrorist and criminal groups have used Thailand for this purpose."

He said a specialist organisation or task force to combat forgery and theft of travel and identity documents needed to be established in Thailand made up of intelligence, military and law enforcement agencies.

"It is important for this organisation not to be just police, it must include military and intelligence services," Gunaratna said. "It would be a huge mistake to make it just police; if combined they cannot be easily corrupted. Police can be threatened, the military can kill anyone who threatens them."

Other scholars argue that the southern insurgency is more intranational than international in consequence, and has been poorly managed by the body politic.

Duncan McCargo, author of *Tearing Apart the Land: Islam and Legitimacy in Southern Thailand* and most recently *Mapping National Anxieties: Thailand's Southern Conflict*, is dismissive of any attempt to link the southern insurgency to the trade in false passports.

---

[73] *The Terrorist Threat from Southern Thailand: Jihad or Quest for Social Justice?* Rohan Gunaratna and Arabinda Acharya, Potomac Books, 2012.

[74] Interview with author, 29 April, 2014.

He said writers suggesting Thailand's southern provinces were a training ground for international jihadist networks did not appear at academic conferences and were dismissed by serious scholars because their work relied on "intelligence sources" which could not be checked or verified.

"The Pattanis are genuinely provincial," he said. "They don't care about papers and passports and have no desire to travel. I am one of a small group of experts who has tried to convince people and especially the Thai elite that this is a political problem in need of a political solution, but it is a message that Bangkok would generally rather not hear."

McCargo said the southern insurgency was provoking discontent in Muslim minorities across Thailand. In a speech to the Lowy Institute for International Policy in April, 2014, he argued: "Thailand has seen a resurgence of ethno regionalist tensions across the country, most recently in the North and Northeast. Grasping the nettle by addressing the root causes of the southern insurgency will be crucial in turning back the tide of regional resentments and allowing Thais everywhere more political space to manage their own affairs without constant interference from Bangkok. The deep south must not become a model for a larger nationwide civil conflict."

With Thailand hungrily eyeing the booming Muslim tourist market, expected to be worth $US192 billion by the year 2020, up from $126 billion in 2011, the potential radicalisation of mosques becomes of significance to millions of travellers. Thailand ranks eighth in the world as the most popular tourist destination for Muslims, with more than 200,000 Indonesians visiting each year.

The Thai Tourism Authority has an office in Dubai and has been promoting Islamic travel packages, including halal spas, transportation and hotels, which require strict privacy. Bangkok's Suvarnabhumi Airport is rated the most Muslim friendly in the world outside an Islamic country.

In December, 2013, a car bomb with enormous potential to damage the nation's tourist industry was disarmed on the tourist island of Phuket.

The improvised explosive device (IED) consisted of two components with a combined payload of 33kg which failed to explode. A smaller 5kg device had exploded nearby, drawing the attention of security forces.

The Phuket attack used comparatively sophisticated twin bomb methodology similar to attacks conducted in Iraq and elsewhere. Security experts suggested the incident was indicative of the growing capabilities of ethnic Malay Muslim separatists. The attack was also notable in that it represented a significant out of area operation in one of Thailand's prime tourist regions. Its explosion would have seriously harmed the Thai economy.

In July of 2014 three people were killed and 30 injured in a bomb attack at Betong in the southern province of Yala, which is popular with tourists from neighbouring Malaysia. A Malaysian tourist was amongst those injured.[75]

In their 2014 Asia Risk Assessment Steve Vickers & Associates warned that extremist activity in southern Thailand could intensify, with political instability in Bangkok undermining security in the south and posing a direct threat to tourists. [76]

The report pointed to an upsurge in activity by groups such as the Pattani United Liberation Organisation. Recent bombings had been sophisticated in nature, suggesting southern insurgent groups were increasing their capabilities.

"The risk of further such acts is growing; government capacity in southern Thailand has slipped as the Thai intelligence and security forces have withdrawn assets to Bangkok. An associated concern in this regard is that elements engaged in the Thai political dispute may carry out bombings in the name of Malay separatists.

"Signs of growing capacity and determination to attack tourist targets are discernible, even as government capacity in the south is falling. Risks of increased attacks in Thailand's south, including in tourist locations outside the traditional conflict zone, are thus rising."

---

[75] Three dead, dozens wounded in Thai car bomb, AFP, 26 July, 2014.

[76] Car bomb explodes at hotel in Sadao district of Songkhla province in Thailand, News, December 23, 2013.

The recurrent exposure of Thailand as a hotbed for fake and stolen passports led once again to criticism of the nation's laissez faire attitude to criminal operations, many of which impacted on or were a direct part of the tourist industry.[77] The Kingdom's location at the centre of Southeast Asia and its sophisticated transportation infrastructure meant that international syndicates of all kinds, including arms and narcotics traders, human traffickers, sex businesses, money-laundering operations and terrorists, had used Thailand as a hub.

"So, why Thailand? *The Nation* asked. "Those who are in trouble at home can easily seek shelter, lead easy lives and even run businesses here. Gangsters of all sorts, be they from Asia, Russia or anywhere in the West, always feel at home in Thailand.

"Nowhere is it as easy to make a deal as in Thailand, as the country's laws and law-enforcement operations are very weak. It is easy to bribe officials and pave the way for illegal businesses, not to mention the high-ranking officials who also have a hand in this grey business. Since Thailand is also close to places where guerrilla warfare is ongoing, the demand for small arms is very high. Plus, it is the land of narcotics producers and drug lords are still very active in the country.

"Some of these drug traffickers also double as warlords, using the money they make from narcotics to finance their battles back home."

At the same time as Thailand acted as a major crime crossroads, the daily news cycle was cluttered with a burlesque display of the last, the lost and the least. They were usually addicts, small time dealers and the dissolute, those who had simply stayed too long at the party. They were usually people without the social connections to protect themselves or the financial resources to bribe their way out of trouble. Before being found guilty in a court of law they were paraded before cameras and microphones as fodder for television stations, news websites and newspapers.

The noise creates an unworthy air of business.

---

[77] Thailand's location a boon for international criminals, Supalak Ganijankhundee *The Nation*, 12 March 2014.

Often the most public arrests are for the most minor of offences.

In April of 2014 Martin Curtis Taylor, originally from Manchester in England, had his face paraded in the media[78] for all to see for the alleged possession of one gram of marijuana, a quantity which would not attract attention in most of the Western world. The drug was no doubt purchased locally.[79]

Renowned Thai journalist Chutima Sidasathian describes Phuket, with its international orientation and plethora of news stories, as a reporter's paradise.

While questioning the Phuket police at a press conference about the number of stolen passports being traced to the island after the disappearance of MH370, she was castigated for raising a subject which could damage the reputation of the island and of Thailand itself.[80]

She declared she was just doing her job and shot back to the senior officer: "Yes, but what is the answer?"

As she recalls: "There was no answer."[81]

Indeed, to the charge against the Thai political, military, police, social and business elites of allowing racketeers to trade freely in doctored, stolen and forged passports, along with a wide variety of other false documents, thereby fuelling criminal and terrorist networks and endangering the world's travelling public, there is no answer.

And no defence.

Chang Island.

---

[78] Martin Curtis Taylor. Courtesy of The Phuket News.

[79] Nigerian, Briton arrested on cocaine and weed charges in Phuket, *Phuket Crime*, 14 April, 2014.

[80] Interview with Chutima Sidasathian conducted by the author at Sydney University's conference on Thailand in the World, 21 April, 2014.

[81] Interview with author at Sydney University, 27 April, 2014.

MAYHEM

Suvarnabhumi Airport has high arching roofs, clean, minimalist lines and facilities handling more than 50 million passengers a year.[82] It is one of the world's busiest airports, and one of the world's most efficient; with processing times short and visitors promptly funnelled into taxis, trains or out into its vast car parks.[83]

Suvarnabhumi means "Golden Land".

Not always so.

In March of 2014 airport police claimed that Canadian Raymond Mark Campbell, 64, committed suicide by throwing himself from the fourth storey of the airport.

On the surface the man had everything to live for. A tribute recorded his love of the outdoors: "He lived for golf, boating and having beer and BBQs with all his buddies in Whitehorse (Inn), Thailand and with his family at home. Mark worked for the past 15 years in the Yukon and wintered in Thailand and Mill Bay. We are devastated at his loss and he will be remembered for his cheerful personality and huge grin." [84]

There are widespread doubts about the veracity of police claims concerning the suicides of foreigners in Thailand. It is a device often used to massage crime statistics, preclude the requirement for further investigation and cover up the murders of foreigners.

Newspaper accounts of Campbell's death were couched strictly in terms of what the police "assumed" had happened. No relatives, friends, bystanders or airport staff went on the record. The truth about the Canadian's death will probably never be known. One commentator on the expat website Thai Visa Forum observed the obvious: "Thailand = hub of farang suicide."

Casual observers find the communal nature of Thai society and the fun loving nature of its people appealing. Old Asia hands have

---

[82] Airports of Thailand

[83] Airports Council International.

[84] Times Colonist, Raymond (Mark) Campbell (1950-2014), March 6, 2014.

no such illusions; and are more likely to make bleak jokes about the gullibility of new comers, who, as the saying goes, "leave their brains at the airport". The latest rorts being perpetrated against expatriates are standard conversational fodder. There are many variations on the standard wisecrack: "Found at the base of a 24-storey condo. His hands were tied behind his back. His wallet was missing, as was his girlfriend. Police classified the death as suicide."

Raymond Campbell was not the first foreigner to have allegedly suicided at the unlikely location of Bangkok's famous airport. In October of 2013, following yet another death of a foreigner; Airports of Thailand announced that it would begin installing glass shields on the top floor of Suvarnabhumi Airport in order to prevent people from taking their own lives and damaging the country's reputation.[85]

Airport director Raweewan Netarakavesana said many people committed suicide by jumping over the handrails on the fourth floor, including three in the previous five months.

Indeed any surveillance of expatriate news websites throws up an endless series of unusual or unexplained foreign deaths, many of which the authorities blame on suicide and broken hearts.

Regulation and self-regulation means that most Western media outlets do not cover suicides, theoretically to prevent copycat cases and protect the individual's privacy. But like all state control of information, there is a downside. Such policies conceal the frequency of incidents, their most probable locations, as well as the times of year at which they most frequently occur. Contributing factors, and the gender breakdown of those killing themselves, are also effectively concealed. The policies have the effect of keeping the public ignorant and contribute to lax behaviour by workers and the community who might otherwise spot aberrant behaviour and respond appropriately.

The Thai media has none of the reservations of Western counterparts. Many stories follow the deaths of foreigners with a

---

[85] Frequent suicides lead to new protective shields at Bangkok airport, *The Washington Times*, 9 October, 2013.

sometimes ghoulish attention to detail and moralistic commentary on the deceased's inability to deal with life on life's terms. Or at least life on Thailand's terms.

The day before Valentine's Day, in February 2014, a 45-year-old Australian man "abandoned by his Thai girlfriend" allegedly leapt from the 6th floor of a Surin Beach Hotel.[86] In quaint English, *Pattaya Daily News* recorded: "At the scene, police found the severely injured body of the foreign man on the concrete surface. There was a big wound on his head that was bleeding heavily.

"Police inspecting the scene saw a big hole in the roof of the restaurant near the swimming pool that was made by the falling body. Police questioned the hotel maid. She told police Mr Anthony was not a guest at the hotel, but he was knocking on the door of every room on the 6th floor, looking for his Thai girlfriend but he could not find her.

"Then he jumped off the balcony before the maid could try to stop him. Later that day at 5.50pm Mr Anthony could not endure his severe wounds so he died. The doctors and nurses tried to keep him alive but he had severe wounds at many places of his bones and his lung was pierced by a broken bone, which made him lose a lot of blood."

Links to the story indicated the daily mayhem of tourist Thailand: "Brit Leaps To His Death After Thai GF Splits"; "Russian Conked By Ladyboy For Copping A Feel"; "Crazed Elephant Kills Thai Wife on Rayong Beach"; "Drunk Beach Ruffian 'Jack Soi 6' Stabbed in Fight" and "French Tourist Stabbed By Thai On Pattaya Beach".

The "Brit Leaps To His Death" story recorded that the body of a 63-year-old man "despondent after being dumped by his Thai girlfriend" was found at the base of a Pattaya condominium in December, 2012.[87] The *Pattaya Daily News* recorded: "At the scene, police went to the back of the building and discovered the mangled body of the victim. He was lying on his back in a

---

[86] Aussie Abruptly Leaps To Death After Thai GF Splits, *Pattaya Daily News*, 14 February, 2014.

[87] Brit Leaps To His Death After Thai GF Splits, *Pattaya Daily News*, 6 December 2012.

grotesque twisted position, and there was a lot of blood on the ground. He was identified as Mr Timothy Bertram Durrell, 63 years old, nationality British.

"Police questioned the security guard at the condominium. He testified that while he was near his desk, he heard a sound of something big hitting the ground hard. At first he thought it was a garbage bag."

The previous month a 39-year-old German man allegedly committed suicide by jumping from the 56th floor of the Pattaya Park Resort Hotel. Police reported that the man, Hyde Stephen Weiner, had left a note asking that his mother and child be informed, but gave no explanation.[88]

Pattaya Daily News record that police attended the scene at the back side of the hotel: "They discovered the body of the foreign man that had been severely damaged from the impact, with blood and internal organs scattered on the terrace... After their investigation, the police assumed Mr Hyde had to be stressed from something, and he could not find a way to solve his problem, so he came to Thailand to kill himself to run from his trouble."

Once again linked stories gave a feel for the chaos of Pattaya: "Unknown Foreigner Killed in Fall At Jomtien Hotel", "Russian Tourist Hangs Himself After Beating Wife", "Pattaya Hotel Maid Finds Dead Russian In Room", "Korean Tourist Jumps To Her Death in Sattahip".

In late April Pattaya police found the corpse of an Irish man, 71-year-old Kenneth Fulcher, who had allegedly jumped out of a sliding window above the ladder on the 7th floor. He had suffered broken arms, legs and skull. He had been staying in Room 707 of the Diana Estate Hotel for the previous two months.

In early May, 2014, the body of an Italian man was found hanging from a rooftop steel bar at the Happy Apartment building in Patong.[89] Roberto Becchetti, 46, was last seen in the building carrying a coil of nylon rope about two hours before his body was

[88] German Leaps To His Death at Pattaya Park Resort, *Pattaya Daily News*, 9 November 2012.

[89] Italian man found hanged in Patong, *Phuket Gazette*, 3 May, 2014.

discovered in a narrow gap between the apartment building and the building next door. "We searched the body and found a receipt for the rope, which was bought from a shop in Patong," a police spokesman said. "We believe that he committed suicide, as we saw no signs of a struggle."

Travel website Holidays Guide Thailand noted the high number of suicides by tourists: "Although Thailand is a major tourist destination and there are plenty of things to keep anyone happy here, there are many suicides that are committed by tourists. One has to think why many tourists feel the need to end their lives in Thailand as it is a tropical paradise with many things to see and do."

Holidays Guide observed that the suicides were almost all male and could be related to issues with a Thai girl friend, or running out of money, mental illness or struggles with addictions. The most common way for a tourist to end their life in Thailand was by jumping off a building. A survey of online news sites would confirm this was a common occurrence.

"There are rumours that some tourists and foreign expats are thrown off some of the balconies and that this is a way that Thai Mafia kill foreigners without having to worry about getting in any trouble, but there is no proof that this happens on a large scale, or at all, but having said this, there is no way to know for sure because none of the falls are ever investigated properly as the police are lazy."

The Guide concludes with an observation on one of the most peculiar aspects of the coverage of suicides in Thailand, officials posing with the body for the media: "When a foreigner does die after falling off a building, you will likely see it reported in the Thai – English online news sites and there is usually a photo of a dead person that is blurred out, but you often see Thai officials pointing at the body with smirks on their faces. Why they think this is funny, who knows, maybe they hate foreigners that much that they like to see them dead? It sure is odd to see."

Not all the deaths of foreigners are a result of violence, misadventure, accident or at their own hand. As a destination beloved by some retirees, some are dying simply from old age or natural causes.

But even in the heavily censored Thai media, and despite the best efforts of authorities to dampen down the flow of negative stories and reports of dead foreigners, the most cursory observation of Thai newspapers and online outlets reveals total mayhem. Too many people are dying unnatural deaths simply because of their naivety over their choice of travel destination; and by Thailand's failure to implement even the most minimal safety protocols within their tourist industry; or to even cursorily investigate the utterly improbable number of deaths of foreigners allegedly "falling" from balconies.

The scandal over the abysmal safety record of Thailand's tourist industry has been building throughout the 21st Century.

Way back in 2009 the now defunct news website CDNN published the following sample list of headlines:

THAILAND - Two female tourists die mysteriously at same Koh Phi Phi resort

THAILAND - Widow of murdered tourist returns to UK

THAILAND - Fishermen find body of murdered British tourist

THAILAND - Pirates attack, kills British yachtie near Koh Dong

THAILAND - Crippled UK diver warns tourists not to visit Thailand

THAILAND - Thai man arrested, charged with murdering tourists

THAILAND - Police double reward for capture of Thailand tourist killer

THAILAND - Game show winner helping to track down tourist killer

THAILAND - Tour guide key suspect in Thailand tourist murder case

THAILAND - $3k reward for capture of gunman who killed tourists

THAILAND - Two female tourists shot dead on Thailand resort beach

THAILAND - Murder in Thailand: another tourist shot dead

THAILAND - Thai men who raped, killed British tourist escape death

THAILAND - Paradise lost: Another tourist raped at Thailand resort island

THAILAND - Increasing violence against tourists threatens Thailand's tourism industry

THAILAND - Thai killers get death sentence for murdering tourist

Some of the expatriate commentary following the publication of that list was vitriolic: "They love foreigner's money but don't care if you are raped or killed. It is very sad that Thailand turns a blind eye to this because of the profits of tourism. There is no heart here."[90]

Just as with Australians, British and other nationalities, the deaths of Swedes, including from falls, murders, fires, drug overdoses, drownings, road accidents and unexplained deaths was hitting record levels by 2010.

Influential Swedish newspaper *Aftonbladet* highlighted the issue in an article Dangerous Thailand, labelling the country a death trap. The paper commented that Phuket had been the subject of crude exploitation and now reality was beginning to catch up with those responsible.[91]

Aftonbladet claimed greed and corruption in a place where everyone and everything could be bought had driven Phuket to the bottom, and politicians, investors, novelty vendors and taxi drivers all faced a poor future as a result. Thailand's dire reputation was driving tourists to choose safer holiday destinations.

Drugs, accidents and murders took the lives of at least 20 deaths of Swedes on Phuket in 2011, about one fifth of the total deaths in Thailand that year.

The deaths included:

Traffic accident: A 32-year-old Swedish man on a motorcycle collided with a power pole in Patong. He died instantly.

Traffic accident: A 54-year-old Swedish hotelier killed after he drove off the road on his motorcycle.

---

[90] Growing List of Westerners Murdered in Thailand, Forum, Topix.

[91] Phuket Labelled 'Death Trap for Swedes' by Tabloid, Alan Morison, Phuket Wan, 21 October, 2012.)

Murder: Swedish man, 25, from Gothenburg knifed outside his home by fellow Swedes following dispute.

Mysterious death: A 21-year-old woman from Skane found dead aboard a private yacht at Patong Beach.

In 2012 Swedish deaths on the island included:

Motorcycle accident: A 48-year-old Swedish military man lost control of his motorcycle on a curve and went straight into a house. He was dead when police arrived at the scene. The man had served in the NATO force in Afghanistan but was on vacation when the accident occurred.

Traffic accident: Four young people in their 20s from Varberg, on their way to a diving site, collided with a truck in Phang Nga, north of Phuket. The Swedes and their driver died instantly. The truck driver escaped the scene but was arrested later.

Fall accident: A man in his 30s fell three stories from a hotel balcony in Karon Beach, on Phuket. He fell through a metal roof before he landed on the ground.

Motorcycle accident: A man, 45, was killed when he collided with a passenger car on a sharp curve near Karon Beach.

Overdose: A 35-year-old man found dead in his hotel room. The autopsy showed a drug overdose.

One of the worst car accidents involved four Swedish youths aged 20 and 22.[92] They were killed whilst travelling from Phuket to Koh Tao. They had hired a car with a private driver but were hit by an oncoming vehicle. The driver fled the scene.

Many foreign tourists underestimate how dangerous the Thai traffic can be, news website for Scandinavians in Asia, *ScandAsia*, declared. Recent figures showed 26,000 dead on Thai roads, compared to less than 300 in Sweden for a similar period. In 2011, the last year for which figures are available, 119 people were killed on Phuket roads alone; and 15,000 people required hospital attention. Most incidents were as a result of motorbike accidents.

Mirroring the experiences of other nationalities as the 21st Century progressed and the chaos in the tourist industry increased, 2012 was a tough year for Swedes in Thailand. A record number of

---

[92] Picture courtesy of ScandAsia

105 Swedish citizens died. The number represented an almost 100% increase from the 55 deaths in 2007.₉₃

Swedish Embassy spokesman Pär Kågeby said 41% of all deaths in 2012 involved a vehicle. He expressed concern over the high number of traffic accidents. About 400,000 Swedes visit Thailand each year and a large proportion of them travel to Phuket, Phang Nga and Krabi.

"Many Swedes are not used to the left side traffic. They also leave Swedish traffic precautions at home and often drive without a helmet, which they would never do back home," said Kågeby.

But even if people do their part to travel safely on the roads, traffic behaviour was poor and speeding was common, as was driving under the influence of alcohol.

"Only half of the Swedes who lost their lives in 2012 were insured. Many believe that the same rules apply in Thailand as in the EU, but that is not the case and casualties and injuries can become an expensive affair."

The escalating number of deaths amongst Swedes in Thailand continued, with 28 deaths in the first three months of 2013. Accidents, natural deaths and suicides were among the most common causes.

In 2011 a mystery illness killed seven foreigners in Chiang Mai and hospitalised several others. Four of the dead had stayed at the subsequently demolished Downtown Inn.

Authorities, including the Chiang Mai governor Pannada Disakul, initially tried to dismiss the deaths as coincidence. [94]

The dead included Sarah Carter, 23, from New Zealand and Canadian Bill Mah, 59, who had been in perfect health prior to his arrival in Chiang Mai. Other affected tourists were from Britain, France and the US.

Incensed, Sarah's grief stricken father Richard Carter claimed the Thai authorities had covered up details relating to his daughter's death. He told the Australian Broadcasting

---

[93] 2012 was record year of Swedish deaths in Thailand, *ScandAsia*, 13 May, 2013.

[94] Thai mystery: seven tourists die after falling ill, Clio Francis and Stacey Wood, The Sydney Morning Herald, 26 April, 2011.

Commission: "There are other deaths that have been discovered in the same hotel; one in the room next to my daughter's, another British couple in a room below my daughter's. There are now other deaths being reported, now that the story has gotten out, of other people in other parts of Thailand being hit with the same thing. It seems beyond coincidence that there should be three deaths or four deaths in rooms adjacent to each other over a very short period of time and I just hope we can get some answers for the benefit of all travellers to Thailand."[95]

Following the international outcry, Thai authorities eventually launched an investigation utilising the services of local university and pathology services and the World Health Organisation.

Without biological samples, the Thai authorities having acted so slowly that the bodies had already been flown home, the findings were inconclusive, but suggested commercial pesticides, chemicals or gas might have been involved.

Optimistically, distinguished Australian born Thailand based journalist Alan Morison declared that Thai authorities appeared to be in the process of recognising that every tourist and expat death —whether in Chiang Mai, Phuket, Pattaya, Samui or Bangkok— needed to be properly investigated and an accurate cause of death determined.

"Too often, local investigating police make the only decision on the cause of death," he wrote. "The report by the investigating body is likely to resonate on Phuket and in Pattaya and among envoys from many countries who would like more thorough investigations of all deaths of expat residents and tourists."

In the wake of his daughter's death in a Thai hospital at 3.30am in the morning, Richard Carter set up the now defunct website Thailand Travel Tragedies. There have been a number of such initiatives over the years, but few of the bereaved have the heart or the resources to continue.

---

[95] Thai police pressed on mystery tourist deaths, The World Today, Australian Broadcasting Commission, 8 March, 2011.

Many hundreds of tourist deaths followed that of Sarah Carter. Almost none of them were ever properly investigated.

Even when there was little if any doubt about the causes of deaths or identity of the perpetrators of violent crimes, foreigners often found themselves frustrated by lack of action or inadequate sentences.

Thai policeman Uthai Dechawiwat, who had pleaded guilty to the killing of Canadian Leo Del Pinto, 25, in January 2008, was finally handed a 37-year prison term — reduced from life – more than five years later.

Del Pinto, from the Rocky Mountain town of Calgary, was shot dead[96] and his girlfriend Carly Reisig, 24, hospitalised with a bullet wound after the policeman tried to break up an argument between the couple outside a restaurant in Pai in the far north of Thailand.

The remarkably beautiful mountain village is known to backpackers and New Agers the world over as a place where the Earth's Ley Lines, a kind of spiritual and mystical energy grid, intersect. Pai has traditionally been a place to party and relax. It became fashionable amongst Thais after a television series of the same name.

Local police claimed Del Pinto had accused his girlfriend of having an affair with a local man. When the argument among the Canadians and the Thai man turned violent, restaurant workers asked off-duty police sergeant Uthai to intervene. Uthai's gun went off three times during the scuffle and he initially claimed it was an accident. He later pleaded guilty to attempted murder of both Del Pinto and his girlfriend.

Three years after Del Pinto's murder, Bangkok based British journalist Andrew Drummond recorded the family's frustrations: "Justice still seems a long way away after a series of delays which might be regarded as Machiavellian to people unfamiliar with the workings of the Thai justice system."

---

[96] Headline Dad's Grief, Sunday Sun, Calgary, Canada 11 January, 2008.

While on bail for murder, Sergeant Uthai Dechachiwat was arrested for bashing to death his 18-year-old wife with a piece of wood.[97]

Pai Landscape by Claire Backhouse

On the 15th of April in 2012, three male tourists died in a single day from a reputed combination of heat and alcohol. Temperatures were only in the 30s.[98]

Russian man, Kiselev Igor, 59, was sent to hospital for medical treatment after he passed out at Karon beach. Medical staff tried for one hour to revive him before he was pronounced dead.

His death was followed by the death of Walter Federick Bell, 62, who passed out on Patong's notorious Beach Road and subsequently died in the local hospital.

Later a Burmese man, aged about 45, was taken from Karon to the hospital after fainting, and was pronounced dead.

[97] Police impunity stalls inquiry over Canadian's murder, Andrew Drummond, Freedom Against Censorship in Thailand, 9 January, 2011.

[98] Phuket Heat and Alcohol Kill Three Men on Phuket, Says Hospital Chief, Chutima Sidasathian, *Phuket Wan*, 16 April, 2014.

Despite the large number of deaths of foreigners on the island, Patong Hospital does not have the capacity to perform full autopsies.

Hospital director Dr Sirichai Silpa-Ar-Cha said the mix of alcohol and excessive heat was probably the cause: "People must make sure that they can adjust to the combination of factors on a holiday island. The alcohol and the heat make for a deadly combination in the wrong circumstances."

The Tourism Authority of Thailand regularly flies travel writers to Thailand on industry junkets. In mid 2012 one such trip went savagely wrong when an Australian travel agent Michelle Smith, 59,[99] was knifed to death during a robbery just near her five-star hotel.[100] Another woman was injured. They were both part of a group of 10 travel agents who had travelled from Perth to inspect the new five-star Katathani Beach Resort. Smith was walking back from dinner, when two men on a motorbike swooped, attempting to steal her handbag. She was stabbed twice in the heart with a seven inch knife and then staggered towards the hotel, collapsing and dying at the staff entrance.

A friend described Mrs Smith as "fun-loving and just one of those people you thought—I'd love to be like her when I'm her age—just so full of life. I'm not surprised she fought back—she was an experienced traveller and worked hard for her money—most of us would have done the same thing. It's just tragic."

While there is no similarly available information for the rest of the country, the Phuket Police produce lists of foreign deaths to which they have been called. The lists are by no means comprehensive. Police, for instance, often don't attend drownings; and therefore don't record those deaths. There were at least 35 deaths on Phuket's beaches in 2013. Tourists who die in hospital after the precipitating event are also often not included; and there are a significant number of oversights. That there are no comparable lists for the rest of the country is of grave concern. In a

---

[99] Michelle Smith, 59. Picture courtesy of *Phuket News*.

[100] Phuket Tourist Murdered: Aussie Woman Knifed to death in Failed Bag Snatch, Phuket Wan, 21 June 2012.

rapidly developing country little is being done to stop the carnage on the roads and at sea, in the streets, bars, clubs, hotels and condominiums of Thailand. Embassies worldwide need to ensure that their citizens are safe. Travel companies need to accept responsibility for the welfare of their customers. Every action has a consequence, including choosing a travel destination. To deliberately conceal information which would enable people to make informed decisions on where they would like to spend their holiday money is, as Alan Morison puts it, "beyond unacceptable".

Below are partial lists of some of the tourists who have died in Thailand in recent years; imperfectly recorded and from only one single island. The full truth of the outcomes for tourists travelling to Thailand, shamelessly concealed by the Thai authorities and compounded by the complacency and complicity of foreign governments, is considerably worse.

Phuket Expat Deaths Between February 16 and May 18 2011

Patrick Emilienne Belgium heart attack Thalang Hospital February 16
Riccardo Carafa Italy heart attack Patong Phuket Palace Hotel February 24
Makhail Shirokov Russia drowning Chalet longstay Chalong February 19
Dennis Joachale Michael Dahl Sweden motorcycle crash Chao Fa Road February 26
Julian Mathie Britain suicide leap Patraburi Mansion Kathu March 5
Lindberg Fjarne Sigurd Finland diabetes Patong March 1
Luciano Butti Italy murdered in shooting Pa Klok March 15
Campbell Philip Mickael Britain drowned at Expat hotel Patong March 18
Woolier Martin William Britain motorcycle crash Patong March 19
Jeffrey Stuart Buck Britain heart attack Thara Patong March 30
Stephen John Hatcher Britain heart attack at Karon March 30
Rolf Billy Nilsson Sweden motorcycle crash Rawai April 28
Goh Shing Cheong Malaysia motorcycle crash Chao Fa West Road April 28
Ms Hitomi Shibata Japan diveboat propeller in face Raya island May 4 (pictured)
Paul Alexander Thurlow Britain motorcycle crash beach road Patong May 12 (pictured)
Frank Michael Sinel German heart attack Patong May 18

Expat Deaths on Phuket from January to June 2012

Knpeeba Kireeva Russia January 1 Phuket City Motorcycle crash

Mahmood Sultan Safi Sweden January 5 Kamala Motorcycle crash

Erna Dahlan Indonesia January 8 Patong Motorcycle crash

Kyle Mark Horo New Zealand January 8 Patong Overdose

Dr Dreve Fitzherbert Germany January 15 Patong Merlin Illness

Daniel Andre Bertholet Switzerland January 15 Thalang Car crash

Nielsen Eva Denmark January 17 Patong Heart Attack

Paul Brian James British January 20 Patong Illness

Jari Matti Ihattumen Finland January 29 Patong Motorcycle crash

Sven Gunnar Sweden January 9 Patong Heart Attack

Christos Liouliacs Sweden February 10 Patong Illness

Ulrich Hans German February 11 Kamala Illness

Mark James Robson South Africa January 25 near Freedom Beach Suicide

Christor Osca Linryuist Sweden February 19 Karon Cause Unknown

Leanoard Vinsent Young Britain February 19 Rawai Illness

Manfred Borwsky German February 16 Chalong illness

Einar Jan Frederik Bergstrom Sweden February 26 Chalong motorcycle crash

Jukka Tapio Olkinuora Finland February 26 Patong heart attack

Robert Francis Mullally Australia March 6 Patong fall from height

Fedor Samsonnov Russia March 7 Chalong electric shock

Lars Jimmy Karlsson Sweden March 14 Karon no cause determined

Gary Meadows Australia March 16 Phuket City no cause determined

James McIntosh Crawford Britain March 20 Patong heart attack

Von Amelyn Klaus German March 21 Rawai Cancer

Jose Luis Landin Ugarte Spain March 21 Rawai Cancer

Boris Falkovskiy Russia April 3 Patong Suicide

James Desmond Hodkinson Britain April 4 Chalong Natural causes aged 92

Jens Houe Denmark April 16 Patong Blood loss

Rudolf Otto Paul German April 24 Rawai Illness

Franz Simmit German May 4 Patong Illness

Marcus Ralf Burghardt German May 18 Patong Suicide

Paul James McNeil Australia June 7 Thalang no cause determined

Sergey Mukurdumov Uzbeckistan June 15 Thungtong Motorcycle crash

Michelle Elizabeth Smith Australia June 20 Kata Noi Stabbed

Trek Atlas Ingram America June 21 Patong Illness

Mohammed Abdulliah Oman June 26 Patong Illness

Audrey Belanger Canada June 28 Phi Phi Island Excessive insecticide in drug/alcohol cocktail

Noemi Belanger Canada June 28 Phi Phi Island Excessive insecticide in drug/alcohol cocktail

Expat Deaths on Phuket September-December 2012

Kan Chen China 28 October 6 Nai Harn resort pool drowning

Terje Iversen Norway 68 October 11 Patong Hospital heart attack

Ganaeson Subramaniam Malaysia 57 October 21 Patong Hospital heart complaint

Didier Jean Robert France 45 October 26 Kamala motorcycle crash

Roger Stuart Wells British 46 October 29 Patong Hospital heart attack

Javier Ruesta Garcia Spain 23 October 31 Vachira Hospital Phuket motorcycle crash

Fredericus Johannes Netherlands 58 November 1 Cherng Talay chronic illness

Kenne Caldwell British 64 November 2 Tourist Police Phuket City suicide

Hayden William Reynolds Australia 56 November 2 Patong suicide

Roar Olsen Norway 57 November 4 Patong Hospital heart attack

Christopher Ian Hart British 44 November 6 Srisoonthorn motorcycle crash (pictured)

Arvidsson Per Ak Ingvar Swedish 67 November 9 Chalong suicide

Peter Zavyalov Russia 27 November 13 Patong Hospital personal illness

Katie Ellis British 30 November 15 Phuket International drowning

Jacobus Thesnaar South Africa 42 November 15 Boat Lagoon heart attack

Andrei Pavlov Russia 31 November 17 Patong Hill motorcycle crash

Mikhail Bogdanov Russia 70 November 19 Patong beach drowning

Yuan Dingrong Russia 57 November 20 Racha island drowning

Mahnken Hans-Dieter German 59 November 25 Rawai illness

Tomas Dewi Wyn British 64 November 27 Thalang heart attack

Peter Reisz Hungary 64 November 30 Kathu murder

Alvin William Aitchison Australia 81 December 5 Patong illness

Mr Konstantin Russia 46 December 10 Rawai

Aleksei Piuro Russia 56 December 10 Racha island drowning

Michael Richard German 52 December 15 Patong illness

Sopiyev Shihnazar Turkmenistan 28 December 16 Kathu motorcycle crash

Theodore Paul Roe American 51 December 20 Rawai motorcycle crash

Alfred Michael Switzerland 64 December 21 Phuket City motorcycle crash

Chooraman Gayaparsad South Africa 55 December 22 Vachira Phuket Hospital illness
Moegamad Kaashief Savahl South Africa 33 December 27 Patong no cause given
Ivan Berestnev Russia 29 December 29 Cherng Talay motorcycle crash
Ekaterrina Emglianova 28 December 29 Cherng Talay motorcycle crash
Clavaud Gilles France 42 December 31 Kamala illness
Sebastian Faulkner Australia 45 December 31 Patong (pictured)
Robert Sven Arthur Swedish 29 December 31 illness

Expat Deaths on Phuket January-February 2013

Matthew John Docherty Britain 31 January 3 Patong Hospital drowning (pictured)
Herve Jean Periard Switzerland 54 January 3 Karon drowning
Jean Delais Belgium 80 January 3 Kathu illness
Donald Edward Copley Australia 44 January 5 Phuket City illness
Hugo Prodano Britain 50 January 10 Patong illness
Mathew Lucas Thornhill Australia 45 January 11 Patong overdose
Stephan Henricus Maria Buczynski Netherlands 26 January 13 Patong drowning
Pietro Fedrigoni Italy 71 January 13 Patong illness
Kim Leonhardt Denmark 60 January 13 Patong illness
Gunther Bugnyar Australia 67 January 13 Patong illness
Pertti Juhani Miettinen Finland 72 January 14 Bang Tao drowning
Yin Ling Lai China 35 January 15 Mai Khao drowning
Nebel Thomas Britain 76 January 15 Patong drowning
Anton Wagner Australia 74 January 19 Patong illness
Dimitrios Gkarlis Greece 34 January 19 Patong Hospital illness
Markku Tauno Olavi Perkkio Finland 62 January 22 Karon no cause known
Richard Ernest Spraggs New Zealand 59 January 235 Chalong drowning
Hiroshi Sasaki Japan 70 January 26 Patong drowning
Neil Gray, 35. January 27. British. Phuket. Drowning.
Nel Gae Britain 36 January 27 Rawai drowning
Gerd Annicka Oscarson Sweden 66 January 28 Kata illness
Jens Nikias Kring Sweden 42 January 31 Vichitsongrkran motorcycle crash
Eveginee Redcove Russia 44 February 4 Rawai fall
Bo Gunnar Kjellstrom Sweden 66 February 4 Srisoonthorn illness
Ivan Maylyukov Russia 53 February 6 Patong illness

Joseph Grant Harmon US 23 February 8 Cherng Talay no cause given (pictured)
Franciscus Josephus Coch Netherlands 73 February 19 Patong illness
Frank Robert Gulbensen Norwegian February 8 Patong illness
Ashley Simon Australia 32 February 10 Patong motorcycle crash
Alexey Babenko Russia 25 February 12 Thepkasattri hit by truck wheel
Stafan Switzerland 47 February 15 Rawai car crash off pier
Robert Leroy Meclurg 63 February 13 Chalong illness
Vandecan Jean Claude Louisroger 70 February 18 Kathu illness
Marcel Switzerland 60 February 23 Patong illness
Geir Age Skogvold Norway 56 February 23 Vachira Phuket Hospital illness
Connie Jensen Denmark 28 February 28 Kata-Karon drowning

Expat Deaths on Phuket March-August 2013

Johenn Schob Switzerland 48 March 5 Chalong Collapsed at home
Niall William Walh Ireland 34 March 8 Chalong car crash
Graziano Cagnato Italy 56 March 8 Chalong car crash
Mrs Linda Brooks Jewell British 51 March 14 Chalong personal illness
Oleg Udaloi Russia 43 March 22 Karon drowning
Adriano Favaretto Italy 64 May 11 Tung Thong Hit head in fall
Gunter Anton Fuchs Germany 56 May 13 Chalong personal illness
Peter Loots Triebner Germany 57 May 17 Karon personal illness
Loh Zhi Wei Malaysia 29 May 21 Tachatchai motorcycle crash
Mrs Semon Cherie Winters New Zealand 47 May 26 Vichit personal illness
Beat Albert Siegerst Switzerland 66 May 29 Chalong personal illness
Joseph Spiteri Malta 70 May 30 Kathu personal illness
Yoann Dieu France 24 May 30 Chalong suicide by hanging
Miss Faetra Augustina US 29 May 30 Chalong no cause determined
Sheng Sheng China 27 June 2 Chalong drowning
Rainer Hellemann Australia 61 June 16 Tung Thong personal illness
Ginnadii Magazinov Russia 54 June 19 Karon personal illness
Jeremy Thomas O'Neill British 37 June 21 Kathu drowning
Yun Zemin China 43 July 1 Chalong drowning
Mrs Aino Marianne Seeppala Sweden 56 July 9 Chalong personal illness
Khudhair Abbas Mansoor Iraq 46 July 16 Kathu personal illness
Li Ran China 31 July 18 Chalong drowning
Park Boksoon Korea 85 July 20 Vichit old age
Aleksandr Poleshchemko Russia 29 July 20 Kathu drowning

Vancher Roojan Belgium 40 July 20 Kamala drowning
Ramesh Chand Singhal India 49 July 22 Karon drowning
Joshua John Smits Australia 25 July 24 Kathu suicide jump
Tsuchida Masahiko Japan 48 July 26 Vichit personal illness
Clifford Nelson Bamford Dominican Republic 69 July 1 Vichit personal illness
David Jay Goin Canada 47 July 3 Tung Thong personal illness
Mark William Carroll US 51 July 7 Karon drowning
Zhao Yi China 92 July 16 Kathu personal illness
Dmitry Onishchenko Russia 32 July 22 Karon drowning
Wael Zakhour Syria 45 August 5 Karon drowning
Peng Yu China 22 August 9 Chalong drowning

Expat and Tourist Deaths August-December 2013

Waladimia Soballdeeyork Russia 29 August 17 Chalong hanging suicide
Vladimir Slobodenyuk, 29. August 17. Russian. Hanging.
Ethan-jade Lascelles Williams British 14 August 18 Patong Cashew nut
Graeme James Philip British 45 August 23 Kathu personal illness
James Condon Jerred Australia 61 August 24 Rawai personal illness
Nari Sadarangani Canada 76 August 31 Patong personal illness
Mrs Tracey Ann Walton Australia 51 September 1 Patong personal illness
Brodie Myers Australia 34 September 8 Patong fall in bathroom
JimmyChan Kai Hong Kong 33 September 8 Patong hill motorcycle crash
Schol Tyssex David Ruddle Sweden 44 September 8 Kamala personal illness
Donald Gordon Louis New Zealand 81 September 12 Karon personal illness
Alexey Tysbalyuk Russia 46 September 17 Patong drowning
Carlo De Roja Austria 60 September 18 Kamala no cause given
Mrs Jacquelline Susan Prior British 51 September 24 Karon personal illness
Denis Lipatov Russia 37 September 28 Racha drowning
Sheng Caoliang China 31 September 30 Kata drowning
Huiseng Lin China 30 October 1 racha drowning
Yury Kiryukhin Russia 36 October 12 Karon personal illness
Ilya Vitovtov Russia 27 October 15 Karon motorcycle crash
Oleg Ozerskikh Russia 52 October 24 Karon drowning
Haifeng Liu China 33 October 24 Karon drowning
Alexander Dekhand Russia 38 October 30 Patong drowning in hotel pool
Mrs Marrine Elenor Jagee Sweden 58 November 2 Karon fall in bathroom
Marshall William British 55 November 3 Cherng Talay personal illness
Kim Doryeong Korea 32 November 5 Vichit car crash

Lee Dongyun Korea 31 November 5 Vichit car crash

Sergey Taruraev Russia 38 November 7 Cherng Talay personal illness

Paul Simon Windler British 49 November 10 Rawai personal illness

Choi Yon Ho Korea 41 November 15 Kathu splashboard fall

Bennewitz Klaus Dieter Hermann German 76 Patong November 17 Patong drowning

Phillip Thomas Schoneok Swiss 43 November 19 Rawai personal illness

Gao Yang China 20 November 20 Cape Promthep fell and drowned

Li Ming China 41 November 25 Rassada murder

Mrs Jiang Chengyue China 42 November 26 Rassada suicide

Paul Anthony Dark British 80 December 5 Rawai natural causes

Per Torben Lindgren Sweden 58 December 11 suicide

Vladimir Petrunev Russia 70 December 15 Kathu personal illness

Im Soojung Korea 44 December 15 Vichit suicide

Jorg Manfred German 44 December 18 Patong drowning

Michael Frederiksen Denmark 56 December 25 Karon personal illness

Pavel Khristict Russia 29 December 26 Tung Thong motorcycle crash

In April of 2012 officials on Phuket stopped issuing monthly updates on drownings and road toll deaths, the two activities that claimed the most tourists' lives.

Eleven foreigners died in January of 2013 in just 10 days on the island of Phuket, including four unrelated deaths on a single day.[101]

The deaths occurred between 11 January and 20 January, 2013 and were revealed at a police press conference. Among the dead were an Italian man reported to have a chronic illness, a Dane who allegedly suffered a heart attack and an Austrian found at Patong Condo apartments.

The deaths of two British men were claimed to be linked to alcohol, while an 87-year-old Swiss man drowned off the beach at Patong. An Australian was suspected to have suffered an overdose.

On the same day that the series of deaths began an additional 100 police arrived on the island with the stated aim of making the island safer during the peak tourist season.

---

[101] Phuket's Biggest Losing Streak: 10 Foreigners Die in 10 Days, Chutima Sidasathian, Phuket Wan, 22 January, 2013.

One death which never had a conclusive cause established was that of Stephan Henricus Maria Buczynski, 26,[102] who was found in the ocean off Patong. He had a fresh four-centimetre cut to the back of his head, indicating a strike from a blade. An autopsy by doctors at Patong Hospital quickly concluded that they were "fairly certain" drowning was the cause of death. Phuket police had regularly criticised the hospital for the rapidity of their findings when foreigners were the victims. Police requested the autopsy because there was a deep gash on the back of his head, arousing suspicions he had been murdered. The body was transferred to Bangkok for further examination. Bangkok doctors backed the findings of Patong Hospital that Mr Buczynski drowned.[103]

No explanation of the cut to the back of his head was forthcoming and in official reports foul play was never ruled out. No witnesses to the young man's death came forward.[104]

"I was informally told by an officer at the Institute of Police Forensic Medicine in Bangkok that the cause of death was drowning," Lt Col Akanit said. "The officer there explained to me that the wound on the back of Mr Buczynski's head was caused by a hard, sharp object. However, forensic doctors were unable to determine if the wound was sustained before or after the drowning, which makes it impossible to know if it was a factor in Mr Buczynski's death."

The Dutchman was remembered fondly on the gaming board Xenimus: "He was always a very intelligent person and very respectable. There was truly never a dull moment with Stef around. We started as enemies and became very close friends as Time went by. Even though I never knew him outside of Xenimus, he will be sorely missed."

---

[102] Stephan Henricus Maria Buczynski, 26. Source: Facebook.

[103] Phuket Riddle of Dutchman's Death, Chutima Sidasathian and Alan Morison, Phuket Wan, 15 January, 2013.

[104] Autopsy results unclear about role of head wound in drowned Dutch tourist's death, Phuket Gazette, 31 January, 2013.

Junior stockbroker Stephen Ashton, 22,[105] was killed on Kho Phangan in the early hours of New Year's Day, 2013, earning him the unfortunate distinction of being one of the first foreigners to die in Thailand that year. He was caught by a stray bullet during a fight between two local gangs outside the Zoom Bar.[106]

Ashton's murder provoked another tirade from one of the editors of the opinion oriented online newsletter *Meebal*, headlined STOP Thailand Murdering Tourists: "It is reported in the national press that the killer, Ekkapan Kaewkla, is likely to serve just two years in prison for Stephen's murder – that's how much the Thais care about justice for those unfortunate tourists who are murdered while on holiday in Thailand.

"You can clearly see from the face of Ekkapan Kaewkla, as he is being led away by police, after his arrest, that he (sic) quite happy, with not an ounce of remorse for killing another innocent person. Why? Because Stephen was a Farang and a Farang's life is considered inferior to a Thai."

Often Thailand is painted as a place of relaxation, beautiful beaches and a carefree way of life and yet the ugly truth is that it has one of the highest violent gun crime statistics in the world.

"The U.S has a population nearly 5 times that of Thailand and yet Thailand has over twice the amount of violent gun crime. Add to this the Rape, Muggings, Assault and Corruption and you have a country that should be avoided at all costs. If only Stephen had been aware of this it is likely he, and his friends, may have chosen an alternative tourist destination.

"All foreign Ambassadors and Honorary Consuls in Thailand are fully aware of just how violent and dangerous Thailand is and yet do very little to warn their citizens of the dangers. It basically all comes down to diplomatic back-scratching in order to preserve Diplomatic Relations so that the flow of trade and money can continue – the Foreign Ambassadors, including that of the British Embassy, are totally ineffectual in providing sufficient and factual

---

[105] Stephen Ashton, 22. Picture Facebook.

[106] Stray bullet kills Briton, 22, as New Year's Eve party on Thai beach explodes into violence, *Daily Mail*, 29 April, 2014.

information to its citizens with the necessary warnings that would save lives.

"As far as I am concerned the British Government are perpetrators of the murder of Stephen Ashton, due to their ineptitude and unwillingness in taking appropriate action to stop their citizens from visiting Thailand and force the Thai government into action to put an end to these murders.

"The problem is, when it comes to Thais they will do everything it takes to prevent the loss of tourism, other than stemming violent crime and murder."

In an unprovoked attack backpacker Nathan Sharpe, 23,[107] was speared at the same location by a six-inch blade which tore through his stomach, liver, pancreas and kidneys before grazing his spine.

In July of 2013 the British government released figures showing a sharp jump in the number of deaths and accidents of British travellers in Thailand.

Deaths jumped from 296 in 2011-2012 to 389 in the year ending April 1 2013. Hospitalisations rose from 217 to 285 in the same period, the official statistics showed. Although fewer British citizens were dying worldwide, the increase in both deaths and hospitalisations was a sharp rise of 31 percent. In 2013-14 there were 362 deaths and 267 hospitalisations.[108]

Proportionally, taking into account the number of residents and visitors, Thailand ranked second only to the Philippines, beloved by elderly retirees, as the country where its citizens were most likely to seek consular assistance.

Thailand ranked second only to Spain as the country in which the most British citizens died. Spain had 17 times the level of visitation.

An email obtained by the BBC under the Freedom of Information Act testified that the trouble with giving the murder rate was "that it would effectively highlight the number of murders over the past year or more here, which in the current circumstances

---

[107] Brit knife terror on Thailand death isle. The Sun, UK. 7 January 2013.

[108] Foreign and Commonwealth Office British Behaviour Abroad Report 2014.

could have a disproportionate impact on Thailand's reputation and legitimate commercial interests."

Thailand's status as one of the world's deadliest destinations had been a long time coming. Way back in 2008 *The Independent* asked why, with so many Britons murdered in Thailand, there were no government warnings that the Land of Smiles was one of the most dangerous places on Earth for British citizens. Official inaction characterised the years to follow.

The paper complained about the refusal of Thai authorities to release data on British deaths in Thailand. It recalled the story of Toby Charnaud, an English expat living in the upmarket seaside resort of Hua Hin, wrote a fictional story about a British man planning to murder his Thai wife. Two years later, Charnaud himself was murdered by thugs hired by his Thai wife. After a gun failed to kill him, he was beaten to death. His body was then partially cremated in a fire pit, cut into pieces and scattered around a nearby forest. What emerged from the death of Charnaud and many others was "the fact that Thailand, despite its popularity with the British, is among the most dangerous places in the world for UK visitors—a fact that the Foreign Office has been reluctant to publicise."

Other cases at the time included a sexually motivated killing of a young British woman, a Thai police officer executing two backpackers in a crowded street, shootings, throat cuttings and several cases of Thai wives or their families murdering British husbands.

There are more reasons than just bar mayhem and youthful indiscretion as to why Thailand is one of the world's most perilous tourist destinations. One of them is simply safety standards, with an endless string of reports on bus, van, train, bike and ferry accidents. Clapped out ferries, dangerous buses, dilapidated facilities, all continue to be used without the mandatory safety checks common in the West.

In March of 2013 some 100 people, mostly tourists, were rescued from a sinking ferry off Phuket. The next month the Royal Thai Navy had to rescue more than 400 tourists, most of them speedboat passengers, because the drivers ignored warnings of

severe storms. Also in April, the crash of two speedboats left 14
injured tourists in hospital. One Korean tourist had a leg ripped off
on impact and another had two legs almost severed.

In November, 2013, six people died after a crowded double-
decker tourist ferry sank off Pattaya, three Thai tourists and three
foreigners.[109] Fifteen people were also seriously injured.

Television footage showed stunned tourists being plucked from
the sea and led to safety on shore, where they were met by dozens
of ambulances along Pattaya's neon-lit beachfront. About half the
passengers were believed to be Russian.

Media reports said engine problems on the overcrowded ferry
forced passengers to one side of the boat, which caused it to list
and take on water.

The Australian Network News observed that that Thailand was
struggling to shake off a reputation for lax safety standards after a
series of incidents—many of them fatal. There had been a "slew of
high-profile cases of foreigners being murdered, drugged or caught
up in tourist cons. Diplomats from China and the European Union
have voiced concern at the number of fatal incidents involving
their tourists."

Less than six months later 47 European and Asian tourists
bound for famous "James Bond" Phi Phi Island were rescued from
a sinking Phuket tourist boat.

With its burgeoning economy, China had in the modern era
become the country providing the largest number of tourists to
Thailand, with numbers escalating rapidly. Some 4.7 million
Chinese tourists visited Thailand in 2013, up from 2.7 million the
previous year, according to figures supplied by the Thai Ministry
of Tourism. China eclipsed Malaysia as the single largest supplier
of tourists in 2012.

In May of 2013, on the eve of a visit by the Chinese
Ambassador Guan Mu to discuss the safety of Chinese citizens on
the island, a young man died during a snorkelling accident. It was
just one in a string of such deaths which had outraged Chinese

---

[109] Six dead after tourist ferry sinks off Pattaya resort in Thailand, *Australian Network News*, 4 November, 2013.

diplomats. There were more than 35 deaths of foreigners on beaches and one-day trips during the year.

The Ambassador said not enough was being done to fix the problems and the time for speaking softly was past. He accused the Phuket police of being corrupt and taking advantage of tourists: "Police and Immigration do not have justice in their hearts. They are not moral and professional. Police are corrupt in Thailand. Some of them use their positions of power to rip off tourists.

"This is not true of every tourist but there are enough cases for this to be a serious problem. We have to sort this problem out immediately. When it comes to fraud in Thailand, there is a lack of quality among investigators. Some cases will never be resolved. Chinese tourists are not satisfied.

"There are food poisonings and accidents. Tourists' documents and money are stolen. Drownings happen too easily on Phuket and Samui. These problems need to be solved.

"I believe tourists have certain basic rights. And Thailand needs to support the large number of tourists that we send with a matching degree of investment in facilities." [110]

Law enforcement was needed when agents cheated customers, the Ambassador said. The Royal Thai Tourist Police needed to have Chinese speaking officers and a hotline service should be added. Prevention and protection from accidents and rip-offs was key to the safety of Chinese tourists and signage needed to be dramatically improved.

"Our people drown on the beaches here because they cannot tell what a red flag is," Ambassador Guan Mu said. "More work needs to be done to educate tourists and save lives."

The admonitions and calls for action went unheeded.

Less than three weeks after the Ambassador's visit to Phuket, a 23-year-old man by the name of Ran Li (pictured[111]) died while on a snorkelling day trip. He drowned at exactly the same site, Koh Racha Yai, where other Chinese tourists had drowned. He had been

---

[110] Phuket Corrupt, Says Chinese Ambassador, Chutima Sidasathian and Premkamon Ketsara, *Phuket Wan*, 29 May, 2013.

[111] Ran Li, 23, drowned off Phuket. Picture *Phuket Wan*.

one of a group of 45 holiday makers when he was hit by a large wave. He was rescued but then dragged out to sea again. Friends in tears accompanied his body back to the mainland.

Phuket Wan commented that boat boys rarely paid attention to the safety of their passengers and Chinese tourists were the nationality with the greatest number of needless drownings: "Many of them are not skilled swimmers or cannot swim at all. Sometimes they are not given basic instructions on how to use a snorkel safely."

The day after Ran Li's death, another Chinese tourist was killed off Phuket, this time by a speedboat propeller near the James Bond island of Phi Phi. Photographs showed Chen Peng's anguished wife grieving over his body. There were contradictory accounts as to the exact circumstances of the 36-year-old's death.

The next day there were two drownings within one hour, the Belgian Laurent Wanter, 42, and Russian Aleksande Poleshchenko, 29. With three metre high waves, a number of other people were rescued on the same day. News commentary blamed travel companies for luring tourists to Thailand's beaches during the monsoon season.

Two days later an Indian tourist Ramesh Chang Singhai drowned at Kata Beach. The following month, in July of 2013, there were five drownings in four days.

In late August of 2013 two Chinese tourists were killed and three people were injured when their speedboat crashed into an anchored long-tail boat.

The incident sparked accomplished journalist Casey Hynes, writing for *Asian Correspondent*, to comment that as someone who had spent time enjoying life in Thailand and appreciating its virtues, it was tragic to read the multiple stories of muggings, attacks, murders, needless deaths and avoidable accidents coming out of Thailand every week. For a place which could be so instantly appealing, and so ravishingly beautiful, the lack of security oversight and absence of safety measures, resulting in multiple tragic deaths, was disconcerting.

One recent horror story had been of a bus crash in which 26 Russian tourists were injured. Another involved a train derailment where 23 tourists of several nationalities were hurt. High crime rates, including muggings, robberies and random attacks, along with appalling safety records, were giving the travelling public pause as to whether Thailand was a desirable destination.

The speedboat crash was yet another in a string of cases: "If you follow news in Thailand at all, you'll have noticed a spate of recent reports on grisly deaths and attacks on tourists and expats in the country. While Thailand is often seen as a paradise for vacationers and expats, these instances raise questions about exactly how safe the country is for foreigners. Anyone who has spent time at many of Thailand's beaches and participated in some of the attractions has seen the lack of safety precautions. People can rent snorkel equipment and boats without demonstrating any competence at all, and transportation not infrequently involves trucks loaded far beyond their capacity with drunk tourists hoping to make it to a party destination.

"To read expat forums in which people comment about the state of affairs here paints a grim picture indeed, one in which little punishment is likely even in the case of violent assaults and murders. So what incentive is there for people to refrain from drunkenly attacking people, robbing them or stabbing them to death?"[112]

Yet despite the high number of deaths and diplomatic condemnation Thailand continued to aggressively lure yet more high-yield Chinese visitors. In September of 2013 the Tourist Authority of Thailand opened up a new office in China's Guangzhou City, in addition to the pre-existing offices in place in Chengdu, Shanghai and Beijing.

The safety of facilities remained a major issue across a range of tourist activities.

In October of 2013 an Indian newlywed was killed in a parasailing accident off the coast of Pattaya.[113] Mrs Shilpi Agarwal had been married less than two weeks when, witness statements

---

[112] Is Thailand still safe for foreigners, Casey Hynes, Asian Correspondent, 2 September, 2013.

[113] Indian newlywed killed in parasailing accident off the coast of Pattaya, *Pattaya One*, 3 October, 2013.

declared, adverse weather conditions led to her parasail ditching into the sea. She was being towed by a speedboat known as "Mr Chang 9", driven by a 25-year-old driver. The driver initiated a U-turn to retrieve Mrs Agarwal from the water, catching the parachute lines which then pulled her headfirst into the rotating blades. The driver was detained by the Port authorities and handed over to Police.

The blog Staying Safe Abroad noted a number of other drowning deaths off Thailand's beaches and called for diplomats to pressure Thailand for greater safety measures to be implemented.

In response to mounting pressure from embassies, tour companies and other stakeholders business interests on Phuket established a campaign Safer Phuket, which brought together the British Embassy, the Office of the Phuket Governor and the Sports Authority of Thailand with major sponsors including the famous Le Meridien Phuket Beach Resort and media outlets including Phuket Gazette and Phuket Radio. A website was launched.

Phuket Wan released a list of 13 deaths between June and November on three of Phuket's best known beaches; Karon, Katai and Katoi Noi, emphasising that these did not take into account fatalities on any of the island's other famous, or drownings on day-trips to nearby islands:

1.. Mr. Ramesh Chand, 56, Indian. June 22, 2013 at 11:33 AM on Kata Beach.
2. Mr. Kho Kaay Gym, 31, Russian. June 23, 2013 at 5.10 PM on Kata Beach.
3. Mr. Carroll Mark William, 61, American. July 7, 2013 at 5.50 PM on Kata Beach.
4. Mr. Dmitry Onisshenko, 32, Russian. July 22, 2013 at 3.56 PM on Karon Beach.
5. Mr. Pruetpol Mookdasanit, 34, Thai. September 7, 2013 on Kata Beach.
6. No name, Burmese. September 19, 2013 at 2.30 PM on Karon Beach.
7. No name, Chinese. September 30, 2013 at 3.50 PM on Karon Beach.

8. Mr. Ozerskikh Oleg, 52, Russian. October 24, 2013 at 10.08 AM on Karon Beach.

9. Mr. Liv Feng Hai, 33, Chinese. October 24, 2013 at 2.50 PM on Karon Beach.

10. No name, Norwegian, 50. November 14, 2013 at 12.10 PM on Karon Beach.

11. No name, 50. November 14, 2013 at 12.40 PM on Katanoi Beach.

12. Mr. Edward Brookes, 63, British. September 20, 2013 at 2.45 PM on Karon Beach.

13. Mrs. Ann Gorli Teres Fjellner, 59, Swedish. September 27, 2013 at 10.30 PM on Karon Beach.

The news site, whose personnel were later to give a presentation to the World Health Organisation on the subject, editorialised that with an increase in Russian and Chinese tourists, many of whom could not swim, there had been an accompanying increase in drownings and needless deaths. Local personnel, including day-trip speedboat crews, had never been trained to act as lifeguards. The sooner beach safety became part of the culture at the island's resorts the sooner their reputation as a safe family destination could be restored: "In response to growing anxiety about beach drownings and marine safety on Phuket, European Union countries—especially Britain—have urged authorities to begin an awareness campaign.... Already, some newspapers are calling for travel agents to warn tourists in advance about the dangers on Phuket—a move that will probably lead to people choosing other destinations. The answer is to fix the problem, not to send tourists home in boxes and urns. An urgent program must be started to educate all resort staff along Phuket's west coast about the beaches so they can properly warn guests about the dangers, from the time that tourists arrive."[114]

Following on from the Chinese Ambassador's visit, in mid-June 2013, European Union Ambassadors and representatives based in Bangkok also made the trek to Phuket. They met with the

---

[114] Phuket's Deadliest Beaches, Where 13 Swimmers Have Drowned in Seven Months, Premkamon Ketsara and Alan Morison, Phuket Wan, 13 December, 2013.

Governor of Phuket Maitri Inthusut and local officials, tour operators and other Honorary Consuls.

An official statement said citizens from their 28 member states made up a large proportion of foreign tourists visiting Phuket. Their per capita spend was high and they made an important contribution to the local economy. The ambassadors said tourists needed to feel safe and that they were being treated fairly. European Union embassies in Bangkok believed that concerns over the safety and welfare of their citizens were widely shared by the diplomatic and broader international communities in Thailand.

In this respect, European Union embassies were keen to see:

- An efficient and fairly priced public transport system in Phuket which was available to foreign tourists and residents alike.
- An end to intimidatory and violent behaviour by an element of tuk tuk and taxi drivers.
- Strict enforcement of marine safety standards, including flags on beaches to indicate when it is safe to swim.
- Strict enforcement of standards of behaviour for public officials, including police and immigration, to ensure that foreign visitors and residents feel protected, treated in a fair way and never at risk of extortion.
- An end to scams involving hiring of equipment such as jet-skis or motorbikes.
- Strict enforcement of road safety regulations.
- Promotion of environmental issues, including monitoring of water quality.

Head of the EU delegation in Thailand David Lipman said there had been many problems on Phuket: "I don't think that the situation is getting better and that's why we really wanted to pursue this matter. I very much hope that the situation will improve. Many people who go to Phuket have a wonderful time and don't encounter problems, but there are a lot of problems that people do encounter."

Lipman said one common scam was to charge large sums of money for pre-existing damage to jet-skis, using threats of violence against people reluctant to pay.

"It's a racket," the diplomat said. "The same with motorbikes as well. People rent out motorbikes. In the middle of the night they're stolen by the people who rented them out in the first place and the next day they say 'let's have our motorbike'."

Fines handed out by local police to tourists for allegedly parking in the wrong spot was another problem."We expect proper standards of behaviour from public officials," Lipman said. "Let's face it, there is a bit of corruption going on and we hope that will be avoided."

In an opinion piece titled "The Carnival of Corruption" the *Phuket Gazette* declared that one and all tacitly accepted that the situation in Phuket was out of hand. Few were offering any realistic strategies to combat the problem at its roots: the well-entrenched mind-set that "playing by the rules is for suckers". It is easy to dismiss corruption as an "inevitable" part of doing business and to point out that no country in the world is completely free of it. However, it could not be ignored that the problem in Phuket had reached grave proportions and was proving extremely harmful to the island's future.

"The good news is that corruption, the island's most fundamental problem, is finally getting the attention it deserves in the national and international media. Nonetheless, if concrete progress on tackling the problem is not achieved through efforts now underway, the only result will be more negative press for the island's all-important tourism industry.[115]

One of Thailand's leading campaigners against corruption in the tourist industry, clearly loved Thailand, for all its flaws. For years Alan Morison had been walking a tightrope in an attempt to prevent his pioneering website *Phuket Wan* from being shut down by the authorities he so regularly criticised. He had been, in a sense, attempting to save the country from itself. The name is meant to echo the phrase "Sweet Phuket Every Day".

In an opinion piece coinciding with the visit of high level delegations to Phuket, Morison wrote: "Shamefully, there are still people in high positions on Phuket who remain determined to keep

---

[115] Carnival of Corruption, *Phuket Gazette*, 1 September, 2013.

Phuket relatively unchanged, people in denial, people who need to be forced to confront reality. They see the world in terms of us and them and fail to acknowledge that the tourists and expats who visit and live on Phuket are entitled to express their opinions and to receive equally fair treatment. In the simplest of terms, the corrupt and complacent island attitudes must be replaced by transparency and action. Otherwise, Phuket's future will grow even murkier. What has to happen is for Phuket's governor and other authorities to actively seek out and involve international expertise in finding solutions for Phuket's problems."

Following the military coup, Morison suddenly found support, or at least coinciding views, at the highest levels of government. Military leader and by that time Prime Minister, General Prayuth, declared in September of 2014 that corruption, which had been accumulating in Thailand for a long time and had severely damaged the country's economy and reputation, was the government's top priority: "The worsening corruption problem has led to political unrest, a division between people in the country, social inequality, and a bad image of Thailand in the eyes of foreigners."[116]

For Australians, Thailand is by far the most dangerous destination on Earth, close to double the next in line, Greece, where immigrants with dual Australian citizenship often return to retire. An Australian dies in Thailand every three days. Hundreds more require consular help, this level of tourist mayhem costing the Australian taxpayer millions of dollars a year. There were 122 deaths of Australians in 2013 which came to consular attention, up from 105 in 2009, when Thailand was already registering as the world's most high-risk tourist destination.

Despite its $7.1 billion budget, Australia's Department of Foreign Affairs (DFAT) offers no ongoing analysis of the reasons behind the high death rates of its country's citizens in Thailand. Once again leading the charge, Alan Morison attacked the Australian government's secrecy over its dead citizens, saying

---

[116] Fighting corruption is government's top priority: Thai PM, 10 September, 2014, *Business Standard*.

attempts to establish an explanation for the exceptionally high ratio of deaths for visitors to the Kingdom had hit a brick wall. He claimed the country appeared to prefer to let its citizens travel in total ignorance about the causes of the alarming rate of deaths in Thailand: "Both the Australian Embassy in Bangkok and DFAT in Canberra, the Australian capital, have declined to provide any explanation for the exceptionally high death rate. This is in contrast to Britain's Foreign and Commonwealth Office, which sends out an explanation of causes and trends with the annual release of its 'travellers in trouble' figures, and responds to journalists' questions.[117]

Proper statistical analysis is the basis for predicting future trends and warning people about potential dangers. Did the dead fall off jet-skis, get mugged by lady boys or suddenly take to drink driving the minute they were out of their own country? "Australia, it seems, does not view the abnormally high death rate of its citizens in Thailand as a problem, or the need for proper statistical analysis as a priority," Morison wrote.

In response to claims of inadequate analysis the then soon-to-be appointed Ambassador to the Association of South East Asian Nations Simon Merrifield said motorbikes, power-ski accidents and alcohol-fuelled mishaps were the most common cause of serious injuries. "Most died from natural causes, such as illness and age but, sadly, many - the result of accident or misadventure - were avoidable," he said. "At any single time, the Bangkok embassy can be managing 200 active consular cases — including providing assistance to the families of the more than 100 Australians who sadly pass away in Thailand each year. Phuket ... can account for as much as 60 per cent of the consular caseload during peak tourism season."

Almost a third of the 1,000 incidents annually reported to Australian consular officials happen on Phuket. In 2012, 146 Australians sought help after being taken to hospital in Thailand, 57 were arrested, 15 were attacked and nine reported child abduction or

---

[117] Thailand 'Deadliest' for Aussies: Cause is Secret, Alan Morison, Phuket Wan, 22 September, 2009.

custody problems. Most arrests involved drugs, theft and assault, with Aussies often facing penalties or jail, even for seemingly minor offences. Consular officials also investigated 82 missing person reports and made 190 welfare checks and other serious investigations.

Melbourne man Sebastian Eric Faulkner, 21, was the first Australian to die in Thailand in 2013 when he fell from the ninth floor of the four star Andaman Beach Suites Hotel in the early hours of New Year's Day.[118] His injuries included a fractured skull. He died in Bangkok Hospital after being transferred from Patong. A representative from his workplace, ANL Shipping, said Sebastian was about to return to university after 12 months with the company. "I have handled the news with the other co-ops because they were very close knit friends and they are all in shock at the moment," the spokeswoman said. "They heard on Facebook ... we are in shock, he was a very good young person and will be very sadly missed. I must admit...they are all very devastated about the news."

Claiming privacy laws prevents them from doing so the Australian government does not release the names of its citizens dying in Thailand. The legislation has the affect of concealing from the Australian public the chaos on the ground, and thereby endangering those who choose to travel there.

One woman who did not die anonymously was Nicole Fitzsimons, a member of Australia's Channel Nine Footy Show team. She was holidaying with her boyfriend, rugby league player Jamie Keith, in Koh Samui in October of 2012.

CCTV footage captured the moment when a local driver, allegedly travelling at 80 kilometres per hour, careered straight into the couple as they waited to turn into their resort on a motorcycle.

Ramming cars and bikes rented by foreigners is a common tactic used to create situations where money can be exploited.

Fitzsimons died three hours after the accident.

---

[118] Melbourne Man Dies after falling from balcony in Phuket, Michelle Ainsworth, *Herald Sun*, 3 January, 2013.

Although his girlfriend had just died, James Keith soon found himself the victim of the infamously corrupt Thai police.

Channel Nine's *A Current Affair* reported that the local police, despite the CCTV footage providing evidence to the contrary, tried to blame him for the death.

Keith told the program the trauma continued when local authorities took him to a police station about six hours after the accident and asked him to sign a statement written in Thai that said the crash was his fault. Hours before he had been on the side of the road yelling for help and comforting his girlfriend, telling her everything would be alright.

"I was vulnerable and they were obviously after one thing and one thing only, it was my money," he said. "It was a way to bribe my way out of it. They threw that report in front of me asking me to sign otherwise they would take my passport. As much as I was hurting... to have evidence there and still blame it on me – I didn't care if they were going to lock me up, there was no way."

Nicole's grieving family were told it would cost between 480,000 and 960,000 baht, roughly between $AUS15,000 and $AUS30,000, to extract Mr Keith from the situation.

Six days after the death of Ms Fitzsimons, the Thai police decided to return Mr Keith's passport, but on the condition that no one would be charged over the crash.

"To sign a blank piece of paper to say it was an accident and that bloke is over there walking free, it burns inside of me," he said.[119]

Channel Nine described the situation as "bad cops" trying to corner a "vulnerable, innocent man".

After the outcry over the allegations, the Fitzsimons case was reopened and the head of the police investigation, who denied allegations of corruption, was transferred. Chief of the Samui Tourism Association said the death could damage the island's reputation in the minds of Australian tourists, and urged the police to be transparent in the investigation to bring justice to the victim.

---

[119] Thai police tried to blame boyfriend for woman's death, Nine News, 27 November, 2012.

The case must be handled in a straightforward manner and the police should not rush to wrap it up, he said.[120]

Nicole's parents travelled to Thailand to repatriate their daughter's body in October 2012.

In an attempt to explain to an Australian media and public outraged by the Fitzsimons' case Melbourne psychologist Sabina Read said parents trying to piece together the last moments of their child's life and the practical implications of their loss could become extremely distressed: "Part of the human psyche is wanting to know the details around the death. You have to negotiate a whole other country with their values, infrastructure, government and laws. Read said. "You specifically get on a plane where everyone is laughing and talking about where they are going and which hotel they are staying at, and you are going to identify or collect your child's body. That level of pain, distress and trauma is beyond comprehension."[121]

In the wake of the attention given their daughter's death, Nicole Fitzsimons' family was deluged with people saying they wanted to donate to a charity that focused on road safety and the dangers of riding motorbikes overseas. Sibling Kate Fitzsimon said establishing the Nicole Fitzsimons Foundation, which carries a message to schools in Australia of the dangers of travelling overseas, was a way of channelling their grief.

Nicole's sister Kate Fitzsimons left a corporate job to establish the Foundation, travelling to schools in NSW, Queensland and the Northern Territory, raising awareness of travel safety overseas.

Two years after Nicole Fitzsimons death, Kate said the Foundation was now travelling from school to school educating youth about never compromising their personal safety while travelling overseas: "I know in my heart through sharing Nicole's story we are saving lives, one presentation at a time. Many foreign countries do not have the same safety standards as Australia and there can be dramatic differences in culture, rules and regulations

---

[120] Phuket: Australian Samui crash case reopened, Claire Connell, *The Phuket News*, 5 December 2012.

[121] Rite of passage comes with a high risk for those seeking foreign adventures, Lindy Alexander, *Sydney Morning Herald*, 26 January, 2014.

that they need to be aware of prior to arriving in that destination. Nicole would have never jumped on that bike had she known how many people are killed and injured on Southeast Asian roads every day."

According to the World Health Organisation, Thailand has the world's third worst road safety record, after Eritrea and Mauritania. There are an average of 38.1 deaths per 100,000, compared to 5.2 in Australia, 6.0 in Canada and 3.0 in Sweden. Foreigners, with no experience in handling the chaos of Thailand's traffic and usually driving rented vehicles, are particularly prone to mishap.

One life the Nicole Fitzsimons Foundation failed to save was that of Australian tourist Owen Dalby, 20,[122] who died after a motorcycle crash on the party island of Koh Phangan.

The popular body-surfer from the mid-north NSW town of Coffs Harbour was credited with shielding his friend, who was travelling in the bike's side car, from the full force of the crash.

A tribute stated: "Owen was everything he was meant to be. An amazing soul with a heart full of love. May his kind and caring soul find peace."[123]

Larry Cunningham, Australia's outspoken honorary consul in Phuket, said more than 50 Australians were dying on Phuket alone each year. Scams and criminality had increased to such an extent that expatriates wanted to leave the island.

Cunningham said young travellers were specially targeted by gangs and local police. He described one incident of a young Australian man who was involved in a minor traffic accident when riding a rental bike. He was told by police an injured man's condition was serious and was forced to pay thousands of dollars in compensation. An investigation found the Thai man had minor injuries.

In another incident, in June of 2012 a 27-year-old New Zealand man Sean Kenzie was badly injured in a motorbike

---

[122] Owen Dalby, 20. Picture *Coffs Coast Advocate*.

[123] Australian tourist Owen Dalby dies from motorbike impact on the island of Koh Phangan, *Koh Phangan News*, 21 July, 2013.

accident. Despite paying for insurance before travelling, the coverage excluded medical expenses arising from motorbike accidents.

An appeal was called on to help him pay a $A20,000 medical bill for injuries including a split liver, punctured lungs, broken ribs, as well as surgery to reattach shoulder muscles and jaw bones.

Drawing from Kenzie's experience, and many other similar incidents, Mr Cunningham was blunt: "Don't hire a motorbike - period."

The Australian and British Ambassadors joined in the condemnation of tourist scams, warning that tourists should be wary of extortion gangs who were in cahoots with local police.[124]

Australian Ambassador James Wise said travellers needed to be on their guard when they hired jet-skis or motorcycles. "Consider the implications if it is stolen or damaged," he said. "Foreigners are commonly detained by police until compensation, often thousands of dollars, is negotiated between the parties." He also warned travellers never to hand over their passport as a guarantee to a hiring company: "If a dispute arises, it can be extremely difficult or impossible to recover your passport until compensation is settled."

British Ambassador Mark Kent said travellers should be cautious in "crowded markets, tourist sites, bus or train stations and festivals. It is best to avoid isolated neighbourhoods, shortcuts, narrow alleys and poorly lit streets, especially late at night."

Although the scandal over tourist safety ran hot throughout 2013, attracting international coverage and numerous statements of concern from senior Thai officials and international ambassadors posted to Bangkok, nothing, it seemed, could stop the flood of tourists to Thailand.

A report from the Thai Tourism Ministry, in September announced that the number of tourist arrivals for the first half of the year had jumped an unexpected 20 per cent. A government spokesman said there had been 14.9 million arrivals between January and July, a 20.77 per cent increase on the previous year. In

---

[124] Aussies warned about Phuket scamsters, *The Sydney Morning Herald*, 24 December, 2012.

July alone 2.2 million tourists had entered Thailand, an increase of 400,000 persons, or 22.77 per cent, year-on-year.

Thailand's top-ten foreign traveller countries of origin were: China, Japan, South Korea, Laos, Vietnam, Singapore, India, Australia and Russia, in that order.[125]

While tourist numbers defied gravity, travel expert for the British newspaper *The Telegraph* Tom Vater warned that particular care should be taken by visitors: "Phuket has more than its fair share of troubles, from aggressive taxi drivers, to jet-ski operators looking to scam tourists, bag snatchers and young disenfranchised kids out to cause trouble. Much of the island is run by mafias and the police are not always sympathetic to foreigners' complaints. Single female travellers are advised to be vigilant while out at night, as sexual assaults on foreigners in Thailand are on the rise."[126]

In a piece on the dangers for tourists in Thailand, the *Chiang Rai Times* compiled a list of foreigners whose deaths had made it into media accounts over a three month period in 2013.[127]

The English language newspaper reported there was no shortage of tourists who had no understanding of the dangers they could get themselves into.

"The violent attacks against tourists in Thailand are actually quite common and anyone who tells you otherwise is either clueless, or doing this because they are affiliated with the tourism industry and are afraid of a drop in tourist numbers. There are literally violent attacks on tourists daily and the Thai authorities do their best to not report these incidents to other countries as they know it will ruin the tourism industry. The violent attacks are usually the result of a mugging gone wrong, or a tourist misbehaving or being disrespectful.

"It doesn't seem to matter how many foreigners get hurt or killed, there are always new tourists who get into trouble that don't know a thing about Thailand that fall victim to a crime. Remember

---

[125] Thailand News Agency, 18 September, 2013.

[126] Fears over safety of tourists in Phuket, Natalie Paris, The Telegraph, 14 March, 2013.

[127] The Dangers for Foreigners in Thailand, *Chiang Rai Times*, 2 May, 2013.

that life is cheap in Thailand and death isn't as big a thing as it is in most other countries and in particular—the death of a tourist, doesn't mean much to them at all."

The piece concluded that there were numerous reports of men coming to Thailand, falling in love with a bar girl and "then they run out of money on their holiday and the fantastic times come to an end so they jump to their death. . . If you are mentally unwell and you are staying in a high rise building and plan on getting drunk, then this could be a recipe for disaster."

Reports of foreigners being thrown off buildings could not be checked as the deaths were often classified as suicides.

Below is the list of deaths of foreigners compiled by the *Chiang Rai Times*:

February 2013

Marcel Spiess, Switzerland – Phuket, 23 February 2013
Henri Antonova, Russia – Koh Phangan, 22 February 2013
Unidentified male, 50s – Pattaya, 20 February 2013
Stefan Braunwalder, Switzerland – Phuket, February 16, 2013
Hans-Jurgen Umbreit, Germany, Phuket, 15 February 2013
Anthony J Scarrabelotti, Australia – Surin, 14 February 2013
Peter Root, UK – Chachoengsao, 13 February 2013 (pictured with Thompson)
Mary Thompson, UK – Chachoengsao, 13 February 2013 (pictured with Root)
Alexey Babenko, Russia – Phuket, 13 February 2013
George John Bishop, UK – Pattaya, 12 February 2013
Rustem Sadri, Turkey – Pattaya, 11 February 2013
Simon Ashley, USA – Phuket, 11 February 2013
Frank Robert Gulbensen, Norway – Phuket , 9 February 2013
Unidentified male, 23, USA – Phuket, 9 February 2013
Paul Porter, Canada – Chiang Mai, 8 February 2013
Delphine Jofette Raene Kiesser, France – Chumpon, 6 February 2013
Ivan Malyukov, Russia – Phuket, 6 February 2013
Evgenii Pozhitkov, Russia – Phuket, 4 February 2013
Rudolf Urbain, Belgium – Chiang Rai, 3 February 2013

March 2013

Male, Austria, 70 – Phuket, 29 March 2013
James "Jimmy" Madigan, USA, 64 – Phuket, 29 March 2013 (pictured)

Christian Klasky, Germany, 34 - Pattaya, 27 March 2013

Michel Rooer Edmond Harnisch, France, 58 – Chiang Mai, 26 March 2013

Oleg Udaloi, Russia, 44 – Phuket, 22March 2013

John Pickin, UK, 52 – Koh Samui, 24 March 2013

Derek Rodney Gent, UK, 69 – Koh Samui, 23 March 2013 (pictured with Holmes)

Michael Holmes, UK, 68 – Koh Samui, 23 March 2013 (pictured with Gent)

Jorg Frings, Germany, 44 – Pattaya, 9 March 2013

Wade Mckee, UK – Isaan, 8 March 2013

Aleksei Iasev, Russia, 34 – Pattaya, 7 March 2013

Dan Bubis, Israel, 56 – Pattaya, 7 March 2013

Theo Schitz, Germany, 56 – Pattaya, 6 March 2013

Martin, UK, – Ban Chang, 6 March 2013

Andrei Komarov, Russia, 39 – Pattaya, 6 March 2013

Ian Blackburn,UK, 61 – Pattaya, 6 March 2013

Male, Australia, 53 – Phuket, 5 March 2013

Male, Sweden, 30s – Koh Phangan, 5 March 2013

Mikko Ulevt Mantere, Finland, 41 – Phuket, 2 March 2013

April 2013

Faetra Petillo, USA, 29 – Phuket, 30 April 2013 (pictured)

Male, Malta, 70 – Phuket, 30 April 2013

Dieu Yoann, France, 26 – Phuket, 30 April 2013

Paul Otto Norbert Richter, Germany, 70 – Bangkok, 30 April 2013

Mark Anthony Woodward, Australia, 45 – Pattaya 30 April 2013

Lane Raphael Woodren, Germany, 21 – Chumphon, 27 April 2013

Paul Ancell, UK, 33 – Phuket, 22 April 2013

Eino Olavi Ahlfors, Finland, 73 – Pattaya, 18 April 2013

Male, 40-50 – Pattaya, 17 April 2013

Peter Lutz Teubner, Germany, 57 – Phuket, 17 April 2013

Hans Peter Hermann Stamminger, Switzerland, 65 – Pattaya, 15 April 2013

Colin Callanan, Ireland, 29 – Koh Tao, 15 April 2013

Oyvind Holmen, Norway, 57 – Khon Kaen, 11 April 2013

Timothy Joseph Carr, USA, 57 – Pattaya, 10 April 2013 (pictured)

Sofia Marain, Belgium, 21 – Phitsanulok, 8 April 2013

Tor Per-Erik Hedberg, Sweden, 65 – Pattaya, 7 April 2013

Hans Kunne, Germany, 84 – Pattaya, 6 April 2013

Lief Anders Lonvik, Norway, 68 – Pattaya, 6 April 2013

Every month another list.

If anybody bothered to compile or publish them.

In an environment where the press is heavily censored and negative stories about the fates of foreigners discouraged, The *Chiang Rai Times* piece was exceptional for its rarity.

Despite the record number of deaths, with the exception of data released by the British Foreign Office, no proper statistical analysis of tourist deaths is available. The travelling public are being kept in the dark by a collusion of government and private interests. Academic studies are non-existent. As in many fields of human endeavour, researchers only find what they are funded to find. But the deaths of tourists in Thailand has become so common that the phenomenon is now the subject of black humour.

The website Living Thai promoted an unscientific list of the Top Ten most common ways to die in Thailand:

1) Vehicle accident. Thailand ranked high in the list of countries where tourists die from vehicle accidents. "Keep your eyes on the road."

2) Murdered by a Thai. There are so many different ways foreigners have died at the hands of a Thai they couldn't possibly all be listed here. Stabbing is named as a favourite.

3) Murdered by a foreigner. Lately there has been a swing in trend of Thai murders Farang. It's now Farang Kills Farang. Swedes will kill Swedes, Brits will beat up other Brits, and Russians will kneecap other Russians. It's the way of the future here in Thailand.

4) Suicide. There is something magical about Thailand isn't there?

5) Killed by Your Thai Girlfriend.

6) Being a Successful businessman in Thailand.

7) Heart attack from sex with a young woman.

8) Food Poisoning.

9) HIV/AIDS.

10) For reasons unknown and unexplained. "Many deaths in Thailand go unexplained and some conspirators say it's a cover up by the Thai police, the authorities might bring in experts and like most farang bodies get sent overseas for more tests all of them

inconclusive. While we might never know why they really died, we do know that we don't know how they died."[128]

Not all Thailand's personal tragedies end in death.

While there had been a few homeless Westerners on the streets of Thailand for decades, their rising numbers prompted a spate of media stories during 2013.

The stories were a novelty to Thais, accustomed to thinking of foreigners as affluent.

Homeless foreigners[129] number in the hundreds, sharing the same streets as an estimated 30,000 homeless Thai nationals, as well as an indeterminate number of Lao, Burmese and Cambodians.[130]

In widely reported comments, Natee Saravari, Secretary-General of the Issarachon Foundation, a non-government group focusing on the homeless, said a growing number of foreign tourists and retirees were ending up on the streets of Thailand and the country should change its mindset to help them.[131]

Charity groups estimated that there are some 200 to 300 foreigners living on the streets in Thailand, most of them in large cities such as Pattaya, Phuket, Chiang Mai and Bangkok.

"We are starting to see more and more homeless foreigners, many of whom have separated from their Thai wives and now have no money," Natee said. "They walk or sit in shopping malls during the daytime and scavenge through garbage for food at night. Of every 10 homeless foreigners, five will say they have been cheated by their Thai wives or families, three would put it down to business partners, while the rest would offer other reasons."

In some cases, these foreigners—mostly male Westerners—arrived as tourists or retirees and fell into poverty or neglect after settling down in Thailand, often having being duped or robbed.

---

[128] Top 10 Most likely ways to die in Thailand, Living Thai, 31 January, 2013.

[129] Picture of homeless man courtesy of Meebal.

[130] Hundreds of Westerners Living on the Streets of Thailand, *TIME*, 13 September, 2013.

[131] Special Report, Homeless foreigners 'lack assistance', *The Nation*, 19 August, 2013.

There was no Thai government agency or even a policy in place to help them.

When arrested or found by the police, most of the homeless were deported.

In one of the few stories to get media coverage, a Greek man was found lying in a street in Phuket, outside a property he claimed his girlfriend had swindled from him.[132] Konstantinos Vardas's mid-road protest caused a traffic jam. Police found the 56-year-old man in a distressed state shouting he wanted his property back. He said he had bought a house for them to live together in. "When I came back from my trip to the USA, I learned that the document of property ownership had been transferred," he said. "Moreover, about two million baht had gone missing from my bank account. Now I have no money to buy any food. I'm in a desperate state, and would like my embassy to help me."

Left penniless by Thai girlfriends, or wrestling with drinking or substance abuse problems, many have nowhere else to go, freelance Irish writer Paul Garrigan, author of *Dead Drunk: saving myself from alcoholism in a Thai monastery* said: "Some people come to Thailand and they already have a drink or drug problem but they have it under control in their own country, but then the restrictions have gone and that addiction can blossom. [133]

Despite the numerous cautionary tales on the consequences of compulsive or incautious partying in the densely atmospheric world of Thailand's night life, pitiful tales of lovelorn foreigners continue to emerge.

Legal advisor Rhys Bonney says a wealth of books have been written about the folly of tangling with Thai bar girls, but foreign men are unable to separate the truth from what they are being told. He told *Time* "Foreigners seeking a little companionship become easy prey. Unfamiliar with Thai bureaucracy, they get pressured into buying cars in their girlfriend's name. The reality is that there's no difficulty to do it in their own name. Next they buy a house in her

---

[132] Greek claims Thai girlfriend swindled him out of Phuket property, two million baht, *Phuket Gazette*, 15 September, 2013.

[133] Hundreds of Westerners Living on the Streets of Thailand, *TIME*, 13 September, 2013.

name with the proviso that they will share everything equally, but no legal documents are signed to that effect. And when they've paid the money the girlfriend can just kick them out."

Without a social safety net, embarrassed about returning to their own countries or without any real home to return to foreigners ended up homeless on the streets. A spokesman for the US Embassy in Bangkok said requests for repatriation from Americans who had run out of money was "more than a trickle".

The stories sparked a wave of commentary and self-analysis on the subject of the trickeries of Thai wives. An editor with the opinion based newsletter *Meebal* wrote that he was not surprised foreigners were ending up homeless and relayed one account:

"I was one of those trusting foreigners who put the land and house in my Thai wife's name. Little did I know that she was gambling and she used the house and land as collateral for her mounting debts. In the end I lost 15 million Thai Baht, nearly $500,000.

"She said she was too ashamed to tell me of her habit which is why she kept silent. I came back from my work offshore to find that the house had been taken by a certain police officer for just a 2 million baht debt. I tried to discuss this with the now new owner; but he wasn't interested, after all why would he be, he now had a 15 million baht home for 2 million. Foreigners need to be careful and my advice would be to rent, it's just easier and will give you peace of mind."[134]

One Thai woman, married to a German and with two children, wrote: "I've read so many horror stories about how foreigners are treated in Thailand and it saddens me deeply and often makes me totally ashamed to be Thai. It often saddens me that many foreigners view all Thai women as bar girls. Yes, Thailand does have a very bad reputation for being a country whereby sex can be bought easily but that doesn't mean all Thai girls will readily sleep with a foreign man for money.

"I have little or no time for the Thai Government, they are all crooks and anyone believing they are there to help the people are

---

[134] Foreigners Being Financially Ruined by Thai Wives, *Meebal*, 19 August, 2013.

simply delusional. The Thai Government does nothing more than sweep important issues under the carpet; issues that affect both Thai citizens and foreign nationals residing here. Thais are often perceived as xenophobic, nationalist, greedy and corrupt and this is yet another reason why I am often so ashamed of my heritage. We seem unwilling to put aside for one moment personal gain and look to the greater good and what Thailand could really achieve on the world stage if only we could look beyond our own greed.

"I know, as a Thai, that Thais often look upon foreigners as being rich but also second class citizens; this is another attitude the Thai people must change. Just because someone is rich does not give others the right to think it is acceptable to fleece them.

"I am ashamed to be Thai for these reasons and others but I do love my country and hope that one day we will have a better understanding of the world and those in it and through this bring about change that will allow both Thais and foreigners to live together whereby respect is mutual and upheld.

"For all those who have been robbed or duped by a Thai woman I can only apologise but also say that not all Thai women are the same."[135]

It is common knowledge to the Thais that at any one time tens of thousands of foreigners briefly dwelling in the kingdom are being cheated out of their life savings in relationship scams. The foreigners believe they are in a genuine relationship. The local population know better. The intimate nature of the scam and the chorus of laughter from the surrounding Thais makes the results all the more devastating for foreigners thus caught.

Tourist Thailand's terrain of incident throws up multiple peculiarities and studies of human behaviour, some of them funny or burlesque, including drunken foreigners leaping from hotel windows when they discover their "lady of the night" is no lady at all. There is always some sort of mayhem; not all of it life threatening, some of it just delinquent, insane, intoxicated or downright bizarre.

---

[135] Ashamed to be a Thai Citizen, *Meebal*, 20 August, 2013.

But with murder by "intimates" aka sex workers a common event, along with road accidents, drownings, poisonings, knifings and numerous other mishaps, most of them avoidable, much of it is just desperately sad.

In February, 2013, Belgian tour leader Rudolf Urbain, 63, died in his hotel room in the northern city of Chiang Rai. Police assumed he died of a heart attack. Also in February, a Russian man, Ivan Malyukov, 53, was found dead sitting upright at a restaurant table. He was discovered by staff from the hotel Aloha Villa at around 7am. His glasses and keys were on the table next to him. He was said to be a heavy drinker. In the same month an American carrying an Australian driver's licence, died in a motorbike accident on the steep curves near Phuket's famous Le Meridien Beach Resort. Roses were found strewn at the site of the crash and police believe he may have been on his way to visit a girlfriend.

Also in the same month a British couple from Guernsey in the Channel Islands, on a round-the-world cycling trip, died in a traffic accident 70 kilometres east of Bangkok. Thailand was their 23rd country. Peter Root and Mary Thompson were both artists, both aged 34 and had been together since they were 20-years-old. Root's devastated father described them as a golden couple who loved life.

Again in the same month, Anthony Scarrabelotti, 44, from Australia, died after plunging from a hotel balcony in Surin, in northeast Thailand. Hospital staff said he thought his Thai girlfriend had someone else in the room and died of a broken heart. Police attempted to contact the girlfriend.

In March well-known expat James "Jimmy" Madigan, 64, the first volunteer coordinator for the Phuket tourist police, died from what appeared to be severe food poisoning. He was the founding president of the US Navy League in Phuket. A spokesman for the League said: "There was no hesitation in Jimmy's step. He loved life to the hilt." A Tourist Police spokesperson said: "Everyone who knew Jimmy will remember him as a person with a passion to help others."

On the 30th of April two tourists were found dead on the same day and in the same street in Rawai, Phuket's first tourist beach. Longtail boats for hire line its shores. The first to be discovered was Frenchman, Dieu Yoann, 26. His body was found by the owner of the house after she smelled something bad. Looking through a window she saw the corpse hanging from a door frame by a length of telephone cable. Police estimated the man had been dead for about 10 days. There were reportedly no signs of a disturbance and no suicide letter.

Five hours after the discovery of Yoann, the body of a 29-year-old American woman, Faetra Petillo, was found in a guesthouse in the same road. A freelance writer, editor and playwright from Brooklyn, she was found lying face-down on her bed, wearing just a singlet and underpants. There were no signs of violence, but police said her face was "very white". 142

On the same evening, but in a different part of Phuket, the naked body of a 70-year-old Maltese man was found at the Maximum Guesthouse. His girlfriend said the man was a heavy smoker and an asthmatic.

In July of 2013 the body of Robbie Robinson, 32, (pictured)[136] was flown home to Ireland. He had been in a coma for four weeks after falling from the fourth floor of an apartment complex in Bangkok. His devastated family refused to turn off his life support in the hope of a miracle. In a statement his family said: "Robbie has gone on to save lives, by donating his organs, so even in his passing he was amazing and touched even more hearts." The family was saddled with a six-figure hospital bill.

In bar and street fights, random bashings and other altercations, the hostility of ethnic Thais to foreigners, particularly Westerners, often boils out into the open.

In mid-2013 a video of a machete attack on an elderly American on the streets of Bangkok was put up on Facebook and promoted on one of the most popular internet forums for expatriates, Thai Visa Forum. The CCTV footage showed a Thai

---

[136] Robbie Robinson Fund Facebook Page.

taxi driver, who was later charged with murder, waving a large blade as he hunts down his frightened customer.

The argument was over a $2 taxi fare.

While many assaults occur off camera, or at least are not posted on Facebook, the video was remarkable for the fact that it demonstrated the schism between visiting foreigners and the local population. The incident barely received any coverage in the Thai media.

In late July of 2013 another American was stabbed to death on the holiday island of Krabi during a dispute with three local musicians about his behaviour on and off the stage. At about 3am Bobby Carter sustained a fatal knife wound to the stomach, while his son Adam, 27, was severely beaten. According to police the two tourists visited the Longhorn Saloon, where father and son joined the musicians for a jam session on stage. Carter senior allegedly refused to leave the stage after the jam session, leading to an argument.

In August 14-year-old British boy Ethan-jade Williams died in hospital after what was thought may have been an allergic reaction to cashew nuts. "I miss your husky little voice as you ran down the path calling my name… We will love you and miss you forever," one family member wrote.

In September of 2013, two suspects aged 19 and 22 were arrested for allegedly murdering an American, Stefen Morfiella, 70, in an internet cafe in South Pattaya.

It was yet another in a string of killings of foreigners by young Thais.

Travel operators, bloated by a multi-billion dollar industry and deluding their customers with glossy brochures, take no responsibility for the welfare of often gullible tourists entranced by the easy availability of everything from alcohol and drugs to massage girls and ladyboys.

Certainly no such warnings emanate from Thailand itself.

The cautions that do exist on various travel websites or are contained in official travel advisories have little impact. Family oriented tourists are not warned that many of the facilities catering for them and their children, including buses, boats, ferries and jet-skis, are not safe; and that the stringent occupational health and safety guidelines that apply for any company interacting with the general public in their own countries simply don't exist in Thailand.

Hollywood Nightclub, Patong. Phuket.
Courtesy of Bangkok Private Party

It is, of course, Thailand's reputation as a place to party for which it is most famous, or infamous. But tourists are not warned that the majority of bars, clubs, brothels and other places they find so fascinating are in fact run by the Thai or Russian mafia, in other words by some very unpleasant, unprincipled and dangerous people indeed. While the interlinking criminal groups known collectively as the Thai mafia are known for their bluster, close relationships with the police and tendency to operate in packs, the Russian mafia are known for their ruthlessness and stealth. The arrival of the Russian mafia in Asia, a group closely associated with smuggling of all kinds, particularly drugs, has transformed Thai nightlife. A number of areas now cater exclusively to Russians.

The pleasure dens tourists so eagerly seek are not safe. And the more travellers relax in the false bonhomie of the bars, the more unsafe they become.

Often drunk or off their guard while on holidays, fooled by the marketing of Thailand, trusting people they should never have trusted, sightseers are not warned of the very high probability of having their drinks spiked, or that they stand a very real chance of being bashed and robbed by mafia run gangs.

A relaxed attitude to prostitution is all very well and good, and despite the moralising from various quarters not a cultural trait to be criticised. But with the inherent dislike and distaste for foreigners, which is a national trait, often comes zero respect from sex workers for their customer's welfare or safety, and zero respect for their property, at a time or in circumstances when those individuals are most vulnerable. The attitude of murderous indifference to the welfare of strangers is ingrained enough in the Thai psyche for it to justify formal government warnings to the many hundreds of thousands of tourists venturing into the bars and clubs of Thailand on a nightly basis.

It is standard operating procedure in Thailand for the bars and clubs to pay bribes to the local police and municipal authorities in order to be able to open their doors. If a bar, club or parlour does not make this payment in all likelihood they will be closed down. The police are not acting in the best interests of the visitors making complaints for the simple reason that they are being paid by bar and club owners; the commonplace complaints of tourists about being robbed are simply shrugged off.

Those who don't understand the system, that almost every Thai policeman is on the take and expects to be paid, could well find themselves in jail. Or killed. One common saying from the locals sums it up: "Bangkok police same same Bangkok mafia." The saying can be adapted for the whole of Thailand.

The lack of warnings, or education of tourists visiting the kingdom, means that many visitors are under the illusion that there is a legal apparatus and judicial process to which they can turn for assistance. The lack of education on the dangers of Thailand is little more than criminal negligence on the part of the travel operators peddling their wares, and a clear breach of a legislated duty of care on the part of many countries supplying tourists to Thailand.

Tourists are not warned that if they are robbed and bashed in the bars and nightclubs, there is little use complaining to the local police. Indeed, if they persist in their complaints, the tourists may well find themselves being seriously harassed, entrapped, threatened or murdered.

It is a well oiled machine, made possible by the fact that most tourists stay less than a fortnight; are in a country which they do not understand and are powerless to take any action.

The same sex worker that robbed a tourist one day and was the subject of a complaint to the police will be back working at the same club the next night, primed and ready to fleece another customer. For both the police and the bar owners themselves benefit from these robberies. In essence, the bars are running organised gangs of thieves masquerading as sex workers.

Below, courtesy of the Phuket Police, is a list of 47 foreigners who died in Phuket in the first six months of 2014, the latest available at the time of writing.

Phuket Wan editor Alan Morison noted, "Police only list the cases in which they were involved. Many people die without the police being notified." As shocking as the available evidence is, there are widespread concerns that the official lists of the dead constitute only a partial record of the true situation on the ground. Thai authorities, for example, are rarely called to and do not attend most drowning deaths of foreigners, which therefore do not show up in the official records. As well, there are many obvious omissions. In 2012, two foreigners and two Thais were killed in a fire at the well known Tiger Disco fire in Patong. Despite the incident receiving international media coverage the deaths of a British tourist, Michael Tzouvanni, 24 and a French tourist Emmanuel Bacard, 30, did not appear on any police records of deceased foreigners.

It is also worth emphasising that these are just the officially recorded deaths of tourists on one Thai island. There were many more deaths of foreigners spread across the country.

All of these people had parents, siblings, children, friends, colleagues, other lives, people who loved them.

And then they made the decision to holiday in Thailand.

Expat, Tourist Deaths on Phuket January-July 2014

Paul Norris, 46, Britain, January 12 Vichit motorcycle crash (pictured)
Mariwan Qader Salim, 27, Iraq January 13 Naka Island drowning
Peter Richard Hofmann, 77, Germany January 19 Patong Bathroom fall
Daniel Burkhard, 72, Switzterland January 23 Patong personal illness
Adin Medzic, 47, Australia, January 30 Patong Hosptial steps fall (pictured)
Gregory Tanqueray, 37, France, February 3 Karon motorcycle crash
Georg Erwin Bach, 55, Germany, February 5 Laem Ka Rawai flying machine crash
Karl Peyer Huch, 71, Germany February 7 Phuket City no clear cause
Gulaker Tore, 52, Normay February 8 Patong personal illness
Timur Ivanov, 43, Russia February 9 Cherng Talay personal illness
Yafet Matahelumal, 24, Indonesia February 10 Rassada murder
Stefan Hans Dressel, 55, Germany February 12 Patong Hospital personal illness
Mrs Rabdall Sadra McIntosh, 72, Britain February 15 Cherng Talay personal illness
Lars Gunnar Roland Hasselberg, 58, Sweden February 18 Patong OTOP bar top fall
Miss Julie Andree Helene Humbert, 32, France February 20 Thalang Car, motorcycle crash (pictured)
Guy John Talbot Hobbs, 20, Australia February 20 Rawai personal illness
Mrs Margret Hiller, 73, German February 21 Thalang steps fall
Straka Robin Ulf Mikael, 25, Finland February 24 Kamala pedestrian crash
Oleg Ukraine, 28, Ukraine February 23 Phuket City balcony fall
Cornells Jocobus Van Der Linden, 62, Netherlands February 25 Patong personal illness
Uvarov Vladimir, 55, Russia February 26 Cherng Talay cause undetermined
Josh Christian Ezell, 42, US February 28 Thalang motorcycle crash
Mrs Monkika Finke 57 Germany March 10 Patong personal illness
Wayne Anthony Stone 48 Australia March 13 Kamala motorcycle crash
Reima Juhani Aro 51 Finland March 21 Patong Hospital personal illness
Malcolm William Murdoch 63 Britain March 25 Cherng Talay personal illness
Miss Tiffany Gagnon 22 Canada April 1 Patong Hospital personal illness
Alexey Yanchenko 28 Kyrgystan April 2 Kathu motorcycle crash
Bent Vagnso 54 Denmark April 3 Phuket International Hospital personal illness

Bay Kheng Yeow 43 Singapore April 3 Renaissance Mai Khao no cause recorded

Henning Bargfeldt 57 Denmark April 8 Honey Resort Karon personal illness

Kiselev Lgor 59 Russia April 15 Karon fatal fall

Walter Frederick Bell 63 Britain April 15 Patong Hospital personal illness

Fabrice Boigeol 37 France April 18 Morakot Bungalow Rawai murder

Hu Hehui, 51, China April 19 Vichit motorcycle crash

Mrs Anna Claudia Schmid Groppuso, 59, Switzerland April 26 Vachira Hospital Phuket personal illness

Roberto Bechetti, 47, Italy May 2 Happy Apartments Patong suicide

Neilsen Henrik Ebsen, 64, Denmark May 8 Nili Marina Hotel Patong personal illness

Ronald Douglas Litherland, 67, Australia May 11 Cherng Talay personal illness

David Charles Staddon, 59, British May 19 Patong personal illness

Tommy Joachim Bernholdson, 50, Swedish May 21 Absolute Guesthouse Patong suicide

Jae Joon Lee, 83, Korea May 30 Vichit personal illness

Bates Denis Joseph, 31, Irish May 30 Vichit motorcycle crash (pictured)

Gnyaneshwar Sindol, 57, India, June 3 Star Cruise personal illness

Philippe Wagner, 45, Switzerland June 4 Karon pickup, truck motorcycle crash

Richard Stephen Griffin, 46, Ireland June 17 PTN Apartment Patong personal illness

Matthias Ehlbeck, 48, Germany June 28 Rawai motorcycle crash

Yalcin Dagdelen, 45, Turkey July 6 Le Meridien Resort Karon drowning

Chiang Rai, Northern Thailand.

THE MANY SCAMS

"Thailand: Scam Land."

The expression is commonly repeated by members of the expatriate community in Thailand, and is also the title of a short book.

The energetic author of *Thailand Scam Land: 50 Most Common Scams*,[137] writing under the pseudonym The Blether in order to protect himself from harassment while living in Thailand, has produced a string of short books warning foreigners to be on their guard.

His titles include *Why You Shouldn't Retire to Thailand*, *The Vicious Truth About Thai Hookers* and *Thailand: The Ten Cardinal Sins*.

Without literary artifice, Blether exposes the multiple scams foisted on tourists and the mind boggling levels of corruption within the local police. The attitude of Thais to the foreigners trampling on their soil, that they are nothing but walking ATMs who deserve to lose their money as quickly as possible, is also exposed.

Yet like many other foreigners, he retains an affectionate regard for Thailand despite its obvious pitfalls, and returns frequently.

The books are designed as a warning to the hundreds of thousands of aging foreigners deluded into thinking of Thailand as some kind of luxury retirement village; and the legions of men who come to find love, companionship, sex or a 24-hour party. Thailand may be a magically beautiful country, with every day a pleasurable assault on the senses, but no one should be under any illusions about the reality of the situation they are entering.

As Blether explains it: "There are plenty of books available that sing the praises of Thailand, and I am certainly a great fan of the country. However I'm not a fan of the growing element that sets out to scam tourists and to set people up. I wanted to write

---

[137] Cover image Thailand Scam Land. Supplied by the author.

about the wonderful culture, the nightlife, and the amazing beaches. That's the book that the tourist industry in Thailand wants to see written too.

"They want to project an image that Thailand is a friendly and welcoming country. As too many tourists discover to their cost, though, that's not the case. Some scams can be very expensive, and I mean to the point of people losing their entire life savings. Setting aside the financial implications, there are many occasions when these scams can erupt into devastating violence and worse."

Blether describes Thailand as an eye-opener: "On my first night in Pattaya I thought it was a world-class party town. By the second day I started to notice things that concerned me, and after a week I left and never went back. The industrial level scamming and sexual victimisation that underpins that coastal city is appalling. The more time I spend in Thailand, the further away from the tourist areas I go. I spend my time these days with Thai people that are just as appalled with what goes on in the tourist areas as I am. These people are the backbone of Thailand—hard working, industrious and with a great capacity for friendship.

"They have taken me in, shown me their way of life, and even taken me to live in temples with them. Sitting in a temple in the northern Thai countryside is a compelling and life-affirming experience. I arrived in Pattaya, and the further away I get from it the happier I am.

"This is the Thailand I want people to see, to watch on as 95-year-old head monks head off to distribute medicines to the Hill-Tribe people. To watch as young kids strive to get to university, to celebrate as my friends open small businesses.

"This is my Thailand—I love it.

"I don't have any affection for the parts of Thailand/Thai society that I discuss in my 'rougher' books. I made a mistake going to Pattaya, however I suppose I learned a lot quickly. Phuket was also an eye-opener, and listening to the many appalling stories I heard got me thinking about the serious dislocation between expectation and reality.

"My books are not aimed at the mongers—there's plenty of how to get a hooker books out there. My books are aimed at the innocent tourists that get victimised (*Scam Land*)—the guys that are sitting in the west thinking 'hey, maybe I could go to Thailand and get a wife'—they should be reading *The Vicious Truth*. The bombastic, ignorant and deluded cannot be helped. My hope, and I know that it has happened, is that some people read the books and step away from problematic situations."[138]

Foreigners are often genuinely puzzled as to why the tourist infrastructure they assume exists to protect them, including organisations like the Royal Thai Tourist Police, does nothing of the kind. And why those they have been so kind to can turn around and rob them with such apparent glee. Blether issues a warning to any foreigner unfortunate enough to interact with the local authorities that the Thai police routinely scam, victimise and extort foreigners. And do so with complete impunity; without fear of being disciplined by their superiors.

"Often when they show up at an incident involving a foreigner it's not to see that justice is done, it's to force payment. Their arrival marks an escalation against you that you could do without. You'll find that even if you are in the right, the foreigner always pays. In far too many cases the police are complicit in the scams, and they profit from them."

The endemic criminality of Thailand leads directly into concerns over the safety of foreign residents and tourists; but is also a matter of great concern to local citizens. Blether said police reform had been one of the key demands of anti-government protestors in recent years. One of the first actions of the military junta was to replace the chief of police.

"The level of corruption is abysmal and undermines the entire country. You're probably not interested in the politics of Thailand. However, you may be interested in knowing that millions of Thais are demanding a change to the way the police operate. The Thai police are not a benign force.

"We Westerners are used to being treated fairly by the law enforcement agencies. We know when we call the police they are more than likely to attend our call, listen to what we have to say

---

[138] Interview with author, 26 June, 2014.

and take action accordingly. Well you can forget about that in Thailand."

Among some elements of Thai society, including the poorly paid Thai police, robbing foreigners is little more than a sport. A foreigner in a compromising situation is simply a source of revenue. Travellers can expect no help from either the authorities or the locals they may have once thought so friendly and welcoming. With the cultural divide so great, stealing from overseas guests is not the subject of shame, guilt, regret or remorse. Often enough it is the subject of celebration. There is no embarrassment. The bigger the bribe they have extracted, the better a policeman's family will eat. The more a sex worker steals from a drunken or drugged customer, the more they can transfer to their family back in their home village.

Foreigners can protest as much as they like about being robbed, they will receive no sympathy. Objections, complaints, refusal to pay or failure to understand how the system works marks them as stingy and mean spirited, "jai dum", literally, black hearted. Rather than the empathy they may expect, they will be ridiculed. The service they are expected to purchase is the privilege of not being harassed, entrapped or carted off to jail for real or imagined infractions. It is in essence a tax.

The frequent failure of tourists and expatriates to understand Thai behaviour, including the widespread acceptance of what Westerners regard as corruption, can place them in considerable danger, particularly if they become the target of scams perpetrated by officials and police in conjunction with local sex workers and business operators.

The most obvious source of assistance for tourists in trouble is the Royal Thai Tourist Police, who have a prominent presence in tourist hot spots. The tourist police constitute a mix of local employees and foreign volunteers, usually former Western police or military personnel who have retired to Thailand and wish to remain active in the field of law enforcement. They have close relationships with the endemically corrupt local police forces, and are thus stained by the same levels of misconduct and the same poor attitudes of service that infiltrate the local authorities.

The quickest, simplest and safest way out of any sticky situation in Thailand is to pay a bribe, and in the process of their arrest and incarceration for real or imaged offences tourists will be given ample opportunity to do just that. They will be repeatedly asked variations on the question: "How much you pay fix this problem?" By failing to warn tourists that they are not dealing with a police force that bears any resemblance to what they may be used to at home, tourist police often make the situation worse. Indeed, foreigners who report an incident may well find themselves being framed or set up by a combination of opportunists from both the local and tourist police.

The tourist police endanger travellers by creating the dangerous illusion that there is a mantle of justice and due process protecting tourists, who would be better advised to avoid them just as assiduously as they would other Thai authorities. Unfortunately too many visitors have discovered that expatriate volunteers for the Tourist Police can be just as unethical, intimidatory, prejudiced against them and indifferent to the welfare of foreigners as their local counterparts.

Tensions between foreign volunteers working for the Tourist Police and local forces boiled into the open in 2014. Following a dispute, Phuket's expatriate police volunteers went on strike for a fortnight.[139] The action followed allegations ordinary police were using the volunteers to extort money from tourists. Five volunteers resigned over the issue.

Head co-ordinator of the Phuket division of the International Volunteers Group Wal Brown said he was tired of being subjected to "shady situations". The dispute which triggered the walkout involved a tourist who was ordered to pay a higher compensation for damage to a room because he asked for assistance from a Thai Tourist Police volunteer. "The tourist was also threatened with a greater fine and jail if he were to talk with the volunteer again," Brown told *Phuket News*. "This is one of a number of issues where the International Volunteers have been used against a tourist."

---

[139] Phuket expat volunteers back to work after successful negotiations, Phuket News, 8 March, 2014.

Corruption is not just widespread in Thailand, newspapers, magazines and websites regularly report on it, "almost revel in it".[140]

A significant percentage of the Thai population despise their own police forces and take their corruption for granted. They assume, usually correctly, that the policeman pulling them over on the side of the road to inspect their vehicle or their license simply wants money. Thais being pulled over will pay 100 baht, less than five dollars, to be allowed to drive on, whether or not they have a license. A foreigner is expected to pay ten times as much for any real or imagined infraction. When it comes to drugs, fights, visa infractions or other misdemeanours, the price climbs rapidly. There is a common wisdom that the only people in jail in Thailand are those who can't afford to pay their way out. Like many popular beliefs, there is a good degree of truth in it.

One of the driving forces behind this is the low pay rates of police.

A senior police sergeant gets a monthly salary of about 10,000 baht, around $US300 depending on the exchange rates of the day. They are expected to find other sources of income. Policemen below the level of senior sergeant must buy their own guns, which start at around 20,000 baht. Many must buy their own motor bikes because of the shortage of government provided machines. Radios cost officers around 7,000 baht. All must buy their own uniforms.

Many other countries have had to eliminate the corruption in their police forces by forcibly retiring the old cadres while raising pay rates and thereby elevating officer's social status and sense of responsibility to the communities they serve.

Thai police only have to look across the Malaysian border to see police who are paid twice what they are; and where the government pays for uniforms, equipment, housing and even furniture. While there is corruption within the Malaysian police, it is on a far smaller scale than in Thailand.

---

[140] *The Merchants of Madness: The Methamphetamine Explosion in the Golden Traingle*, Bertil Lintner and Michael Black, Silkworm Books, 2009.

The more tourists and expats frequent the red light districts, the more likely they are to come in conflict with the interlinking networks of mafia and the police who run the nation's nightlife. Foreign men, most of whom would regard themselves as street-wise in their own countries, would do well to understand the system of patronage which lies behind the bars they love so much.

Western writers and foreign governments commonly assert that while low level corruption may be rife in Thailand there is no evidence of such conduct at higher levels of government. As Southeast Asian experts Bertil Lintner and Michael Black, co-authors of *Merchants of Madness: The Methamphetamine Explosion in the Golden Triangle*, point out, this represents a complete failure to understand the Thai system.

They write: "A traffic policeman in Bangkok might stop motorists—especially trucks and other commercial vehicles—and demand bribes to ignore real or imaginary traffic offences. In this way a policeman can collect thousands of baht a day. But he can only keep a small portion of the money in his own pockets. Most of it goes to the chief of his police station, because the traffic policeman wants to make sure that he is not transferred or demoted. The chief, naturally, collects money from all the policemen in his station, and thus ends up with a substantial amount of money—which he, in turn, has to share with his superiors."

This system ensures that some areas are prized by police, particularly red light districts.

Some of the most prized are the interlocking police districts which cover the red light district of Patpong and its surrounds; where the streets are jammed with foreigners frequenting the night markets or ogling the goings on inside go-go bars such as "Super Pussy".

"Officers would have to pay their superiors a fortune to be posted there, but then the superior officers would also be able to collect huge sums of money from the street cops, who, in turn, would have to pay weekly visits to the owners of Patpong's go-go bars and sex shows," Lintnel and Black write. "The police generals don't stand in the streets and stop motorists, or visit massage parlours to collect monthly 'fees' from, for instance, wealthy commercial sex tycoons or sometimes even drug traffickers. But most of the money still ends up at the top of the pyramid, not at the bottom."

In their book *Corruption & Democracy in Thailand* academics Pasuk Phongpauchit and Sungsidh Piriyarangsan point to another factor behind the phenomenon so often observed with disbelief by foreigners: that with almost every encounter they have with a Thai policeman they are expected to pay a bribe. In the traditional Thai system of government "officials received their appointment from a higher authority but were not remunerated by any flow of income from the same source. They were expected to remunerate themselves by retaining a reasonable portion of the taxes they collected, and by exacting fees for services rendered."

These sources range from Thai drivers unfortunate enough to be pulled over and "fined" for alleged traffic or vehicle infractions; to the foreign tourists and residents who represent such a rich source of income.

There are six different words for corruption in the Thai language.

The most widespread form is sin nam jai, literally a "gift of good will" such as a bottle of whisky or some money to a government official who has been helpful. Khan nam ron nam cha, "tea money", is the term used for payment to police or officials over issues such as license or traffic violations.

Lintnel and Black observe: "Few Thais would object to those kinds of practices, and it would be hard to find any government official in the country who has not demanded, or accepted, 'gifts' and 'tea money' from the public and private companies. The bitter reality is that without such gifts few law enforcement officers would be able to survive."

Blether was discouraged from writing his books by members of Thailand's expat community, many of whom see it as some sort of character test to assimilate into Thai culture. They look down on foreigners who find themselves in trouble and aggrandise their own experience, compatibility and understanding of the complexities of Thai culture. Often enough their assimilation extends only as far as their money; and in reality most of the Thais they deem as friends are directly or indirectly in their employ.

Like other commentators Blether notes the peculiar tone in the expatriate cliques lack of compassion for new comers in trouble. Europeans walk past each other in the streets without acknowledging the other's existence, lost in their own Asian adventures, or stand next to each other in lifts studiously staring straight ahead as if they were back in their own crowded, unfriendly cities: "They reckon that people get scammed everywhere and it's no worse in Thailand. These are the same people that look on tourists and new arrivals with contempt. They take a salacious delight in watching people get ripped off. To me it's some kind of self-affirmation that these people are after. It's a sad day in life when that is the highpoint of your existence. There are far too many expatriates in Thailand with that mind-set. Many of us are carrying the battle scars caused by these scams. What we pass on to you is to prevent you suffering the same fate."[141]

The contributor to the British based opinion oriented newsletter *Meebal*, who wishes to remain anonymous, just like others contributing on the subject of Thailand, also observed the lack of collegiality between different groups of foreigners; with those falling on hard times treated disparagingly by successful expats.

"Any foreigner falling foul of the system simply attracts a multitude of abuse from other expats; I've seen this on a number of Thai based news websites targeted at foreigners," the *Meebal* contributor wrote. "There are many expats that troll the likes of Thai Visa looking to voice their worthless opinions. They appear to relish the idea of any foreign national falling foul; it's like they have the upper hand of being intellectually superior because they have been here for so long and understand how the system works. It's deplorable in many instances how anyone could be that cold but when you live in Thailand for many years and spend most of your days sitting in a bar it's understandable how these people have become bitter and disenfranchised and so take to mocking other people's misfortunes."

---

[141] *Thailand Scam Land: 50 Common Scams*, The Blether, Amazon Australia.

Many travellers coming to Thailand bring with them the illusion that they are entering paradise, a nirvana they cannot find in their own countries. The marketing of the country as inhabited by warm, welcoming and peaceful people lulls visitors into a false sense of security. The fact that Thailand is an intensely Buddhist country also beguiles tourists into thinking they are in safe hands. The brazen violence, thefts and scams perpetrated on visitors are at apparent odds with the Buddha's precepts against killing and stealing.

These activities are also against Christian teachings, but the same tourists who would never trust the people they met casually in bars, restaurants or on the streets of their own home towns are happily charmed into thinking they are amongst friends. It is a mental state called the suspension of disbelief, or cognitive dissonance. They are well advised to wake up, quickly.

Speculation over the Thais indifference to the literal truth of any given situation is common amongst expatriates; their lack of respect for the private property of others, defiant lack of guilt when caught out thieving or defrauding foreigners and their clear lack of remorse or concern at the discomfit or even death of visitors to their country.

"Don't Thai to me", as in "Don't lie to me" is a byword across Asia; but many Westerners have never heard the expression, and if they have don't understand it.

Award winning author Timothy Mo puts it a little more elegantly in the following repartee from his superb novel of Thailand, *Pure:*

"Why are Thai people such fucking liars?"

"What?"

"Come on, you know damn well what I mean."

"Well, depends. Could be to be polite and avoid mutual embarrassment and hurt feelings."

"Yeah. I heard that 100 times. But it can be damn malicious and when money comes into it, it's downright dishonest. I'm not insulting you about the cash you've borrowed from me, baby."

"And that I've never paid back. Well, we're a very money-minded, mercenary people, Avril. It's the Chinese in us. And, yah, we are sneaky sometimes, I admit it. Not just to farang but ourselves as well. I guess we don't respect truth as much as you guys do. I mean, intrinsically. It's not something that's solid for us, it's not such a big deal."

"I swear to God people give me the wrong street directions just for the fun of it."

Foreigners often appreciate the traits of communally oriented peoples that Thais display: an ability to enjoy the day and to laugh freely at the behaviour of themselves and others, a lack of career orientation, a dismissive attitude to what is sometimes called "higher" learning and a tendency to share whatever they possess, including food and whisky. But there are other sides to communality. Some of the speculation over the Thai's lack of respect for private property is simply racist and offensive in tone, further deepening the dislike between visitors and the host population. Others point to the traditionally poorly educated villagers' aural based traditions, which focus on storytelling and saving face rather than specific, evidentiary truth, traits which lead to a great many misunderstandings between foreigners and Thais.

There are more controversial theories.

In *The King Never Smiles*, Paul Handley writes that while the Thai people's belief in a divine king has destroyed the country's fledgling democratic institutions and underpinned the country's political instability, "the other main conflict ascribable to Bhumibol's reign, over which rules should govern men's behaviour, is far more deleterious. By advocating a broad, flexible, and ultimately self-enforced dhamma-based moral system, Bhumibol has helped undermine the rule of law. Violent crime, vice, and corruption are wide-spread in Thailand, as is a highly casual view of law among both offenders and enforcers. While such problems are common in developing countries, Thailand's collective indifference toward law stands out as boldly as its open sex industry, narcotics networks, and murder-for-hire rackets."

Handley wrote that modern laws designed to prevent criminal activity were ineffective because there was no link between modern and dhammic law. "By ignoring or condemning the modern statutes, advocates of the dhamma-based system abet the many wrongdoers who are unafraid of karmic retribution. The lack of law enforcement, and the resultant massive criminality in the country, vexes the Thai people. Often, the powerless turn to the king's morality system of dhammic fate and suffering and karmic retribution; others take the law into their own hands, adding to the problem."

Peoples around the world romanticise, mythologise and even celebrate their criminal milieus. But the Thais respect for wealth no matter what its source, their overt fascination with the soap opera lives of their criminal classes, and their obsession with criminality itself has a peculiar national characteristic, a shrugging acceptance of the transgressions of their own authorities and a joyful appreciation of deception, of the double double-cross.

The most famous rort in Thai history, the so-called Blue Diamond Affair, with its trail of murders, gems and links to the highest reaches of Thai society, has fascinated the country for more than 20 years.[142]

The story, which spanned a quarter of century, began in 1989 when a Thai gardener climbed into the palace of a Saudi prince, busted open a safe with a screwdriver and stole some 90 kilograms of jewellery. As the story goes, the gardener stuffed "rubies the size of chicken eggs" into his vacuum cleaner bag, along with a nearly flawless blue diamond which, at 50 carats, was larger than the Hope Diamond.

The Thai worker, Kriangkrai Techamong, sent the gems he stole from the palace of Prince Faisal bin Fahd to his home village in Lampang Province, Thailand. Techamong had little understanding of the value of his heist. Some of the gems were sold to a local jeweller for as little as $US30, around 1,000 baht.

A Thai Police investigation led by Lieutenant-General Chalor Kerdthes resulted in the arrest of the Thai worker and recovery of some of the jewels. Chalor headed a deputation of officials to Saudi Arabia to return the stolen jewels, but upon his arrival Saudi officials soon discovered that many of the jewels being returned

---

[142] Thailand's Blue Diamond Heist: Still a Sore Point, by Christopher Shay, *Time*, 7 March, 2010.

with such ceremony were in fact fakes. Shortly thereafter a businessman close to the Saudi Royal family, Mohammad al-Ruwali, travelled to Bangkok to resolve the matter. Instead he was abducted and murdered. At around the same time three officials from the Saudi Embassy who were suspected of having specific knowledge on the whereabouts of the gems were also killed in Bangkok. Their murders were never solved.

Thai media organisations reported that women amongst Thai's elite, including members of the royal family, had been seen wearing new diamond necklaces at society functions, further incensing the Saudis. Trade was cut. Saudi tourists were banned from travelling to Thailand.

Chalor was subsequently convicted of ordering the 1995 torture and murder of the wife and son of the local jeweller, and sentenced to death. Six other policemen were also found guilty of involvement in the murders. On the occasion of his 84th birthday King Bhumibol commuted Chalor's death sentence to 50 years imprisonment.

As a result of the imbroglio following the heist the Saudi government stopped renewing the visas of more than a quarter of a million Thais working in Saudi Arabia, bringing to an end a major source of income for hundreds of rural villages.

A ban on Saudis travelling to Thailand was also imposed.

An estimated 77,782 Saudis visited Thailand in the year before the ban came into effect in 1989.[143]

Time summed up the story, saying "the alleged theft eventually cost Thailand billions of dollars in lost revenue, left people dead in its wake and put an Elvis-impersonating Thai official (Chalor) on death row. More than 20 years later, the ripped-off Saudis still want their jewels back, and relations between the two governments remain strained."

By 2010 many of the original characters involved with the Blue Diamond Affair were dead. But with the statute of limitations about to expire, Thailand's Office of the Attorney-General announced that five policemen were to be charged over the murder

---

[143] 17,000 Saudis visit Thailand despite ban, *Gulf News*, 3 September, 2013.

and kidnapping of the Saudi businessman Mohammad al-Ruwali. The men denied the charges. Appropriately, on April Fools' Day in 2014 came the news that the charges had been dropped.[144]

In 2013 police announced the results of a six-week crime crackdown operation involving local divisions in the red-light town of Pattaya.

The crackdown came in the wake of representations to the Thai government from senior diplomats, including from China, Britain, Australia and the European Union and took place between 12th August and 20th September. There were 5,185 arrests involving drugs, firearms and visa overstays.

Police General Wutti said similar crackdowns were taking place in all of Thailand's major tourist destinations to demonstrate to Thai and foreign tourists that they were serious about solving crime and keeping the tourist destinations as safe as possible, especially during the high season when millions of domestic and international tourists visit destinations such as Pattaya, Phuket, Koh Samui and Chang Mai.[145]

Foreigners often complain that they feel they are being robbed from the minute they arrive. With so-called "taxi mafias" operating at every major airport, it is literally true.

In 2013 the Thai government announced that illegal tour operators, taxi drivers and chauffeurs previously caught scamming tourists at Bangkok's Suvarnabhumi Airport would be forced to wear electronic ankle bracelets to prevent them entering the airport precinct.[146]

The devices were intended to alert security when offenders returned to the airport precinct.

Those judged guilty of offences such as pick pocketing, theft, and illegal taxi operators and tour guides would be ordered to wear

---

[144] Thai Court throws out murder charges in 'Blue Diamond Affair', Lindsay Murdoch, Sydney Morning Herald, 1 April 2014.

The decision had been reached following discussions with the Probation Department and the customer service's division of Suvarnabhumi Airport. [145] Thousands arrested in Pattaya Crime Crackdown Operation, Pattaya One, 23 September, 2013.

[146] Airport Criminals Get Tags, *Bangkok Post*, 28 March, 2014.

ankle bracelets. The bracelets enabled the authorities to track the wearers through the use of GPS technology.

Spokesman for the scheme, Chief Justice Awirut Chanchaikittikon, said crime at the airport had damaged the country's tourism reputation. Far from being a human rights abuse, the electronic bracelets would help rehabilitate offenders back into society.

Deceiving travellers is not a recent phenomenon. From the 1970s, before cheap flights from Bangkok to the resort islands in the south of the country became both frequent and cheap, one of the only ways to get there was via an extremely uncomfortable overnight bus.

The 1998 Lonely Planet's guide *Thailand's Islands & Beaches* warned that tourists taking the then narrow bumpy road to the islands should take extra care: "On the long journey south, well-organised and connected thieves have hours to comb through your bags, breaking into (and later resealing) locked bags, searching through hiding places and stealing credit cards, electronics and even toiletries. This scam has been running for years..."

The pilfering operation could not have lasted for so long without the cooperation of the bus drivers, bus companies and the authorities, all of whom benefited financially. Lonely Planet sarcastically queried why the Thai police seemed incapable of stopping the scam: "Ask yourself, how hard could it be? It's a crude but very effective scheme; while you are (hopefully) sleeping your way south on the overnight bus, a man is hiding in the luggage hold and slowly working his way through all the bags, stealing whatever takes his fancy. One traveller reported that his stolen credit card was used to pay for the trip's petrol. Locks are no great deterrent as these guys can pick one faster than you can tie your shoes. By the time you realise you've been robbed, you're far away and the thieves are long gone."

Fifteen years later nothing had changed. In August of 2013 police arrested two Khao San tour bus company owners who stole cash and goods from passengers. The married couple, who specialised in stealing credit cards and, rather oddly, brand name shoes, operated the Saipanya Tour Company bus from the

Bangkok backpacker mecca Khao San Road to the holiday island of Koh Chang.

As is the Thai custom the police paraded the thieves before a press conference and explained their modus operandi: on departure the couple would hop into the bus storage compartment and then sift through tourist's suitcases for valuables. They would exit when the bus stopped on the motorway. Police found credit cards, 12 different kinds of currencies and a collection of shoes in the couple's possession.[147]

Comedic, sad, chaotic, or just further proof of the truth behind the advertising slogan "Amazing Thailand", every day brought more colourful stories involving foreigners. In August, 2013, four Bangkok-based policemen were suspended for allegedly extorting two million baht from two Italian tourists after making a false allegation against the victims and holding them captive.

Two officers were arrested and warrants issued for a further two who were on the run.

The Nation observed: "While it may sound like another instance of police misconduct well familiar to Thais and foreigners alike, this case has resulted in immediate action by their superiors and abrupt suspension of the four police suspects, thanks to an INTERPOL inquiry conducted after the victims' families lodged a complaint. The case therefore potentially brings shame upon the entire police force, due to its global exposure."[148]

The mug shots of the police were made public. Border checkpoints and immigration offices at airports and seaports were alerted.

Senior personnel at Lumpini Police Station, which is located close by Bangkok's world famous Lumpini Park, assisted in negotiations with the two tourists. Police threatened to charge the two Italians with using a false ATM card, although INTERPOL confirmed the card was genuine. The two tourists successfully halved the amount that was being demanded of them down to

---

[147] Khao San Crocs crooks arrested for swindling tourists, Bangkok Coconuts, 21 August, 2013.

[148] Police officers suspended over alleged extortion of tourists, *The Nation*, 24 August 2013.

25,000 Euro and were kept in a motel overnight before being taken to an ATM the next morning.

INTERPOL was alerted to the case by the families of the two men.

One of the most colourful and most truly hypocritical of all the famous scams perpetrated against foreigners in Thailand is busting revellers for small amounts of drugs at the Full Moon Party on Kho Phangan, a once picturesque island in the Gulf of Thailand in the south east of the country known since the 1970s for its relaxed attitudes towards recreational drug use.

Revellers dance at Haad Rin Beach during the Full Moon Party.
Picture courtesy of Samui Times.

The Full Moon Party began at an improvised wooden disco not far from Haad Rin beach in 1985; and quickly became a must-have experience for youthful travellers.

Hotels soon took over from the cheap dilapidated guest houses which had once characterised the island; and a new breed of traveller took over from the junkies once drawn by the island's high quality, inexpensive heroin. By the 1980s so-called party drugs, particularly ecstasy, took over.

In an expose of the Full Moon Parties, *Time* recalled the words of one of their reporters a quarter of a century before. The year was 1988: "The skies were star-spangled and phosphorescence would spray like diamonds in the sea ... the sand glowed silver and the waves danced alive as they hit the shore. Hippies from across the globe used to gather quietly at this idyllic enclave, drifting in on marijuana smoke to sit on a beach, strum a battered guitar and simply be. Today, however, the only blue spray you'll see might be the lurid Curacao cocktail expelled from the guts of a retching 20-something. This onetime Eden has degenerated into a modern-day Gomorrah awash in tawdry techno, cheap fast food and wasted millennials."[149]

Embassies and travel advisors around the world now warn of the life-threatening dangers of the Full Moon Party. To little effect, the event remains as popular as ever.

Paul Dillon, the director of Drug and Alcohol Research and Training Australia says a whole new industry in high-risk tourism has emerged in the past 20 years that encourages young people to push the boundaries. "The evidence is very clear that young people are aware of the risks and know what the consequences can be, but they think it won't happen to them."[150]

The website Full Moon Party Booking describes the latter day experience thus: "The party begins at dusk, when the round yellow moon makes its appearance over the white sand beach. In twilight, small tables are lined up on the beach and thousands of lamps are lit . . .

"As the evening progresses the beach explodes into a dancing frenzy.... There is something for everyone here, trance, techno, drum and bass, commercial dance and reggae, no-one is disappointed. Jugglers and fire-eaters entertain the crowds.... All around people are doing the same, there are no barriers here, no inhibitions, just people enjoying themselves with one unified intention, to rejoice in the magic that is."

---

[149] Thailand's Full-Moon Parties Have Become a Trashy Disgrace, Charlie Campbell, 8 July, 2013.

[150] Rite of passage comes with a high price for those seeking foreign adventures, Lindy Alexander, *Sydney Morning Herald*, 26 January, 2014.

In his piece "Thailand's Full Moon Parties have been taken over by Yolo Idiots", blogger George Henton recalls standing on a crowded Haad Rin beach: "Hours before, 20,000 bodies writhed together in motion to pulsating house music, fuelled by cheap alcohol and magic mushroom milkshakes. Now, among the rapidly sobering hardcore who continue to dance, a smattering of those bodies dot the beach, their semi-conscious, half-naked torsos slowly roasting in the Thai sun. They lie surrounded by beer bottles, shattered glass, and plastic buckets."

Since the Full Moon Party's halcyon days, chaos has set in. Each party sees dozens ferried to the mainland hospitals with a litany of inebriation related issues; while drownings, unsurprising given the number of intoxicated revellers on a beach with no life guards, are a common event.

What began as an event all about peace, love and New Age consciousness has become a potentially deadly event, with a number of governments issuing formal warnings, including the Canadians: "Be careful at night in entertainment areas throughout the country, particularly during Full Moon parties in Koh Phangan and similar events in other popular tourist locations. Robberies, injuries, drug abuse, arrests, assaults (including sexual assaults) and deaths related to these parties have been reported. Passport thefts and losses are extremely common at these parties and their replacement may cause significant travel delays. Foreigners have been targeted in incidents of drink spiking, often combined with sexual assault or theft. Never leave food or drinks unattended or in the care of strangers, and pay attention when drinks are being prepared and served. Seek immediate medical attention if you suspect that you have been drugged."

Australian Ambassador to Association of South East Asian Nations Simon Merrifield said the parties often sparked calls for help: "Consular officers regularly assist young Australians who have been arrested, robbed, assaulted, sexually assaulted or injured. Tragically, Australians have also died as a result of full moon party accidents."

The British government mirrored the concerns of other governments, issuing warnings that Western tourists had been victims of "vicious, unprovoked attacks by gangs".

The Holiday Guides Thailand website warns solo travellers to be particularly careful at the Full Moon Party, where drink spiking, as in so much of Thailand, is rife. At least one person was estimated to die at every monthly party. It is not uncommon for hundreds of people to have their drinks spiked at sometime during the night. There are buckets of alcohol that are served up at the party and although the majority of the buckets aren't spiked, some most certainly are.

"The drugs that can go into these buckets are tranquillisers and sleeping pills which make you fall asleep not long after you consume a bucket. The spikers usually watch you and follow you around until you fall asleep and once you do, they act as though they are being a good Samaritan to other punters and look as though they are attending to you, when they are actually picking your pocket.

"If you have any doubts about how rife drink spiking is at the Full Moon Party, then just ask one of the foreign volunteers who work at the party and they will tell it to you like it is. Remember, the Full Moon Party is held on an island which is almost lawless and the only laws that seem to get enforced here are against the tourists for money making opportunities.

"It should be noted that the police don't have to find drugs on you for you to go to jail, they only have to suspect that you have had drugs and ask you to have a urine test and if that test shows up positive, you could potentially go to jail, or pay a large amount of money to stay out of it.

"There are also special shakes at the Full Moon Party and these shakes contain magic mushrooms and a concoction of unknown ingredients. These shakes could potentially be spiked too and it would be best to avoid these drinks, as they could have anything in them."

There is zero doubt that the Thai police are involved in preying on tourists, many of whom are on their first major overseas holiday without their parents. *Time* noted the obvious: "Thai police have a well-documented corruption problem and many people get caught in stings arranged with local drug dealers, with steep 'fines' demanded to secure their release."

Aimed at a UK audience, the eight-part series of one-hour tabloid-style television documentaries called *Big Trouble in Tourist Thailand* began screening in 2009, when British deaths per year were still under 300. While sensationalist in tone, it was useful for documenting and placing on the visual record several common scams.

The Thailand Film Office did their best to block production of the series. All releases and permissions required for filming were withdrawn.151

Big Trouble documented the established routine of Thai police arresting the first suspects at a Full Moon Party they could easily pin for possession, acting duly outraged that a foreigner should be so disrespectful as to take drugs on Thai soil. They then proceed to extract as much money as possible from their victim, the alleged wrong-doer.

In reality there are only a small number of police cells on the island and no genuine will to crack down on recreational drug use at the parties, where up to 30,000 Westerners gather each month. While the threat of the Dickensian Thai prison system hangs over those arrested, outside the police station thousands of foreigners, stoned on drugs purchased from local dealers, dance until dawn. The few foreigners who do get caught act as sacrificial lambs for the rest of the tribe, who get smashed with impunity.

In the tight-knit island communities of Thailand it is common knowledge who is selling what to whom. And as every drug dealer in Thailand knows, you cannot operate without paying the police. At the time of the broadcast of the Koh Phangan episode of *Big Trouble* authorities announced plans to make the island "drug-free". They might as well have been writing science fiction. If the authorities and the community genuinely wanted to stop foreigners taking drugs and partying on their island, they would crack down

---

151 Koh Phangan News, September 14, 2009.

on the local dealers. They do no such thing. For exactly the same reason as drives every other scam in Thailand, money.

The many tens of thousands of youthful Western travellers flocking to Kho Phangan each year with the simple aim of having the time of their lives provide a significant boost to the island's economy, filling the hotels, guesthouses, bars and restaurants; lining the pockets of not just local business people but drug dealers and thereby the police. And enabling many of the local families to have a standard of living they could otherwise only have dreamed of. Without the ready availability of "recreational" drugs, those very same visitors would choose another destination with more lax or liberal attitudes towards recreational drug use. And the locals would be forced to go back to fishing for a living.

Big Trouble in Tourist Thailand followed the case of a distressed young English woman picked up for possession of a mere three grams of marijuana, which she had not even partaken of. As it turned out, the marijuana had been purchased by her boyfriend, which made no difference to the fact that the young woman was threatened with the full force of the Thai justice system, including time in the nation's infamously harsh prison system. The young woman's bail was set at more than $US2000, the equivalent of four months pay for a Thai bank manager, money which she did not possess. Ultimately, as for so many other young foreigners caught in the scam, the money was sourced from her parents. Once the woman faced court she was released.

While in her case, with the cameras trained upon her, bail was refunded, essentially the scam had been successful, if not in this specific case as lucrative as normal. On camera, tourist police warn that foreigners paying bail should get a receipt or otherwise the money was likely to disappear without account. So much for due process. The brutal nature of the Thai prison system encourages both foreigners and Thais to promptly settle any outstanding police matters with a "fine", or more precisely a bribe. Thailand has proved indifferent to the international coverage on the human rights abuses occurring within its jails. The numerous books written by expatriates who have survived the inhumanity of the Thai prison system should act as cautionary tales to anyone travelling to Thailand. There have been no attempts to reform conditions.

Alan Morison, recorded the conditions inside Phuket Prison: "Inside the cell I look around, and it's not pleasant. I do a quick count. There are 36 men I can see, and one I can smell. He's on the toilet, one of two with half-doors that don't hide a lot. Most of the men are in Phuket Prison garb. The inmates all have shackles around their ankles. Heavy metal makes movement difficult, so most use a string attached to the chain that runs between their ankles to make getting around easier.

"With 2700 prisoners in a jail built to hold 750, there is little room for sleep. Inmates in Phuket Prison are kept in their dormitories for 15 hours a day. Food and water are not easy to come by."[152]

Conditions are so cramped inmates, in order to sleep, are forced to lie on their sides in a long row, so when one person turns over, everyone has to turn over.

Thai jails are no better for women.

Morison's colleague Chutima Sidasathian, wrote: "Being held a prisoner on Phuket is no fun. This is a grim place. The jail is hugely overcrowded, say all the women, with so little space that women and men have to lie on their sides at night so everyone has room to sleep on the floor. The space is frighteningly small."[153]

These are the jail conditions police on Koh Phangan were threatening to send a naive young British holiday maker; unless, of course, she paid up.

There are numerous warnings, both governmental and on tourist websites, about travel in Thailand. The Canadian government, signalling the out of control criminality afflicting the Thai tourist industry, states in its official advisory: "Petty crime, such as purse snatching, pick pocketing and theft, is common. Do not leave bags unattended. Ensure that your personal belongings, passports and other travel documents are secure at all times,

---

[152] Democracy is What A Free Media Means, and What Real Warriors fight to Defend, Alan Morison, *Phuket Wan*, 24 April, 2014.

[153] Behind Bars With Woman Who Sold Her Daughters, Chutima Sidasathian, *Phuket Wan*, 19 April, 2014.

especially in tourist areas, crowded markets, and bus or train stations. Thieves sometimes use razors to slit open purses or bags to remove the contents. Use only reputable transportation companies. Thefts have been reported on the buses and vans that provide transport services throughout the country. Personal belongings, including passports, have been stolen from luggage compartments under buses, especially on long distance journeys. Break-ins occur at budget guesthouses, sometimes while guests are asleep in their rooms."

But, unfortunately for the many dead and injured, travel advice by governments is largely ignored; the warnings not being couched in dramatic or attention-grabbing enough a style to impact on most travellers.

To combat the tide of tourist complaints and growing Mafioso presence, in 2012 the Thai government made Patong the flagship of its "Zero Crime Area" experiment.

Much good that did.

In its safety advisories travel service World Nomads suggests that the red light district of Patong in Phuket, typical of other red light districts in Thailand, "is a total circus. Whether you are playing Connect 4 with a bar girl off Soi Bangla, getting your photo taken with a beautifully festooned ladyboy, or find yourself searching for your missing scooter there is plenty to keep an eye out for. Patong is a haven for all manner of scam artists, stand over touts, crazed farangs, drink spikers, pickpockets, bike gangs and other nefarious individuals conspiring to challenge the safety and wellbeing of the budding Bangla Road adventurer."

The tourists who so eagerly make their way to Thailand's bars and fleshpots are often unaware that the so-called "rape drug" Rohypnol, along with a variety of other sedative drugs, are readily available in Thailand, and regularly used by bar owners and sex workers to drug and rob their customers. Often drunk or off their guard while on holidays, fooled by the marketing of Thailand, trusting people they should never have trusted, travellers do not understand that there is a very high probability of having their drinks spiked. Many tourists, young men in particular, fail to realise that their rite of passage, waking up hungover in a dishevelled Thai hotel room with little memory of what happened the night before, the prostitute of their choice nothing but a blur, missing along with their wallet, is an experience more likely to be the result of their deliberate drugging than from excessive alcohol consumption.

The practice of drink spiking remains so widespread that many missions have begun issuing formal warnings. The Australian Department of Foreign Affairs, for instance, formally warns travellers: "Tourists may be exposed to scams and more serious criminal activity in Thailand. Be aware that food and drink spiking occurs in Thailand, including around popular backpacker destinations such as Khao San Road in Bangkok the night-time entertainment zones in Bangkok, Pattaya and Phuket, and during the Full Moon Party on Koh Phangan."

Australian volunteer with the Thai Tourist Police Wal Brown tells numerous stories of the consequence of drink spiking, including one group of Italians stumbling out of bushes not having just lost their wallets but their clothes as well. They could not remember anything that had happened in the previous three days. In another case two young Australian men awoke in an alley behind a bar about 30 hours after their drinks were spiked. All their valuables were gone. It is a very common story across all nationalities. "There are a lot of people who get drugged here," he says.

Brown also cautions visitors to beware of "ping pong" shows, where two beers could cost $100, with touts becoming extremely aggressive if the customer refuses to pay. Bag snatching and robberies are also a regular occurrence with visitors on motor bikes targeted on dimly-lit roads. "One French girl hid in the bushes for three hours," Brown says. "Another Swedish girl stayed there until daybreak. They were on motorbikes and stopped by people with hatchets and screwdrivers and makeshift weapons."

Drink spiking is hardly a problem restricted to Full Moon Parties. It occurs regularly in every major tourist centre. At one point in Phuket's colourful social history, in 2011, Patong Police arrested six bargirls and charged them with spiking drinks and robbing tourists. The arrests only occurred after a string of complaints from holiday makers.[154]

The women all worked in bars on Patong's famed red light district of Soi Bangla, a precinct crowded with bars, discotheques, sex workers and tourists.

"They went back to foreigners' rooms and asked the foreigners to have a drink," Major Thammasak Boonsong of the Patong Police said. "They then slipped a concoction of drugs into the victim's drink to knock them out. When their victims were unconscious, they robbed them."

The women used pills crushed and mixed with water, which they kept in small plastic bottles they carried with them. All six women were charged with illegal possession of prescription drugs. Their initial fines were halved by the court.

A month later one of the women was rearrested at 3.30am in Patong carrying prescription drugs which, she confessed, were intended to be used to drug foreigners. "She put the mix in their drinks and then she stole their belongings," a police spokesman said. "She always chose foreigners on Soi Bangla."

Just before Christmas the same year the Thai Tourist Police issued an alert to visitors, saying two or three cases of drink spiking were brought to their attention each week.[155]

The Tourist Police released the name of a bar in the central gay strip Soi Paradise, but warned the problem was widespread throughout Patong and occurred less frequently in other parts of Phuket. Group Leader of the Phuket Tourist Police Foreign Volunteers Frank Tomensen instructed his patrol units to be on the lookout for victims who appear impaired or disoriented. He said they were aware of two recent cases which occurred on the gay strip known as Soi Paradise where an odourless and colourless substance was added to drinks.

"The effects take about 15-20 minutes to set in, rendering the victim completely helpless," Tomenson said. "In both cases it is

[154] 'Bargirls' nabbed for spiking drinks, robbing Phuket Tourists, *Phuket Gazette*, 1 November, 2011.

[155] Phuket Visitors Warned of Drink Spiking at Some Patong Bars, Phuket Wan, 15 December, 2011.

known the victims were robbed. We see these guys carried out of one particular bar in Soi Bangla. They are incoherent and usually vomiting badly. The police are aware of it; one of the bars where it happens is owned by a policeman. Robbery is usually the motive. If things are a little quiet, some of the hostesses will resort to drink-spiking to make ends meet. Medical intervention is required as soon as possible. In cases where you come across someone who is very impaired and disoriented, the drug loosens inhibitions and paralyses motor control, they may not necessarily be drunk."

Phuket is not the only place with bars owned by police where drink spiking or drugging of tourists is common. The popular late-night gay club G.O.D. in Bangkok, owned by a policeman, is well known for drugging foreigners. Gay men, on holidays and out to party hard in their fantasy kingdom, the City of Black Eyed Angels, are easily sold what they are told is cocaine; and which in fact is a dangerous mix of Grievous Bodily Harm (GBH), the NY nightclub drug ketamine and other drugs; a combination which immobilises the user and leaves them easily robbed. Tourists are asked within minutes of arrival whether they would like to purchase anything; all part of the service. The locals thronging the bar all know what is going on. Nobody warns the visitors.

With the police and the mafia running the nation's entertainment industry, no tourist should ever trust a Thai bar tender. Never ever. Full stop.

Commentary on the Holiday Guides Thailand website declares: "There are mysterious deaths which happen quite frequently in Thailand and most of these deaths don't make the headlines in other countries. There have been many deaths which are declared as suicides by the police and are not investigated properly. One would hate to think about the real statistics of how many of these are from drink spiking overdoses. You don't hear about exactly how many people die in Thailand from the authorities here, as they know it will have a negative impact on tourism, so the best advice would be to be careful at all times while you are on holidays in Thailand."

The best known of all Thailand's many rackets, also effectively filmed on *Big Trouble in Tourist Thailand*, is the jet-ski scam.

Despite repeated diplomatic warnings and international media coverage, tourists continued to be lured year after year.

The scam is all the more effective for its simplicity and involves using threats to extort large amounts of money for the tiniest damage to a jet-ski. A holidaying foreigner hires one of the machines from an operator. On returning the jet-ski, and while the tourist is getting changed or is otherwise distracted, the operator deliberately damages the jet-skis or replaces it with a similar looking one that has already been damaged. The jet-ski owner then puts on a display of outrage that their equipment has been so badly destroyed and demands payment of at least 45,000 baht, around $US1500.

Tourists are threatened with physical harm or jail if they don't pay. The hirers are over a barrel because they have handed over their passports as collateral. Intimidated, bewildered and unfamiliar with the currency, most foreigners end up paying. In reality the damage the operator is protesting so vociferously about would cost perhaps 500 baht to repair. The scam is perpetrated against thousands of tourists each season.

In one case two Australian women injured in an accident were pursued by jet-ski thugs right into the hospital where they were being treated. The blatant scam has persisted for so long for one simple reason: corruption. Both police and local government officials share in the cash extorted from tourists.

Big Danger in Tourist Thailand documents a British soldier, fresh from Iraq and barely out of his teens. He is shown hiring a jet-ski and taking it for a ride in the bay. He is clearly enjoying himself. But on returning and changing into dry clothes, the situation quickly turns sour. The operator, "OJ", one of Pattaya's better known operators, shows the damaged jet-ski and puts on a display of faux outrage while demanding payment. The British soldier protests that he doesn't have the money, and that he did not damage the ski.

OJ, in a well practised routine, acts as if the entire nation has been insulted by the suggestion that he might be lying, and continues to demand payment.

Adding threat to the situation, several of OJ's muscled companions lurk nearby. "Are you a man?" OJ demands to know of the hapless tourist. The soldier continues to refuse to pay for damage he did not do. So OJ escalates the situation by producing a rifle. The soldier and his friends are outnumbered and outgunned, literally.

At this point the soldiers call one of their own military police. While the military police comment sardonically on the number of OJ's jet-skis that wind up damaged, in the end they agree the soldier will pay $US1000. The scam has been successful.

The UK taxpayer, courtesy of the British Army's choice of destination for some much needed rest and recreation, have placed troops direct from a war zone into yet further danger.

Nor are the British military the only victims of Thailand's many scams. American soldiers, on respite from active duty, were captured by the film crew being duped in the same jet-ski scam. Sport loving beach oriented Australians are also frequent victims.

With direct flights from Australia to Phuket, the Thai island has replaced Bali as the most popular holiday destination in Southeast Asia for Australians. In 2013, 880,000 Australians visited Bali and 900,000 visited Thailand.

In their official advisories the Australian Department of Foreign Affairs warn that Australian travellers continue to report harassment and threats of violence by jet-ski operators on beaches across Thailand, and particularly in Phuket, Pattaya, Koh Samui and Koh Phangan. The advice reads: "Carefully consider your safety and the implications of accidents if you hire a motorcycle or jet-ski and seek advice on any restrictions that may apply (such as insurance cover if you are not licensed to ride a motorcycle in Australia). You should check with your travel insurer whether these activities are covered by your policy. You may be detained and arrested by police following jet-ski and motorcycle accidents until compensation, often in thousands of dollars, can be negotiated between parties."

Unstated is the fact that corrupt local police benefit from the disputes by taking a substantial share of the money changing hands. Then Australian Honorary Consul to Phuket Larry

Cunningham, a property developer with a long association with the island, was vociferous in his protests over the scam throughout his eight years of service. Despite international coverage of the scam, Cunningham declares the scam has been running for years and remains rife. He slams what he sees as the authorities wilful sweeping of facts about jet-ski operators under the carpet.[156]

"Just sit on Patong beach and watch the way these thugs behave," Cunningham said. "You're dealing with criminal elements. It's one of the most dangerous beaches on Earth because of those jet-ski operators. It's just disgraceful.

"I have a very extensive contact base and people are telling me that nothing has changed at all. What [the provincial government] is doing now is they're not reporting cases any more. They're keeping everything completely and utterly hidden. They're trying to smother all the statistics by not reporting them."

In March, 2013, only a few hours after a seminar to look at ways of reforming the industry and making jet-ski operators "brand ambassadors" for Phuket, yet another Australian tourist was caught up in the scam.[157] Cunningham intervened and the case quickly escalated. The Governor of Phuket, Maitree Intusut, had previously expressed himself satisfied with the operators' actions to clean up their industry and reduce incidents of threats, intimidation, extortion and violence against customers. On this occasion the Governor met with the jet-ski operator accused of assaulting and deceiving a foreign tourist, but refused to meet with the Australian Consul.

Cunningham said, the rip-offs, scams, criminal activities and bad behaviour were ruining the holidays of scores of Australians, including a new wave of "schoolies". Australian tourists arrived on cheap direct flights from Australia's capital cities, lured by the benefits of a comparatively high Australian dollar, tales of a wild night life and an exotic location. The high cost of vacationing in Australia, along with its comparatively strict licensing laws and

---

[156] Phuket jet-ski intimidation has not gone away, The Phuket News, August 22, 2013.

[157] Aus Hon Con in tense talks over Puket jet-ski incident, 30 August 2013, *The Phuket News*.

high levels of social conformity, also played into people's decisions to holiday in Thailand.

"Many Australians come here behaving as if the same standards and laws apply in Thailand as they do in Australia," Cunningham said. "They have little idea about Thai culture and think that what happens in Australia happens here."[158]

More than 50 Australians a year die on Phuket, half of them from natural causes and the other half from motorbike and car accidents, misadventures or alleged suicides. Cunningham estimated that about 80 per cent of the cases in which Australians found themselves in trouble were settled before he heard about them, often through extorted payments. Tourists sometimes found themselves in situations that made them "scared for their lives".

Similar to the jet-ski scams, the hiring of motor bikes can also be fraught with difficulty.

Cunningham said Australian "schoolies", teenagers who had just graduated from high school, were coming to the island in rising numbers. He said they were being preyed on by Thai criminals, and corrupt police, at full moon parties where they are often robbed after having their drinks spiked, set up and extorted for money or sexually assaulted. Their experiences were very far from the holidays in paradise they had dreamt of; and paid for. "We have also had motor boats coming from the parties crashing, killing and maiming people ... these parties are dangerous and the kids should not attend them," he says.

In another not uncommon instance, Cunningham tells of an Australian man involved in a business dispute who was wrongfully accused of sexually abusing a child. While being held for 84 days in a Phuket jail, the particular man in question was told his throat would be cut if he did not put money into a bank account. He paid up.

Unsubstantiated accusations of paedophilia are a common strategy of the Asian criminal milieu; and of the Thai police. The aim is either to discredit a business rival or critic, and to extort

---

[158] Island a paradise for many, and a hell for others, Lindsay Murdoch, Sydney Morning Herald, 26 March, 2011.

money. Foreigners thus so unethically accused are left floundering, horrified and extremely frightened. It is a tried and true tactic. Before fleeing the country the accused almost always pay.

Not all scams are life-threatening.

The world famous singer Rihanna went to Phuket on a break between gigs for her Diamonds World Tour. And unintentionally highlighted a scam common in Phuket's infamous red light district of Bangla Road in Patong. Tourists are charged to pose with the endangered slow loris, an appealing looking primate native to Southeast Asia.

Two men were arrested as a result of Rihanna's Instagram showing her holding the cuddly animal. As they realised the significance of the picture, the response of her 9.7 million followers quickly turned.

Slow lorises have a toxic bite, a trait unique to the lorisid group of primates. The toxin is produced by a gland on their arm which is then licked, the animal's saliva combining with the secretion to make the poison. It is also wiped on the loris young to protect them from predators. While nature intended their bite to be protective, it has become one of their greatest vulnerabilities. The lorises used in the tourist trade have had their teeth pulled in order to make them safe to handle. They can die of infection or blood loss.

An animal rescue worker involved in educating the public about the trade said her centre had recently taken in a loris for which a tourist had paid 40,000 Baht, about $US1,250. They had intended to rescue the animal. Instead all they had done was further encourage the trade.[159]

"They'd negotiated while they were probably drunk, and they just wanted the best for the animal," Petra Osterbeg said.

She said 40,000 baht was at the extreme end of the scale – the average selling price was around 10,000 baht, about $US300. But obviously touts would try and extort as much money as possible. The animals could not be returned to the wild, and needed long term captive care because of their teeth having been clipped.

---

[159] Drunk tourists 'saving lorises off Phuket streets, says animal rights worker, Claire Connell, *Phuket News,* 26 September, 2013.

Rihanna was "no more to blame than the millions of other tourists" who had their photos taken with lorises.

Nor were loris pedlars the end of the arrests as a result of Rihanna's fame and hyper-connectivity.

Rihanna tweeted of a night out in Patong: "Either I was phuck wasted last night, or I saw a Thai woman pull a live bird, 2 turtles, razors, shoot darts and ping pong, all out of her pu$$y."

The owner of the Season A-Go-Go Bar was subsequently arrested and faced charges of obscenity and operating without a permit. The local district police chief claimed that the police had only found out about the venue the morning after Rihanna's visit. "We were not able to catch them violating the law until Saturday night," he said. "We had been waiting for them and finally caught them red handed."[160]

Councillor on the Patong Municipal Council and President of the Patong Business and Entertainment Association Veerawit Kruesombat said announced crackdowns on loris touts and sex shows were a "flash in the pan" which would fizzle out within a month. Business people and tourists had repeatedly alerted the police to issues surrounding illegal wildlife and sex shows, but there had been no action until a celebrity reported it. He said he was bored with repeating that the raids were just window dressing: "We all know who is being paid. I think after a month, those in authority will stop paying attention, and things will be back the way they always are. If there was any genuine intent to stop endangered wildlife and sex shows the police must get serious. But the police take bribes, even from beggars. All the business owners in Patong pay to the police. You can ask anyone; they will all say the same. The most important thing is intent—wanting to get rid of illegal things."[161]

"In a month business people in Patong have to pay bribes to police totalling not less than 10 million baht. You can ask anyone, they can give you names and point out who. The bribes have been

---

[160] Rihanna's sex show tweets lead to third Thai arrest, Kate Hodal, *The Guardian*, 15 October, 2013.

[161] Phuket loris, ping pong crackdowns after Rihanna's visit 'just window dressing', *Phuket News*, 24 September, 2013.

paid for a long time. The senior officials—they all know, but they do nothing."

Asked to comment, the Superintendent of the local Kathu Police Station told *Phuket News*: "There are no bribes. The police enforce the law. We check Patong strictly every day. I have ordered more thorough checking and patrolling to find the sex shows. But we haven't found them. They do it in secret. They will have a normal entertainment show, but when the number of customers increases, they change it to a ping pong show ... we are being strict with the checking."

Perhaps in his desperate search for sex shows the good policeman should have looked up phuket.com, which provides the following helpful details:"Depending on the time and the place, shows are performed once every 30 minutes or so but you might have to wait a while if the management feels the imminent presence of the law. Sometimes the show might not happen at all, but that is quite unusual.

1. The Ping Pong Show: A classic... A show performed by a naked lady, usually more mature than and not as sexy as the dancers. The show not only involves ping pong balls, but also all kinds of other interesting accessories such as goldfish, birds, unopened beer bottles, balloons and even darts to name but a few. If you visit different Go-Go bars, you might see the same lady again as they seem to rotate as these kind of skills are not acquired overnight!

2. The Bath Show: This will probably involve you, so don't be shy, nothing really seriously embarrassing happens... but stay in the background if you are 'going commando' or not wearing underpants. If one of your friends is selected, you will be disappointed that photos are not allowed.

3. Body painting in black light: the artistic moment of the show. It's actually quite impressive considering an artist will paint complicated floral patterns on a girl's body in three minutes of almost total darkness.

4. The girls shows: Involving two or more amorous girls... enough said."[162]

With bashings, murders, robberies and other difficulties on the streets and in the bars besmirching Thailand's reputation and attracting unwanted attention around the world, in late 2013 the Thai government announced that it would be establishing "Tourist Courts". In reality the courts are largely a use of resources from within the existing justice system. They are intended to fast track tourist related cases and reassure tourists of their personal safety. They handle complaints involving personal security, thefts, robberies, unfair business dealings/services, pick-pocketing, purse-snatching, credit card fraud, scams, conflicts, accidents, injuries and deaths.

Walking Street, Pattaya, Picture by Lyndhdan.

The Tourist Courts were planned for the major tourist and transit centres of Bangkok's Suvarnabhumi Airport, Pattaya and Chiang Mai, the islands of Phuket, Samui and Krabi and

---

[162] Go Go Bars in Patong, Phuket, Phuket dot com.

Bangkok's Dusit District covering the areas surrounding backpacker haven of Khao San Road and Wat Phra Kaew, otherwise known as the Emerald Buddha, the most sacred Buddhist temple in Thailand. Other resources were scheduled to be established around the upscale shopping precinct of Siam Square and the significantly less upscale district of Patpong, the city's oldest and most dilapidated red light district catering to foreigners.

All the Tourist Courts were originally scheduled to open in 2013, but a year later were still largely in the planning stages, with only three operating full time. Each Tourist Court, formally called the Tourist Protection Section under the local regional Administrative Court, required only a budget of 1.5 million Baht, about $50,000, in addition to personnel and refurbishment costs.

Expat website Coconuts Bangkok noted that the opening of tourist courts was a sign of just how overrun with tourists the country had become.

The Courts had a mixed reception from the beginning, with critics querying their many legal and practical problems. *Phuket Gazette* opined "that the sheer number of legal and bureaucratic hurdles that would need to be cleared to establish a new, independent court under Thailand's rather arcane judicial system would probably end up becoming just another 'pie in the sky' dream that would never be realised."[163]

The paper raised questions over whether the tourist courts would operate under a similar framework to small claims courts in the West, what criteria would be used to determine which cases required judicial intervention and exactly who would be able to seek redress: "We have reservations about the ethics of establishing a 'special' court specifically for tourists, especially if cases involving Thais are delayed as a result. The extraordinary nature of this kind of court is itself a cause for reflection on the extent to which Thailand relies on tourism. Theoretical issues aside, if the court functions as hoped it could be a big practical improvement over the existing system that has needlessly

---

[163] Phuket Opinion: Tourist Court vs Holiday Justice, *Phuket Gazette*, 23 September, 2013.

inconvenienced and in some cases wreaked havoc on the lives of both Thais and foreigners, delivering benefits only to lawyers and corrupt officials."

Others were equally sceptical. The travellers news website *Jaunted* said the mere presence of tourist courts might make vacationers feel warm and fuzzy about visiting Thailand, but unless foreigners were genuinely able to recoup losses they would provide nothing more than a false sense of comfort: "Critics have wondered whether it would be better to put the resources into preventing the crimes instead of solving them. An example would be passing tighter regulations on companies within the tourism industry, as France currently does. The thought is that even if the issue is resolved by the court, tourists who are robbed and conned are still going to leave with a bad taste in their mouths regarding Thailand and its people, which impacts tourism negatively in the long run."

Jaunted speculated on how redress could be obtained in the short time available to most tourists. "If you realise a jet-ski operator has ripped you off, do you have to get him to come to court? We're assuming that's not going to happen. So how does it work? Suppose an incident occurs on the last day before you leave Thailand and the person who ripped you off doesn't come to court. You log your complaint, and the government may or may not mail you a check once they sort through the details? And how will they navigate through the inevitable bogus claims, such as from tourists trying to take advantage of the system?"

Thai officials claimed positive feedback for the experiment. Secretary of Justice Virat Chinvinijakul said problems with tourists being harassed at major tourist attractions, including the theft of property, had been a major issue. The fact that most tourists had to travel back to their country of origin and therefore suspects were not prosecuted or punished had severely affected the image of Thailand.

The first case in the Phuket Tourist Court involved a jet-ski operator who attacked two tourists with a "No Swimming" flagpole.[164] The case was resolved in less than 36 hours.

Danaichet Yomjinda, 25, pleaded guilty to charges of assaulting a 66-year-old father and his 43-year-old son. The dispute arose over alleged damage to a jet-ski. Danaichet had told police that after the tourists, originally thought to be Israelis but in fact Australians, returned the jet-ski "I saw that it was damaged. I was angry, and we quarrelled. Then I used the wooden flag-pole to smash them."

Danaichet was fined 1,000 baht, the equivalent of about $US30, and put on two year's probation.

The Pattaya Tourist Court also heard its inaugural case in September, 2013.[165] The case concerned compensation for the deaths of two Chinese tourists in a speedboat accident the previous month. The families of the deceased Chinese travellers originally sought 16 million baht, almost half a million dollars. They accepted $US70,000 each.[166]

Also in the same month, Airports of Thailand (AOT) announced that the tourist court to be set up at Bangkok's Suvarnabhumi Airport was expected to deal with up to 250 cases daily. AOT Spokesman Pongsak Semsan said from January to August 1,980 crimes involving 1,047 suspects had been reported. The establishment of the Court was aimed at reducing crime at the airport and facilitating legal proceedings. The court would be flexible. If aggrieved foreigners wanted to leave the country early they could schedule their cases appropriately.[167]

Many foreigners arrive in Thailand with plans of opening up a bar, nightclub, restaurant, hotel, resort or some other form of tourist oriented business. Equal numbers leave Thailand with their

---

[164] Phuket jet-ski thug gets first taste of swift tourist court justice, Phuket Gazette, 30 September, 2013.

[165] Tourist Court Resolves its First Case, *Sunday Nation*, 15 September, 2013.

[166] Positive Feedback from The Tourist Courts, *Pattaya Daily News*, 16 September, 2013.

[167] Suvarnabhumi to open special airport court for foreigners on Monday, *Coconuts Bangkok*, 18 September, 2013.

fortunes plundered and their fantasies in tatters. There are many variations on the quip, "How do you establish a million dollar business in Thailand? Start with $10 million."

One of the original reasons why the Thai government was once so keen to attract retirees and foreign business operators to the country was not just to encourage investment but to bring entrepreneurial skills to a traditionally agrarian-based economy. The expat fantasy typically involved them playing mine-host to a steady stream of overseas visitors; while loyal and friendly staff made every day a pleasure.

In their dreams.

Relationships between foreign business owners, the police, local authorities and rival business operators are often difficult. The natural resentments between employers and employees are exaggerated by racial tensions and cultural misunderstandings. Many foreigners complain that it is impossible to keep even good Thai staff. The minute they are paid they disappear back to their villages. Careers in the service industry are not where their hearts lie.

Since the escalation of political turmoil began in 2009 hundreds of bars, resorts, hotels, guesthouses, nightclubs, villas and condominiums have seen their values slashed. Businesses advertised for a half or a third of what they cost to establish can languish on the market for months; or not sell at all.

One well known example of why foreigners should think twice before establishing businesses in Thailand is the case of John Gray.

Originally a dive enthusiast drawn to the beauty of Thailand's southern seas, in the 1980s he discovered that many of the limestone islands in Phang Nga Bay in the Strait of Malacca north of Phuket, made famous by the James Bond movie *The Man With the Golden Gun*, are riddled with caves and tunnels. Entry to secret lagoons is through caverns decorated with oyster-encrusted rock gardens, stalactites and shimmering limestone waterfalls. He established a business in 1989 taking tourists to what were then magically pristine places. Eco-tourism was a catch phrase of the era, the enterprise boomed and Gray won many international awards. His company went bust after 13 years when competitors began eying off the tourist territory he had opened up.

Gray says he was victimised by racism, harassed by the Thai government on trumped-up drug and immigration charges, assaulted, robbed and betrayed by employees as well as being strong-armed by local mafia and business interests. His business manager was arrested on a cannabis charge, with the authorities insisting that the company pay the bail. His manager promptly fled the country and the company's cash reserves were wiped out. Gray received numerous death threats. Called to a meeting with the local mafia chief, a .45 pistol was placed on the table between them. One of his key employees was shot three times in front of his office, leaving the man on crutches for a year. On another occasion an employee stole 10 of his boats and held them for ransom. Gray eventually had no choice but to pay. Meanwhile the precious environment Gray had cared so much about fell prey to his competitors. Tourists formed queues outside the caves, stalactites were broken off for souvenirs and the lagoons became filled with rubbish.[168]

There are countless other examples of the best intentions of foreign investors going savagely awry.

A police crackdown on the Phuket dive industry, which saw foreigner boat and dive operators rounded up, highlighted some of the problems of doing business in Thailand.[169] *Phuket News* suggested the crackdown might be more accurately described as a shakedown.

In March of 2014 some 50 expat dive business investors held a public meeting to defy alleged extortion by rogue police. Many had been asked to pay additional "fees" of up to 20,000 baht. Plain clothes police officers had been arresting foreigners found working for a dive company and threatening to charge them with contravening the terms of their work permits. The police claimed that expats were breaking the law by performing jobs specifically

---

[168] *Bangkok Babylon*, Jerry Hopkins, Periplus Editions, 2005.

[169] Questions over crackdown on Phuket dive industry as foreigners arrested over permits, *The Phuket News*, 11 March, 2014.

designated for Thais, such as loading and unloading equipment onto dive boats. The regulations were designed to boost employment for Thai workers.

The business owners were not charged but asked to "donate" money to the police.

One dive operator estimated that the police were snagging as many as 30 people from the industry every day. In a series of emotional speeches, expat dive managers denounced the tactics of police and undertook to pool their resources to end the rip-offs. The gathering was told that raids on Chalong Pier alarmed customers and were damaging Phuket's reputation as a key centre for diving tourism. "It's horrible," one speaker said. "The police come, they don't explain. They don't care. They just want money." [170]

The problems in the diving industry led to the arrival of the Public Sector Anti-Corruption Commission. In a relatively rare circumstance, the organisation took on the dive operators' case alleging extortion by local police. Under the terms of its legislation, acceptance meant there was a prima facie case against the police officers. It was the first time in memory that alleged corruption on Phuket had been resisted by a group of expats to the point where an investigation was ordered. [171]

The Superintendent of Chalong Police Station, Colonel Krittapas Detintharasorn, was transferred. At the time Phuket's top policeman Ong-art Phiewruangnont said he had moved the colonel "because he has been there a long time and developed close relationships with his men, which makes it hard for him to maintain discipline."

The following month Colonel Krittapas was back at his home station.172 Director of Suppression of Corruption in Public Sector 4 Wannop Somjintanakul said formal charges might be laid in the

---

[170] Expat Phuket Dive Operators Fight Alleged Rip-offs by Rogue Phuket Police, *Phuket Wan*, 23 March, 2014.

[171] Phuket Police Corruption Probe to Begin Next Week, Say Investigators, *Phuket Wan*, 21 April, 2014.

[172] Chalong Top Cop back at work in home station, *Phuket Gazette*, 19 May, 2014.

future. Major General Ong-art changed his tune, saying that since Colonel Krittapas had survived the Public Sector Anti-Corruption Commission inquiry there was no issue with him returning: "As for the relationship between him and his men, that is for him to manage. I believe that if he finds any of his men being bad cops, he will control and discipline those officers."

Krittapas declared he would not institute any new measures to stop extortion: "My officers know I won't tolerate extortion. It's a delicate issue and can have a negative effect on Phuket's tourism image. Still, it's difficult for me to control completely. We have about 100 officers in the Chalong Police Station. I can't keep an eye on every single one of them."

The scandals in the Thai tourist industry came as the nation prepared for the establishment of the ASEAN Economic Community (AEC) in 2015, basically an Asian free trade grouping similar to the European Union.

The Thai government spent billions of baht preparing the nation for the advent of the AEC. The countries involved are Brunei, Cambodia, Indonesia, Laos, Malaysia, Myanmar, Philippines, Singapore, Thailand, and Vietnam. Combined they represent one of the planet's most dynamic economies, with nine per cent of the world's population. The AEC aims to make ASEAN a more competitive economic bloc by turning it into a single market and production base, with a free flow of goods, services, including tourism, investment and skilled labour, and freer flow of capital. The creation of a common market with the aims of clean, corruption free industries threatened the future of Thailand's tourist oriented businesses.

One of Thailand's leading corporate lawyers Cynthia Pornavalai wrote that each ASEAN member country was still struggling to align its national laws and legislation to a unified market: "In Thailand, the lack of understanding of the AEC within the private sector, the civil society, and even the government has contributed to delays in implementing the regional agreement."[173]

---

[173] ASEAN Economic Community 2015 and Thailand, Cynthia Pornavalai, *Informed Counsel*, Vol 3 No 1, February 2012.

The impending advent of the AEC came at a time when there had been a dramatic downshift in the tourist industry; underpinned by a prolonged climate of political upheaval and the nation's spreading reputation as an unsafe and unsavoury destination. The Association of Thai Travel Agents estimated tourist arrivals through its member companies would decline by 35 per cent in 2014. The ATTA counts tourists who buy tour packages handled by a member tour company and is calculated on fees paid to the Airports of Thailand for members to gain access to their clients who arrive at the airport and need a meet-and-greet service.

Analysis by the National Economic and Social Development Board showed that millions were staying away. With at least 66 countries imposing travel warnings during the first two quarters of 2014 and the suspension of many internationally issued travel insurance policies as a result of the May 22 military intervention, inbound tourism figures tumbled. There was an overall drop of 12.28 per cent in the second quarter following a decline of 7.8 per cent in the first. Visitors from East Asia abandoned Thailand in record numbers, with arrivals contracting 18.8 per cent. As a result tourism receipts for the second quarter were down 7.2 per cent, while hotel occupancy over the period stood at just 47.5 per cent, the lowest level of average hotel occupancy rate in the previous 15 quarters and 21.23 per cent down on the same period in 2013.[174]

ATTA president Sisdivachr Cheewarattanaporn called on the military junta to rehabilitate Thailand's image and build confidence in top markets such as China, India and the Middle East: "It will take time to recover and there should be positive signs by the fourth quarter but it will not be enough to fully recover what has been lost."[175]

Director of the Centre for International Trade Studies at the University of the Thai Chamber of Commerce Aat Pisanwanich said unfriendly staff and poor services were hitting competitiveness,

---

[174] Thailand 2014 Q2 & H1 GDP—Southeast Asia's Second Largest Economy on Life Support, John Le Fevre, *The Establishment Post*, 8 September, 2014. http://www.establishmentpost.com/thailand-2014-q2-h1-gdp-southeast-asias-second-largest-economy-on-life-support/

[175] ATTA: Big drop in tour bookings, *TR Weekly*, 1 July, 2014.

with Thailand in serious danger of losing ground. A study by the Centre showed that Singapore and Malaysia had significantly improved their tourism and hospitality sectors and were drawing increasing numbers of international visitors. After the AEC crystallised Thailand could find it more difficult to compete because its tourism services had developed less than those in other countries in the region. Foreign visitors were less satisfied than they once were with the "Siamese Smile", as many Thais, particularly people working in service businesses, look displeased, according to the study. The service industry should urgently improve its services and the attitude of its employees or otherwise the country could see fewer visitors in the future. Other issues concerning foreign visitors included political stability and safety.[176]

In March, 2014, pioneering expat news website *Phuket Wan* began a campaign under the banner "Make Phuket a Role Model: End Corruption". [177]

Award winning journalists Alan Morison and Chutima Sidasathian urged the public not to become fearful, declaring they knew the European Union Ambassadors to Thailand for a start wanted an end to Phuket's chronic corruption. They called for the introduction of cleanskin police, immigration officers and officials on the island and severe punishment for anyone caught taking a bribe. They also called for the confiscation of jet-skis of any operator attempting to scam a tourist, the slashing of tuk tuk and taxi fares, arrest and imprisonment for anyone caught polluting the sea, the end of tourist retail rip-offs by imposing set prices on essential items, and the placing of all future condominium developments on hold until the oversupply in the resident property market had resolved.

"We hope people continue to keep blowing the whistle ... everywhere that illegal graft is being demanded and paid," they wrote. "Unless action is taken now, corruption, environmental

---

[176] Warning to tourism sector, Petchanet Pratruangkrai, *The Nation*, 28 August, 2013.

[177] Make Phuket a Role Model: End Corruption, Alan Morison and Chutima Sidasathian, *Phuket Wan*, 30 March, 2014.

degradation and lack of safety on roads and beaches will kill Phuket's tourism industry within 10 years.

"What we are urging is simple: Follow the Singapore example. Introduce incorruptible officers who can provide the foundation for a new beginning on Phuket. Start with just one of Phuket's 10 police stations, fill it with honest officers and expand the corruption-free process from there. Eventually, with 17 organisations or groups on Phuket known to be on the take, according to Patong business people, Phuket and Thailand are certain to be exposed and found wanting."

Phuket Wan had frequently argued that Phuket needed a benevolent dictator to solve its problems, and from what they had seen so far, coup commander General Prayuth Chan-ocha could be the perfect man for the role: "If the coup commander honestly wishes to remove the flaws in Thailand's version of democracy, we would suggest he starts by attempting to obliterate corruption first. Phuket, as an island-province with its mix of long-term residents, workers from other provinces and thousands of tourists, remains the ideal place to start."[178]

Bangkok. Picture by Bobby Jean.

---

[178] Coup Commander an Ideal Phuket Dictator, Alan Morison and Chutima Sidasathian, *Phuket Wan*, 28 May, 2014.

THE VARIETIES OF EXPATRIATE EXPERIENCE

Walter 'Whacky' Douglas looked like he was having a fine old time when he was arrested and deported from Thailand in 2014.

Douglas, known as "The Tartan Pimpernel" and once described as one of Britain's ten wealthiest drugs traffickers, disappeared from official view in the late 1990s after a career linked to narcotics. As one of the world's principle centres for opium trafficking in the 19th Century, heroin in the 20th Century and methamphetamines in the 21st Century, and with easily bribed officials, Thailand has long proven a comfortable hideout for smugglers.

When he was tracked down to the island of Koh Samui in 2013 Douglas claimed stories about him were grossly exaggerated. "No charges are pending," he said.[179]

But early in 2014 police raided The Tartan Pimpernel's villa on the north coast of Koh Samui as well as his nightclub Dreamers, where he went under the name of Bobby Brown.

He was flown to Bangkok and put on a London bound plane which was met at Heathrow by officers of the National Crime Agency.

Bangkok based British journalist Andrew Drummond wrote that Douglas's deportation and arrest in police custody had caused a panic among a group of British expats, known to British police, living in an enclave in Bang Rak, Koh Samui, just five minutes from the airport. Others had been arrested when they returned to the U.K.

Douglas began his working life as a milkman in Glasgow. He didn't stay there for long. His record includes arrest and time served for smuggling 18 tonnes of hash, along with ecstasy and cocaine, as well as money laundering to the tune of £150 million, of which he was acquitted. He was also charged with travelling on a false passport.

Douglas was also one of many people interviewed in connection with the 1990 murder in Marbella of Great Train Robber Charlie

---

[179] 'Tartan Pimpernel' Deported from Thailand, 7 February, 2014, Andrew Drummond website.

Wilson. He spent his time between Thailand and southern Spain, where he also owned Dreamers clubs.

Thailand's courting of foreigners has led to the arrival not just of respectable retirees and senior business people, but to a bevy of colourful characters, many of whom are regarded as criminals in their own countries. Those on the wrong side of the law find, just as do more legitimate investors, the Kingdom's open slather version of capitalism, its easy approach to visas and corrupt immigration offices, along with a compliant officialdom where money greases all wheels, a congenial atmosphere in which to do business.

In April of 2014 alleged British drug dealer Michael France, 53, was arrested in the seaside resort town of Cha-Am, where he had purchased a luxury apartment in 2008. He was wanted on suspicion of masterminding a gang that smuggled hundreds of kilos of cocaine and heroin. He fled to Thailand after gang members were caught in France with 30 kilos of cocaine and 95 kilos of heroin in their car.

The British criminal class in particular find Thailand hugely attractive; a kind of safe house replete with cheap drinks and obliging sex workers.

Head of the fugitives unit at the UK's Serious Organised Crimes Agency (SOCA), Dave Allen, said Thailand was high on the list as a destination of choice among international criminals: "The attraction for Spain is still there, as there is a huge expat British population. The places we're seeing them go to now are Thailand, certainly, South Africa, and the United Arab Emirates."[180]

Thailand has played host to international mafia gangs since the virtually uncontrolled immigration of the Chinese into the country during the latter half of the 19th Century. The Chinese now constitute an entrepreneurial upper-class of Thailand. The ethnic Thais, with the heart of their culture based in rural villages, have in general terms shown few business skills. The Chinese are notorious for treating them with contempt.

With the arrival of the Chinese came the infamous triads. At first, as the opium trade was still legal in the 19th Century, they ran

---

[180] As police arrest fugitives in Spain, are the days of the Costa del Crime numbered? Duncan Campbell, *The Guardian*, 14 July 2013

the narcotics trade, along with opium and gambling dens and other smuggling operations. The gambling and smuggling produced handsome profits, further enhancing their power.

As the authoritative Thai Law Forum reports, the present-day Chinese mafias cannot be considered foreign anymore.[181] Over time, they have become naturalised citizens. Ethnic Thais envy their wealth, but the Chinese now form an integral part of Thai society.

Unbeknown to most tourists, they regularly interact with and financially support the Chinese triads while visiting the nation's entertainment centres. The Chinese criminal class run a broad spectrum of brothels, massage parlours, karaoke bars and escort services. All of these enterprises operate with the full protection of the Thai police.

The red light district Patpong and the interlinking streets running off the thoroughfare of Surawong, has many venues run by the Chinese. Any long-time observer can watch a steady flow of drunken foreigners availing themselves of the mafia run brothels of Bangrak any time of the day or night. With an all pervasive contempt for the gullibility of foreigners, providing value for money is not in the triad's hearts. From outrageous over-charging by the operators themselves to the stealing of passports, cash and possessions by the sex workers thus employed, tourists are routinely fleeced under the noses of, or, more precisely, with the assistance of the local police.

The most profitable of all the Chinese enterprises, particularly in Bangkok, are the gambling dens. Technically illegal, any foreigner can find these sophisticated operations simply by asking a taxi driver. Thailand has some of the cheapest taxi fares in the world. Partly as a result, the drivers form a kind of synaptic link between Thailand's police, criminals and foreign tourists, and make money where they can.

If foreign travellers do not want to take the risks involved in entering the larger operations, where they will be checked for weapons and are essentially powerless, they can easily participate in

---

[181] The Darker Side of Tropical Bliss, Thomas Schmid, 25 February, 2010, Thai Law Forum, 25 February, 2010.)

gambling simply by approaching one of the street based operations. The easily located makeshift "dens", often operating on main thoroughfares, are usually enclosed with plastic. They may be illegal, but are there for all to see.

The games are rigged. The tourist cannot win.

A number of these dens operate in the major tourist areas, and any traveller prepared to lose a few thousand baht or a few thousand dollars for the sake of experiencing a bit of local colour, will be able to find them with ease. One of the most famous, frequented by senior police and known to all the locals, is located in a dilapidated building at the end of the city's most famous gay strip, Soi Twilight.

Soi Twilight by Ryan Lackey.

No foreigner should ever assume that when they enter this netherworld they are not in danger. For a start, if they carry any quantity of cash on them at all, their drinks will be spiked and they will be robbed. In the unlikely event they win at the gaming tables the chances of them leaving the area with any substantial amount of cash in their pockets is more or less zero.

The general cliché is that the Thai mafia talks big and operates in packs. The Russian mafia is far more lethal, operating in silence and killing without compunction. The breakup of the former Soviet Union, beginning in 1989, led not only to the creation of several new nation states but also the eventual dissolution of Russia's dreaded KGB secret service. Suddenly thousands of former KGB operatives or associates had to search for new means of income.

Post-1989, visitor numbers of Russian tourists to Thailand soared. Sensing opportunity, Russian mafia organisations rapidly established themselves. While the fleshpot of Pattaya was once dominated by German restaurants, it soon became flush with Russian eateries – and the Russian mob. Many of those restaurants and bars are little more than money laundering operations. In 2009, according to figures released by the Thai Ministry of Tourism, some 336,000 Russian tourists visited the Kingdom. Subsequent years showed massive increases, rising to 1,736,990 by 2013.

As Bangkok-based journalist Thomas Schmid observes: "With the mob also arrived Eastern European prostitutes, virtually unheard of prior to 1989. Bangkok's downtown area around Sukhumvit Soi 3 to 15 has matured into a 'hub' of which Thailand can hardly be proud."

In 2014 a Russian mafia gang leader wanted for his involvement in scores of killings and other criminal activities, was arrested in front of a supermarket in Thailand's eastern seaside town of Sattahip. Alexander Mutusov was notorious for killings, extortions and kidnappings in the Moscow and Petersburg areas, according to the Russian embassy. He had been living in Thailand on a retirement visa since 2009.[182]

---

[182] Russian Mafia Boss Arrested in Thailand, *The Moscow Times*, 25 June, 2014.

Shortly thereafter five alleged Russian gangsters were arrested in the same neighbourhood, wanted largely on extortion and false passport charges. INTERPOL dispatched a team to Bangkok.

While their mafia had become a uniquely powerful, feared and dangerous force in the Thai criminal ferment, Russia wasn't the only country providing colourful personnel to Thailand's shores.

Contract killer, ex-US soldier Joseph "Rambo" Hunter, was found living quietly in a villa next to the Loch Palm Golf Course on Phuket.[183] Other than visiting acquaintances on the estate itself, Hunter rarely went out and kept his blinds shuttered. He was arrested after a request from the U.S. Government and faced charges of murder and training cross border assassins, as well as trying to kill drug agents and informants for Latin American drug cartels.

The newspaper *Bangkok Post* intoned that Hunter was only the latest high profile cross-border criminal to consider Thailand an excellent place to plan "heinous" crime: "Since the late 20th Century, an almost steady and predictable string of criminals have used the country in this manner. It is known that some of the most important planning for the 9/11 attacks took place among Arab plotters in Bangkok. Foreign criminals of all types, guilty of violent and white-collar crimes, have tarred Thailand with a bad brush. Thailand continues to play host to far too many ill-intentioned, fraudulent or violent foreign criminals."[184]

Hunter revealed to undercover US Drug Enforcement Agents that he had arranged for two female real estate agents on Phuket to be murdered; confirming the often dangerously corrupt relationship between property developers, real estate agents, local authorities and international gangsters.

Thailand's love of the dark side, its multiple obsessions with soap opera lives and criminal milieus, along with its numerous almost satanic appeals to expatriates, has spawned a colourful sub-genre of thriller and detective novels, along with experiential or documentary accounts.

---

[183] Special Report: Is my neighbour a contract killer, *Phuket Gazette*, 5 October, 2013.

[184] Editorial Opinion: Keeping out the rotten few, *Bangkok Post*, 8 October, 2013.

One of a number of serious works, *Blood Brothers: Crime, Business and Politics in Asia*, by Thai resident Bertil Lintner and former president of the Foreign Correspondents Club of Thailand, put it simply enough: "While criminals may live outside the law, they have never lived outside society. In Asia, there has always been a symbiosis between law and crime."[185]

Some works include romantic or dissolute tales of alcoholism or substance abuse in the enervating heat of Thailand; accompanied by a colourful caste of local prostitutes, gangsters and police, with virtually all the characters on the take in one way or another. Others affectionately record the characteristic slippery collisions and collusions of morality in the Land of Smiles, also known, perhaps more appropriately, as The Land of Hungry Ghosts.

Still other books document alarming expat experiences in Thailand's prison system.

The 1999 book *The Damage Done: Twelve Years Inside a Bangkok Prison* by Australian Warren Fellows, recorded how, through a "labyrinth of chance meetings and bad decisions", the author was convicted in 1978 of heroin trafficking and sentenced to life imprisonment.[186]

Fellows[187] was certainly guilty of his crime. He worked for years as a drug courier for one of Sydney's most notorious underworld figures, Neddy Smith, who had close associations with the Australian police of the 1970s.

The days of the Vietnam War, when the CIA was closely linked to the heroin trade through fronts like Lao Air, may be gone. But until recent years, when poppy eradication programs and the rise in popularity of methamphetamines made other drugs more financially viable, Thailand was a centre for the world's heroin trade.

---

[185] *Blood Brothers: Crime, Business and Politics in Asia*, Bertil Lintner, Allen & Unwin, 2002.

[186] *The Damage Done: Twelve Years Inside a Bangkok Prison*, Warren Fellows, Mainstream Publishing Company, 2000.

[187] Picture courtesy South East Asia Backpacker.

Fellows was a pioneer in the heroin trade between Thailand and Australia, which operated with virtual impunity under the protection of senior Thai generals. In the days of primitive customs controls, the routine was well established. Couriers from Australia, usually practising or former addicts down on their luck and prepared to take the risk, travelled to Thailand, where they met up with a fellow Australian. They would swallow a kilogram divided into 30 balloons, and catch a return flight. As the years progressed and screening grew more sophisticated, the criminals grew cleverer; sending several couriers through at the same time, and pointing the finger at one of them. While the authorities were busy with the hapless courier who had been anointed the fall guy, the others walked through scot free.

Also in later years other transit points became popular, particularly union controlled shipping wharves where customs officers were essentially powerless.

Fellows, who went to school in Sydney and whose father was a champion jockey, began his Prologue: "I am going to tell you about the worst thing that ever happened to me. Think about the most wretched day of your life. Maybe it was when someone you loved died, or when you were badly hurt in an accident, or a day when you were so terrified you could scarcely bear it. Now imagine 4,000 of those days in one big chunk."

A vivid opening sequence describes the lancing of "an enormous lump" which appeared to be moving on the neck of a fellow prisoner, a Frenchman who would not stop screaming. "As soon as the blade sliced the skin, the wound opened up like a new flower. And out of the gash in the Frenchman's neck spilled hundreds of tiny, worm-like creatures, wriggling and oozing like spaghetti. It was appalling, a dreadful dream, only real and right before my eyes, happening to a human being... A man who, somewhere, had a mother and a father, family and friends, had been left to become a living nest for maggots... Such visions marked my days like the chimes of a clock."

Fellows claimed that heroin was readily available in Thai prisons, and that he became addicted, "an outstanding case of poetic justice".

Escape: The True Story of the Only Westerner to ever Escape from the Bangkok Hilton, by David McMillan, known for having established the largest drug importation network Australia had ever seen, is better written than many others of its type. As a child McMillan attended Melbourne's elite Caulfield Grammar School, and as a 12-year-old became well known in the fledging television of the 1960s presenting a regular 5-minute news bulletin for children. His drug smuggling career began with hashish from India. At his peak, in the mid-1980s, he owned houses and apartments all around the world. In 1982 he was arrested and charged with heroin smuggling, running houses associated with the business in London, Brussels and Bangkok, as well as using multiple false passports.

Released on parole from an Australian prison in 1993, after a close call at Bangkok's former international airport Don Muang, now reserved for regional flights, McMillan was arrested and charged with heroin trafficking. In *Escape* he records how he watched 600 foreigners in a prison population of 12,000 in Bangkok's infamous Klong Plem prison, aka the Bangkok Hilton, falling prey to disease, violence and despair. Financially better off than most of his fellow inmates, McMilan had his own chef and servants. For others, up against the brutality of the Thai justice system, death appeared to be their only way out. McMillan, also likely to be given a death sentence if his case ever reached trial, resolved that this would not be the end for him. He escaped in 1996 in circumstances Australia's future Attorney General Robert McClelland described as "really quite an achievement".

McMillan was subsequently rearrested in 2012 in Britain as part of an investigation into the importation of heroin from Pakistan.[188]

Many of the foreigners intermeshing with Thailand's drug trade are so-called "drug mules".

The mules may be judged guilty of moral turpitude, naivety, desperation, stupidity or greed. Some should be classified not as

---

[188] Notorious Australian drug smuggler David McMillan jailed in London, *Australian Times*, 19 September, 2012.

perpetrators of drug trafficking, but as victims of human trafficking, according to the International Organisation on Migration's criteria for trafficking, which includes coercion or trickery, transportation and exploitation.

Sandra Gregory's *Forget You Had A Daughter: Doing Time in the 'Bangkok Hilton'* is one of the few to be written by a woman. She recounts how she went from having a successful life in Bangkok that included friends, two teaching jobs, and her own apartment, into a Thai prison. Her life took a terrible turn when she ran out of money while recuperating from dysentery and dengue fever. With mounting medical bills to pay, she met a heroin addict who offered her $1,000 to smuggle his personal supply of heroin to Japan. It was just enough to pay her medical bills and buy a ticket home, but Gregory was arrested at Bangkok airport before she even boarded the plane.

Forget You Had A Daughter[189] details the four and a half years she spent in prison. She tells of her daily fight for survival, of many women who died with no medical care or loved ones around them, and of her acceptance of her guilt and ultimate redemption.

Sandra Gregory was just one of the many small time mules who, out of their depth and given up by drug smugglers as decoys, find themselves in jail. Bertil Lintner, an expert on the global narcotics trade, says the syndicates recruited several "mules" at a time to carry varying quantities of narcotics. They designated one or two as "decoys or sacrifices" who would be arrested by airport customs after a "tip-off" from the syndicates. Meanwhile, mules carrying larger consignments slip through undetected: "Usually the ones with the smallest amounts get nabbed. The numbers look good for the Thai government's war on drugs and the risk factor is profitable for syndicates because the higher price of the drugs is maintained."

Thando Pendu was from a South African township, had not completed high school and had never left the country before travelling to Thailand. Recruited by a syndicate, she could not

---

[189] Forget You Had a Daughter. Sandra Gregory. John Blake Publishing 2013.

swallow the condoms normally used for smuggling heroin, and instead bound them crudely to her chest.

At the age of 23 she was busted at Bangkok's Suvarnabhumi Airport with heroin strapped to her body like a suicide bomber. She was caught in October 2008.

Bangkok customs officials had been tipped off before she even boarded the plane and, while she was being stripped of her illicit cargo, four other South African mules who had been coerced by the same syndicate slipped through.

"In Pendu's case she was obviously a liability to the syndicate," said human rights lawyer Sabelo Sibanda. "So they had two options—either dispose of her permanently or the kinder option of setting her up."

While evidence that she had been set up was provided both to INTERPOL and national authorities, Pendu's fate had already been sealed: 25 years in prison, with no recourse to appeal or a retrial.

Patricia Gerber, who founded the activist group Locked Up after her own son was caught in a foreign jail, said: "They are the decoys! Deliberately set up by the people who send them, they take the fall while the bigger consignment gets through with the real drug 'mule'. These are not cold blooded murderers. They are people like you and I who may or may not have made a colossal mistake. Do they deserve to rot? Do we, as a 'humane' society throw them away, or do we get our country in line with the rest of the world and bring these people back by extradition to serve their sentences on home soil?"

Sebastian Williams' *Send Them to Hell: The Brutal Horrors of Bangkok's Nightmare Jails*,[190] describes the human rights abuses, murder, drugs, prisoner and child sex slavery, blackmail, extortion, violence, medical maltreatment and unjustifiable death sentences that characterise the Thai penal system. He describes the Thai justice and prison systems as a cartel and accuses Thai officialdom and the Thai mafia of involvement in drug trafficking and "political skulduggery" forming a criminal empire run at the expense of legitimate businessmen and innocent tourists.

---

[190] Send Them To Hell. Sebastian Williams . Mainstream Publishing. 2012.

Almost every foreigner who ends up in a Thai prison is there either due to the complicity or treachery of local drug dealers, or the misconduct of officials. If they are unprepared or unable to bribe their way out, they rot.

Other books recording the experiences of foreigners in Thai jails include: Andy Botts' *Nightmare in Bangkok: The incredible true account of survival in a Thai prison*, T.M. Hoy's *Rotting in the Bangkok Hilton: The Gruesome Story of a Man Who Survived Thailand's Deadliest Prison* and Jon Cole's *Bangkok Hard Time*.

In 2012 Africa's *Mail & Guardian* recorded the impending release of the Bangkok Hilton's longest serving foreign prisoner, South African Shani Krebs.[191] Krebs was arrested in 1994 at the age of 34: "His story carried a familiar refrain: in Thailand on vacation, surrounded by the paradoxical fast foods of sex and drugs that are legally prohibited in Thailand but available on every street corner, with one proviso: 'Don't get caught!' He was holed up in a dodgy backpackers, where his travellers cheques were stolen, he said. He was stranded, desperate. A member of the Nigerian community living in the Sukhumvit area of Bangkok offered him a way to make a quick, relatively low-risk buck. The next thing he knew, he was in Bang Kwang."

Two decades after Kreb's arrest, Nigerians are still closely linked to the drug trade centred around narrow streets in the entertainment areas off Sukhumvit. Organised teams arrived in the city for periods of 12 months before the workers are recycled back to their homeland and replaced by fresh crews. As with every other criminal activity in Thailand, there are close associations with the local police.

New inmates in the Bangkok Hilton wear leg irons for the first three months, whereas those on death row have their shackles permanently welded on. Fates are determined by will or whim—a royal birthday here, a public holiday there. The stroke of a monarch's pen determines who shall live, die or be released.

---

[191] Free at last: Longest-serving farang at 'Bangkok Hilton' is checking out, Mail & Guardian, 3 February, 2012.

Initially condemned to death, Kreb's sentence was commuted to 100 then 40 years. Until his release, he had not spent a second in a democratic South Africa, having been arrested a day before the elections in 1994. Longevity earned Krebs senior ranking in the inmate hierarchy, which meant that the junior inmates cooked and cleaned for him. His self-taught artistic prowess further elevated his status. His portraits ranged from Louis Armstrong to sultry nudes.

Mail & Guardian recorded that on Facebook a 751-strong support group had been established in 2008 and Kreb's messages of support included: "Shani, only 56 days to go ... every day gets brighter" and "Support our friend in the last steps to victory". There were psychedelic artworks and photo-shopped collages of Krebs on an aeroplane, Krebs giving the thumbs-up, Krebs reunited with his family in Johannesburg.

The staff reporter said covering South Africans convicted of drug trafficking in Thailand "was a harrowing assignment... Most of the 12 South African prisoners had been incarcerated in Bangkok for well over a decade, yet were still delicately hanging on to gossamer threads of hope. I had none to give."

South Africa remains one of only three countries—with Ghana and Nepal—that will not sign a prisoner transfer treaty that would enable its citizens, after spending a portion of their sentence in the country in which they are convicted, to be repatriated to serve the remainder of their time in their homeland. Without this agreement they are doomed to remain incarcerated in a foreign country, far from their loved ones, isolated and often forced to endure horrific conditions. In Thailand's case, with the conditions so poor, a prison sentence often meant a death sentence. Kreb was atypical because of his survival skills.

The *Mail & Guardian* editorialised that the South African government appeared indifferent to the welfare of its citizens in Thai jails, ignoring questions concerning the welfare or status of foreign prisoners: "Even recreational drug users—anyone who has smoked dagga, shnarfed a line of cocaine, imbibed an ecstasy tablet—form an inextricable synapse in the narcotics chain of command. It stretches from the producers—usually peasant farmers—to the global drug cartels and middlemen or dealers and is distributed worldwide by the most disposable component of this billion-dollar trade, namely the mules."

Mirroring views widely supported in academe, one online commentator James Stockley wrote: "As long as there is a demand there will be a supply. The war on drugs will never be won. Legalise, and stop putting money in the hands of real criminals whilst incarcerating the poor and desperate."

Put simply, the argument goes that prohibition, just as it did in America in the 1930s prohibition of alcohol and the era of Al Capone, breeds corrupt officials. The huge profits involved empowers and enriches criminal networks, makes the trade almost impossible to police and endangers the health and safety of average citizens psychologically predisposed to addiction, or either stupid, disturbed or adventurous enough to flaunt the legislation.

It is a lesson entirely ignored by Thailand, whose history of corrupt officials, police and military officers' involvement in the drug trade dates back at least until the 1940s.

Heroin use in the West took off in the 1960s. In the decades to follow Thai elites vastly enriched themselves through the heroin trade. At the same time foreigners entrapped or caught with small amounts of drugs and unable to pay the expected bribe, or who had been used as decoys or stooges by Thai drug syndicates, rotted and died in the country's barbaric prisons.

"South Africa is sacrificing its citizens on the altar of diplomatic and trade relations with countries such as Thailand," said human rights lawyer Sabelo Sibanda.

On the occasion of his 84th birthday Thailand's monarch, King Bhumibol Adulyadej, awarded a reduction in sentences for all foreigners convicted of drug offences.

Ironically, throughout his long reign Thailand had operated as a major transport route and one of the world's principal sources of narcotics; a trade which had enriched the country's military, police and royal elites while laying waste to individuals, families and entire neighbourhoods in the West.

The King had long been closely associated with corrupt police and military officers running the heroin trade.

Through the 1960s and 1970s, the seemingly limitless supply of heroin produced in the tri-border area of Thailand, Cambodia and Burma fed a soaring number of addicts in America; and then throughout the Western world. The thousands of addicted GIs returning to America and other allied soldiers returning to their home countries also boosted the trade.

Dr Alfred McCoy's seminal work *The Politics of Heroin in Southeast Asia* puts it thus: "America's heroin addicts are victims of the most profitable criminal enterprise known to man—an enterprise that involves millions of peasant farmers in the mountains of Asia, thousands of corrupt government officials, disciplined criminal syndicates, and agencies of the United States government. America's heroin addicts are the final link in a chain of secret criminal transactions that begin in the opium fields of Asia, pass through clandestine heroin laboratories in Europe and Asia, and enter the United States through a maze of international smuggling routes."[192]

McCoy wrote that Thailand's legacy of god-kings underpinned and enabled the nation's heroin trade: "At the bottom of Thailand's contemporary pyramids of corruption, armies of functionaries systematically plunder the nation and pass money up the chain of command to the top, where authoritarian leaders enjoy an ostentatious lifestyle.... Such potentates, able to control every corrupt functionary in the most remote province, are rarely betrayed during struggles with other factions. As a result, a single political faction has usually been able to centralise and monopolise all Thailand's narcotics traffic."

By the 1950s the Golden Triangle was producing half the world's opium. Bumper harvests were shipped to northern Thailand, particularly Chiang Mai, where they were sold to the Thai police. Commander General Phao Sriyanonda grew immensely wealthy, maintaining 100 mistresses. He was a close ally of the King. Under guard from the army and police, including General Phao, the harvest was transported by train to Bangkok for export. The Venice of the East became Asia's opium capital. The

---

[192] The Politics of Heroin in Southeast Asia, Alfred W. McCoy, Harper & Row, 1972.

King of Thailand became the wealthiest monarch on Earth. And the sight of the police and the military guarding the opium crop on the train travelling down from the foothills of Chiang Mai and across the plains and paddy fields to Bangkok became an annual ritual.

Thanks to its history, Thailand was uniquely placed to take advantage of soaring demand during the second half of the 20th Century. By the early 1960s large quantities of cheap heroin were being refined in Bangkok and northern Thailand, while substantial amounts of morphine base were being processed in the Golden Triangle region for export to Hong Kong and Europe. By the late 1960s laboratories were producing high quality heroin for disenchanted American soldiers caught in the Vietnam War.

The entrapment of foreigners for small amounts of drugs is little more than a blood sport within the nation's law enforcement officials, who in reality control the very trade they are supposed to be policing. But Thailand's hypocrisy on the issue does not end there.

Western governments have long since abandoned the campaign slogan "War on Drugs". As research on former US First Lady Nancy Reagan's Just Say No campaign amply illustrated, such programs are not just ineffective, they are counter-productive, arousing rather than dampening interest and defining margins towards which people are drawn. Thailand's War On Drugs, initiated by former Prime Minister Thaksin Shinawatra, was uniquely brutal.

In their report *Not Enough Graves: The War on Drugs, HIV/AIDS, and Violations of Human Rights*, the prominent group Human Rights Watch found that the campaign had left 2,598 people dead in extra-judicial killings at the hands of the police. Without evidence, local officials put thousands of people on blacklists and forced them to report to the police. Drug users who turned themselves into police found themselves shot and killed on the way out of the police station. The report concluded that Thaksin's policies encouraged extreme violence against anyone associated with the drug trade; or smeared without evidence. After Thaksin was deposed in a coup an inquiry found that some 1,400 people who had no association with drugs were killed in the campaign. Thaksin, who began his career as a policeman, was never charged with murder. About all the campaign had achieved was to discredit the country in the eyes of the international community, rearrange the personnel and power brokers in the lines of supply and kill innocent people.

The duplicity of the Thai government and the Thai police's approach to drugs helps to justify the common entrapment of tourists and foreign residents. And locals also pay a high price; with the Thai police extracting bribes from dealers at the same time as preying on users.

With Thailand's police intimately involved in the drug trade, no foreigner should be under any illusion that if they purchase drugs in the Kingdom they will not be expected to pay a bribe, often in the thousands of dollars. The entire point of selling drugs to foreigners is to entrap them.

Thailand has marketed itself as party central; and made billions of dollars in foreign exchange out of the tourists thus lured to its shores. But foreigners, primarily coming from countries with relaxed attitudes to recreational drug use, are not properly warned that the minute they let their guard down and indulge they become a target for the police, and for the bar tenders, sex workers and anyone else they choose to spend time with.

Entrapment is the name of the game.

It is where the real money is to be made.

Foreigners routinely make the mistake of assuming that the Thais they are partying with will appreciate their generosity; and want to party just like they do. Nothing could be further from the truth.

Once entrapped, foreigners will pay almost anything to get out of prison. And every Thai, every policeman, every bar owner, sex worker and local conman knows that. There is no such thing as discretion. There is no such thing as a private party.

Putting the morality of drug use to one side, travellers looking to party would be well advised to choose another destination, one where entrapment is not a business, just another tourist scam. Or to stay at home. While Thais can be easily observed consuming amphetamines, in late night bars or in their own homes, any foreigner, addiction prone or just out for a good time, who thinks they can do the same, that they are just partying amongst friends or like-minded people, will soon find themselves the subject of an extortion attempt, with a Thai policeman or three at the centre of the shakedown. And none of their "you happy me happy" friends will warn them, for the simple reason that they all make money off the hapless foreigner.

Opium crops and heroin laboratories have now largely disappeared from the North of Thailand, thanks to official crackdowns and poppy eradication programs. But the eradication of one drug has simply created another, bigger problem. By the turn of the millennium methamphetamines had become a far more lucrative source of income than heroin and opium had ever been.

As many tourists soon discover, often to their peril, millions of Thais, from the poorest villagers of Issaan to Bangkok office workers and fashionable elites, consume a drug peculiar to Southeast Asia known as yaba, the so-called "crazy drug". It is a small usually pink pill produced by the millions in Myanmar and smuggled across the borders into Thailand, with, as always when it comes to the drug industry in Thailand, the cooperation of authorities.

Heroin, once fashionable, is now widely dismissed both in the East and the West by new generations of users as a drug for "losers". No such negative image attaches to yaba, despite the propaganda of authorities. The fact it can be smoked or swallowed, rather than injected, and that its affects are almost instantaneous, is one of the factors behind its contemporary appeal. On the surface, the drug appears to fit perfectly with the Thais love of a good time. But while powerful business interests in the region earn huge profits, scenes on the street can be just as sad and desperate as for any other drug of addiction.

Rumour has it the chemist who invented the drug, a particularly psychoactive kind of amphetamine, aimed to wipe out the heroin market within two years. He more or less succeeded. Heroin, once common across Thailand, is now rarely used, while yaba can be found virtually anywhere.

The drug is popular across a broad range of social groups, but particularly amongst the sex workers with whom foreigners so often interact. The drug is widely believed to boost sexual performance and many prostitutes use it to enable them to perform sexually with foreigners—to "tahm nahm", work, as they call it. It is in these financially based but nonetheless intimate circumstances in which foreigners are often proffered drugs, and thus entrapped. They may think they are just having a bit of fun. They are just being foolish; allowing themselves to be set up for a sting.

From the outside, observers find yaba[193] usage inexplicable.

Snooky, a Bangkok ladyboy dragooned into infiltrating the mujahedeen training camps in southern Thailand, is the principal character in Timothy Mo's 2012 masterwork *Pure*. The book is replete with numerous geo-political references and paints a chilling portrait of fanaticism. Snooky is one of the truly great creations of contemporary literature. This is how she describes her reasons for partaking: "Why did a smart, well-educated chick like Snooky do it? Well, it was like being picked up by a giant trapeze or swing and whirled 600 feet in the air in a rush of utter joy. That lasted a few all-too-short seconds but afterwards not only was your mind fresher and clearer than it had ever been (since your last hit, silly) but the entire skin of your body was a giant, delicious organ of sensation. When you were high, a touch from Frankenstein's monster or Quasimodo could make you swoon with the lasciviousness a meth-less caress from the beloved never could. Even as your partner breached your sphincter (or you hers) you had freeloaded the portals of bliss."

Authors of *Merchants of Madness: The Methamphetamine Explosion in the Golden Triangle* Bertil Lintner and Michael Black dismiss the efforts of international drug agencies to eradicate opium production in the Golden Triangle as merely returning production levels to pre-1990s levels, and encouraging the switch to methamphetamine production. They describe yaba as a more serious threat to society than heroin ever was. "Millions of people across Thailand have become regular or occasional users. And

---

[193] *Bangla Photo News.*

unlike heroin, yaba has successfully transcended socioeconomic barriers, creating a new wave of drug addiction on an unprecedented scale in Thailand."

Heroin and methamphetamines are not the only drugs for which Thailand has been famously associated; as historians of the drug trade Peter Maguire and Mike Ritter attest in their 2013 book *Thai Stick: Surfers, Scammers and the Untold Story of the Marijuana Trade*. In the days before America increased its domestic production, most of the marijuana consumed in the country was imported. Moving a shipment of Thai sticks from northeast Thailand farms to American consumers meant negotiating one of the most complex smuggling channels in the history of the drug trade. During the 1970s Bangkok became a modern-day Casablanca to a new generation of treasure seekers, from surfers looking to finance their endless summers to wide-eyed hippy true-believers and lethal marauders left over from the Vietnam War. Predators, pirates and drug lords; some involved thought making fortunes from supplying drugs would provide epiphanies otherwise unobtainable to a generation keen to step outside social convention; others just liked the money. Bangkok, and Thailand as a whole, is central to the tale.

While more foreigners are in Thai jails as a result of being set up for drugs than for any other reason, there are other means of entrapment.

Welcome to Hell: One Man's Fight for Life Inside the Bangkok Hilton, by Colin Martin, was written inside prison and smuggled out page by page.[194] Published in 2005,[195] it chronicles how, after being swindled out of a small fortune, by Thai con artists Colin was let down by the Thai police. Forced to rely upon his own resources, he tracked down the man who conned him and, drawn into a fight, accidentally killed the man's bodyguard. Colin was arrested, denied a fair trial, convicted of murder and thrown into prison, where he remained for eight years."

---

[194] Welcome to Hell: One Man's Fight for Life Inside the Bangkok Hilton, Colin Martin, Maverick House Publishers, 2005.

[195] Welcome to Hell. Colin Martin. Maverick House Publishers. 2005.

The Liverpudlian originally headed to Thailand with a team of other engineers for work. His company had trumped up deposits, supposedly for work permits, insurance and the like. Through the charade of an apparently legitimate engineering company based in Bangkok, Martin was swindled out of $460,000. As he says, at the time he was completely blind to the dangers.

Martin quickly discovered that Bangkok made an ideal venue for criminal gangs. Mobsters mingled with Bangkok's large expatriate business community of Chinese, Taiwanese, Russians, Koreans, Australians, New Zealanders, Nigerians and Columbians. "If they weren't dealing heroin, they produced counterfeit goods and clothes. Crime mingled like a virus in the blood-stream of Bangkok. I know this now..."

Welcome to Hell records a very common expatriate experience of a journey from innocence to terror. During his first days he felt overwhelmed by the heat, the traffic, the crowds: "Bangkok city fascinated and intimidated me. No one told me that Bangkok was the crime capital of Asia. My knowledge of the city was superficial. I knew nothing of the Thai black market and the implicit dangers in operating there. In time I would learn that Bangkok was a city where everything had its price. I was oblivious to the fact that money laundering and organised crime were the lifeblood of the Thai economy. While bloodletting between gangs was rare, Bangkok had a dark and dangerous underbelly that visitors seldom see. By the time I arrived there, organised crime had discovered the attractions of the city and its corrupt authorities. The city had become a haven for all sorts of criminals. If I had known there was a large foreign criminal fraternity in Bangkok, I wouldn't have travelled there. I always thought Bangkok was an easy-going place. But it wasn't—that was my fatal mistake."

Predictably, Martin's decision to involve the Bangkok Police and the Thai Tourist Police in an attempt to recover the money stolen from him backfired. During the tumultuous years that followed, Martin lost his company and became estranged from his first wife and children, remarried and had a child with a Thai woman who, while he was trapped in a dysfunctional justice system, disappeared with his bail money.

Of his experience in a Bangkok prison Martin wrote that hell was no exaggeration: "Once in prison, I was beaten endlessly by the guards. I went for days without eating because the food was so revolting. I was forced to wear shackles on my legs for two years. I almost died of tuberculosis which the prison officials left untreated.

"I saw things nobody should have to see.

"I saw prisoners murdered. I saw prisoners rape each other. It was a living nightmare—one from which I could not wake up from... The Thai justice system is brutal, but it's also big business. In any way they possibly can, the cops, lawyers, guards and prison directors will cheat you out of your money."

Without the money to buy his way out of prison, around $US12,000, Martin was left marooned. He wrote that the situation was always worse for foreigners. If there was a dispute between a foreigner and a Thai, the visitor always lost. Not because the police were taking the Thai's side, but because expatriates usually had the money to pay their way out. After a brief taste of the Thai justice system, that is exactly what most of them did.

"I now know there have been many cases like mine," he wrote. "In Thailand you don't even have to commit a crime to find yourself in prison. Sometimes they'll bang you up because there's a chance you'll be able to pay them a few baht—or because you can't. You just have to be in the wrong place at the wrong time."

The Internet Revolution has vastly increased the numbers and types of people participating in public debate and storytelling, moving the rich tapestry of the written word beyond professional journalists and writers to encompass the sometimes clumsy and mawkish, often intensely felt or even riveting accounts of ordinary people. The great democracy of the internet has also vastly expanded the range of and style of accounts of expatriate life in Thailand, from cautionary tales of the pitfalls of bargirls to joyful accounts of paradise to woebegone accounts of dissolution and deception, drunkenness and deceit. Most of those joining in the online chorus of clattering opinions on forums such as ThaiVisa are not professional writers. But one who is, and by far one of the most entertaining, is well known Bangkok expat character Jerry Hopkins.

After an early career which included ingesting large quantities of LSD and opening one of America's first "Head" shops selling incense and rock posters, Hopkins spent 20 years writing for *Rolling Stone*. He penned bestsellers including *Elvis Presley: The Biography* and *No One Here Gets Out Alive* about Jim Morrison of The Doors. His books on Asia include *Romancing the East*, *Asian Aphrodisiacs* and *Thailand Confidential*.

Hopkins moved to Thailand in 1993 and stayed.

The tone of his collection of sketches *Bangkok Babylon: The Real-Life Exploits of Bangkok's Legendary Expatriates Are Often Stranger Than Fiction*[196] is set by a quoted exchange from Ernest Hemmingway's *The Sun Also Rises*:

Bill Gorton: "You're an expatriate. You've lost touch with the soil… Fake European standards have ruined you. You drink yourself to death. You become obsessed by sex. You spend all your time talking, not working. You are an expatriate, see? You hang around cafes."

Jake Barnes: "Sounds like a swell life to me."

Hopkins affectionately profiles the often alcoholic cast of expat characters who make the city their home; most of whom had one thing in common, they were escaping their homelands and their pasts, reinventing themselves in their adopted home of Bangkok, Thailand.

As he explains in his final paragraph: "This is a book that celebrates bumpy Bangkok and the concept of escape. My dictionary has twelve meanings next to the word 'escape'. The first one says 'to get away, as from confinement.' That does it for me and, I think, everyone else in this book."[197]

Hopkins writes with a certain philosophical bent about the expatriates drawn to Bangkok, "bolder, more imaginative or more curious, and more heroic or foolhardy or more over-the-top than

---

[196] Bangkok Babylon. Jerry Hopkins. Periplus Editions, Singapore 2005.

[197] Bangkok Babylon: The Real-Life Exploits of Bangkok's Legendary Expatriates Are Often Stranger Than Fiction, Jerry Hopkins, Periplus Editions, 2005.

most—men imbued with an unchecked sense of adventure—or at least a delight in the eccentric (on a slow day), the unexpected (on an average day) and no less than incredible (on a good day)."

At their best they are intellectual and physical explorers adamant in their quest for knowledge and experience. But, "Thailand also attracts the con-men, law-breakers, runaways and what might back home be called sexual deviants. It is a place where erratically enforced laws are written by men who may not intend to stick to them—who, if they get caught, know they will spend little or no time in jail because the fix is almost a political certainty or is, at worse, bargain priced."

With its multiple illicit trades, Hopkins compares the Thailand of the present day, where so many foreigners seek refuge and unleashed fantasy is accessible and affordable, to the Bahamas and Latin America of old, where bank robbers and scam artists once sought escape: "Thailand is South East Asia's prime marketplace. It's not surprising that such an environment has appeal for some of what society deems the best and the worst. Missionaries and NGOs come to fix 'the problem'. Others come to roll around in it."

Portraits in *Bangkok Babylon* range from worthy altruists to dissolute miscreants. Among them is the man thought to be the model for Colonel Kurtz in the movie *Apocalypse Now*, an advertising executive who photographs Thai bargirls for *Playboy*, a Catholic priest who lived and worked in the Bangkok slums for 35 years, a circus dwarf turned restaurateur, three Vietnam war helicopter pilots who opened a go-go bar, a pianist at one of the world's best hotels who ended up on the FBI's 10 Most Wanted list for being a paedophile, an insurance company detective tracking the hundreds of Westerners faking their deaths each year, a documentary filmmaker who became one of the world's experts on the Asian elephant and Stirling Silliphant, the Academy Award-winning screenwriter who wrote *In the Heat of the Night*. The latter moved to Thailand because he couldn't think of a better place to die.

Yet another in Hopkins' collection of characters was James Eckardt, whose book *Bangkok People*[198] preceded *Bangkok Babylon*, which in turn portrays a cast of characters including boxers, business tycoons, bar girls and body snatchers, "from the filthy rich to the just plain filthy".[199]

As he put it: "Bangkok reminds me of what Dr Johnson said about London: a man who's tired of London is tired of life." Having left his family in the provinces, and despite a healthy income, Eckardt lived in a cheap flophouse known as the Peachy Guesthouse.

Eckardt also wrote *Waylaid by the Bimbos: And Other Catastrophes in Thailand* along with two novels set in Thailand, *Boat People* and *Running with Sharks*. He explains: "My journalistic career was launched when my wife tried to castrate me. I was writing the dire details to a friend in Canada when the thought struck—why not polish this gibberish and peddle it to the *Bangkok Post?*"

That was in the 1970s. Born in New York, his "chequered and improbable life" had already spanned five continents. Known for his prodigious thirst and boisterous ways, Eckardt finally settled in Thailand. Between stabs at immortality through the written word he was renowned for wanton weekends with louts and tosspots, as he called his friends: "Just because you're middle-aged doesn't mean you can't be immature. What is the fragile flower of truth before the onrushing steamroller of a good story?"

Many expat tales of Thailand involve excessive amounts of alcohol. Even the most cursory survey of bars throughout the Kingdom reveals a determined contingent of European barflies, some showing a rapid deterioration in the tropics now that they have escaped their responsibilities and roles back in the West. In a piece promoting Alcoholics Anonymous, one member told the *Phuket News*: "I remember being in Patong in 1982, in a bar, saying to the other drunks, 'This is either the best decision or the worst decision that I've made—to come to Phuket.' Coming to

---

[198] Bangkok People. Asia Books. 2009.

[199] *Bangkok People*, James Eckardt, Asia Books, 1999.

Thailand was like a free for all. There was drink, girls, no police, and no one cared what you did. It was like Christmas every night and every night was New Year's Eve."

Talking of drunks, at the bottom end of Hopkins' worthiness spectrum lies Bernard Trink, who for decades was Bangkok's most famous, or infamous, expatriate.

To his critics he represented everything that was wrong with the foreigners who made Bangkok their home.

As a columnist, Trink covered the expatriate Bangkok bar scene for more than 40 years, reaching his pinnacle of gutter-fame in the 1970s in a now defunct newspaper called *World*. He and his column Night Owl migrated to the considerable more respectable *Bangkok Post* in 1987.

Trink was fired from the *Bangkok Post* in 2003 when in his 70s, which in any case was well past the paper's mandatory retirement age. His sacking came during a period when the ruling Shinawatra family were running moralistic campaigns purportedly aimed at cleaning up Thailand. In any case, political correctness had wiped out the racy pictures which once decorated the wall behind his desk, no-smoking-in-the-office rules made him intensely uncomfortable and a lifetime of heavy drinking was beginning to catch up with him.

Trink was both loved and loathed.

Hopkins was one of those who couldn't stand him and his portrait in *Bangkok Babylon* is far from flattering: "It was my belief that Bernard Trink was not only boring, he was dangerous."

To his critics Trink's coverage of bar girls, nightclubs and happy hours may have been irresponsible, puerile and pointless, a crazy patchwork quilt of lechery and self-aggrandisement. None of that stopped Trink from being immensely popular. It was said the circulation of the *Bangkok Post* increased by 5,000 copies on the days it appeared. Night Owl dominated the newspaper's website and led all other parts of the newspaper for the number of overseas hits.

One of the main criticisms levelled at Trink was that he was a misogynist with zero respect for the bar girls with whom he spent so much time. He once wrote: "Prostitutes are anything but sweet young things, their smiles covering a hard-as-nails nature. They didn't choose their profession out of necessity. The vast majority of poverty-stricken girls in the provinces refuse to regard prostitution as an option. Those entering the profession do so because they have the required callousness."

In fact, Hopkins argued, while rip-off stories were common, equally there were many honest bar girls and numerous successful marriages between foreigners and bar girls: "Over the centuries, the arts produced many champions of Trink's 'demimondaine'—from Emile Zola and Toulouse Lautrec to John Steinbeck and Jane Fonda —but the Bangkok columnist stood in the opposite corner of the ring, a man with a heart of lead."

Thailand, and Bangkok in particular, has proven to be fertile ground not just for aging, dissolute expatriates living out their final days in an excess of alcohol and flesh, hurtling down self-destructive sinkholes amidst Asia's colourful criminal milieus. Many fiction writers are drawn to the country's intensely atmospheric feel, its complexities, duplicities and intrigues.

At its best, the largely Bangkok-based genre of Thai crime fiction is an insightful reflection and investigation of Thailand, displaying an intimate knowledge of and great affection for the country. Many authors place the bones of their stories across barely fictionalised circumstance, alleging a level of government and police corruption and socially wide involvement with crime which would get them banned, bashed, jailed or killed if their books were written in the Thai language or aimed at the Thai market.

Long term Bangkok resident Christopher G. Moore, a former Canadian lawyer, is regarded as the grandfather of Thai detective novels writers. He is by far the most popular, successful, prolific and long lived of them all. Dashiell Hammett was the hard-boiled author of *The Maltese Falcon*, pioneer of a sparse, acerbic and highly entertaining style and creator of the enduring archetype of the fictional detective, Sam Spade. Moore is seen as Hammett's Bangkok counterpart. His Bangkok-based Jewish Italian ex-lawyer private eye Vincent Calvino from New York first appeared in *The Spirit House*[200] in 1992, and was still going strong ten books later in

---

[200] Spirit House, Christopher G. Moore, Grove Press, 2008.

Paying Back Jack. He is best known for the trilogy which took a knowing look behind the Thailand's façade, *A Killing Smile, A Bewitching Smile* and *A Haunting Smile*.

Moore has also produced a number of collections of essays reflecting on modern day Asia, and Thailand in particular, including *The Cultural Detective* and *Faking it in Bangkok: Crime and Culture in the Digital Age*. His books bring to life gangsters, gamblers, killers and local and foreign criminals against a backdrop of television images and news reports of demonstrations, deaths, demands, shadowy corporations, organised crime, social chaos and multiple underground cultures.

Moore has also retained a long-term interest in Thailand's expatriate community. In an interview about his book *Fear and Loathing in Bangkok* Moore said the city now had a very different group of foreigners to a quarter of a century ago, when adventurers, journalists, ex-Vietnam veterans and diplomats made up a small coterie who had more in common with the romantic colonialist writers Somerset Maugham and Joseph Conrad than the present day. In the 21st Century the world's discontented middle classes were on the move, providing the present ever-changing, diverse, dynamic crop; many of whom lack the romantic inclinations of their forebears.[201] But the fascination with Thailand from both writers and readers remained: "There are a lot of people with very great stories out there. I think people are interested in the quite different culture, which comes from a different history, a different language tradition, a different religion, a different political set-up. I try to find people who have an interesting story about their experience with Thai culture, living here, brushes with the law, work, study, and give a composite idea of what life is like for people who come here for a fresh start."

There are widespread fears within the tourist industry that the political turmoil gripping the country will turn away tourists, and therefore impact badly on the country's economy. At various times once bustling swathes of Bangkok had been devoid of foreigners: "Tourists, like a lot of people, are fearful and they have many

---

[201] Interview with Christopher Moore, Thai Law Forum, 9 February, 2014.

choices. There is no reason why they have to come to Thailand as opposed to someplace else. So people do a kind of risk calculation. They will look at dramatic news clips. They are going on holiday. They want an adventure, which is finding a unique new sea-shell on a shore. They don't want the adventure of finding a discarded casing for an AK-47."[202]

John Burdett is one of the most successful elders of Thailand crime fiction. Like other writers, his love of Bangkok pervades his work: "From a novelist's point of view it's a gift because you've got so many different things, so many different themes all coming together. It's a crucible."[203]

His much acclaimed books include *Bangkok 8*, *Bangkok Tattoo* and *Vulture Peak*. The blurb for *Bangkok Haunts* sets the tone: "In Bangkok, where holy men, prostitutes and serial killers prowl, nothing is as it seems..."

The books feature the philosophical Royal Thai Tourist Policeman Sonchai Jitpleecheep, the son of a former US marine he has never met and a Thai woman. Regarded as probably the only honest cop in the red light district where he works, the fact that Sonchai is apparently unbribable increases his alienation from his colleagues. He has, more or less, kept his Buddhist soul intact while facing some of Bangkok's vilest criminals. One of his targets in the series is a Thai general running a methamphetamine lab near the Thai Burmese border. Once again Western writers disguise reality in fiction.

Burdett's characters include not just a wide range of acting and retired sex workers, but crooked cops of all ranks, jade merchants, bemused agents from the FBI, local drug dealers and a surgeon specialising in sex change operations. In a sense his greatest character of all is Bangkok itself, a sprawling, chaotic, illogical city full of jam packed bars and impassable streets, a city unique on the world stage, a metropolis with an overwhelmingly powerful presence.

---

[202] TLF Interview available through author's website, cgmoore dot com.

[203] At Home Amid the Red Lights, Thomas Fuller, *NY Times*, 25 October, 2007.

Bangkok 8 was first published in 2003 and sold more than 100,000 hard copies in the US. As one reviewer noted, it seemed to deal with an entire city of prostitutes.[204] One of Burdett's charms was that he did not moralise about Thailand's sex industry: "In a land with few opportunities for women, they have found a way to prosper and be independent. They are models of capitalism and free trade, entrepreneurs who, unlike the sullen Russian prostitutes in Bangkok, are not saddled with pimps."

Burdett's approach to prostitution was often a tetchy point with Western reviewers determined to see it as exploitation akin to human trafficking. In fact the mix of 20th Century academic feminism, which imposes a Marxist analysis of power on gender relations, combined with Christian moralising on sexual relations, produces a kind of prurience which is little suited to understanding Thailand's approach. The US State Department itself urges countries around the world to defuse the need for prostitutes and the link between sex and money as a way of diminishing human trafficking. But while there are many cruelties in the Thai sex industry, there are equally many workers who have proudly provided income for their extended families and bought their parents homes as a result.

New York Times' journalist Thomas Fuller accompanied Burdett to the infamous stretch of go-go bars known as Soi Cowboy, established in the 1970s as an alternative to the dilapidated red light district of Patpong. He observed the anthropological side of the author's work: "Mr Burdett explores a side of Thai society that has long fascinated Westerners: the apparent willingness of large numbers of women here to sell their bodies without obvious shame; and, in a country where brothels are illegal, the willingness of the police, the government and the society as a whole to look the other way . . He explains the improbable presence of Buddhist shrines at the entrance to many sex bars."

---

[204] Red Light, Green Light, David Willis McCullough, *New York Times*, 6 July, 2003.

Soi Cowboy, Picture by Daniel Grosvenor.

Indeed, the prayers said by sex workers before accompanying a client to a hotel, for a kind of grace, the maintenance of personal dignity and the ability to do a good job, for Buddha to bless them with money and riches to help their families, is something that almost invariably surprises foreign patrons.

Thai Private Eye[205] makes no pretences at being an academic dissertation, instead telling common tales of deception with a high degree of humour. Warren Olson, once a real private eye in Thailand, has one central theme: the astonishing naivety of Western men prepared to pay a private detective real money to investigate their Thai girlfriend's conduct. The foreigner is almost

---

[205] Thai Private Eye, Warren Olsen, Monsoon Books, 2008.

invariably back in his home country pursuing his own business interests and sending money to Thailand each month. Almost invariably, the Thai "girlfriend" is back in the bar where the client found them, and he is more than likely only one of several men sending the object of his affection money each month, supposedly to keep her out of the bars and away from the "evils" of prostitution. It is the dream of many Thai prostitutes to develop such a situation, where they are maintained in smart apartments with nice cars and plenty of cash to support their extended families; sleeping with a number of besotted foreigners who in reality only visit a few weeks a year. That is, they achieve an affluent lifestyle for very little "tahm nahm", work, and gain status with their colleagues.

Timothy Hallinan is another expat writer who barely fictionalises the physical, political and cultural backdrop of his stories. *The Queen of Patpong*,[206] *The Fear Artist, For The Dead, A Nail Through the Heart, Breathing Water* and *The Fourth Watcher* all feature the much loved phlegmatic American detective Poke Rafferty, an American expat writing offbeat travel guides before arriving in Bangkok, and promptly falling in love.

While Hallinan's books are thrillers, they are also the story of a "hand-made" family whose characters appear to generate as much affection among readers as the detective himself. Rafferty marries a Thai woman known as Rose, former queen of one of the city's oldest red light district. Many people familiar with Thailand think they know who the real Queen of Patpong was. The couple adopts a Thai girl off the streets known as Miaow, the Thai word for cat. Thai words are frequently onomatopoeic in nature. The word for rain, "plon tok" for instance, exactly echoes the sound of rain hitting the mud in a Thai village.

Hallinan has an intimate knowledge of Bangkok high and low, and writes lovingly of the city. The novels include some of its more down-at-heel bars and havens for washed up veterans from the Vietnam War and other past conflicts. Even when the scenarios are undramatic, his affection for The City of Angels is clear:

---

[206] The Queen of Patpong, Timothy Hallinan, Harper Perennial, 2011.

"Moderate foot traffic average for an early weekday morning in an upscale Bangkok shopping district.... The usual blast-furnace, wet-blanket Bangkok heat, heat with an actual *weight* to it that frequently takes Rafferty by surprise even after more than two years here. It changes the way he dresses, the way he breathes, and even the way he walks. The way everybody walks. It shortens the stride and makes it pointless to waste energy lifting the feet any higher than absolutely necessary; all the effort goes into moving forward. The result is what Rafferty has come to think of as the Bangkok Glide, the energy-efficient and peculiarly graceful way Thai people have of getting themselves from place to place without melting directly into the sidewalk."[207]

Thai women are often regarded as the most beautiful in the world and there is a slew of books on Western men's obsessions and misfortunes as they fall head over heels for them. They range from the professionally written to the amateurish. While the latter might lack literary polish, the 21st Century's revolution in digital publishing has brought a range of authentic new voices to the table.

The first major book in the genre, Jack Reynolds' classic novel *A Woman of Bangkok*,[208] was published to great acclaim in 1956 and to this day is regarded as one of the best books written on the theme of Thailand's fairer sex. After decades out of print, it was finally republished in 2011. Set against a beautifully observed Thailand of the 1950s, this is the story of a young Englishman's infatuation with a dance-hall hostess named Vilai, who all Bangkok knows as The White Leopard. No ordinary prostitute, Vilai is one of the most memorable in literature's long line of brazen working girls. An unmitigated liar and brutally transparent about her desire for money, she unscrupulously milks young Reggie Joyce, the son of an Anglican vicar, with complete frankness. Reggie knows her for what she is yet there seems no folly he will not commit for her, no road to ruin he dares not take. Vilai becomes an obsession for him—an obsession that brings

[207] The Fourth Watcher, Timothy Hallinan, HarperCollins, 2009.

[208] A Woman of Bangkok, Jack Reynolds, Monsoon Books, 2012.

Reggie moments of ecstasy, months of anguish and the threat of complete disaster.

Despite the instant fame which the book brought him, *A Woman of Bangkok* was said to have sold more than one million copies, Reynolds' never wrote another full length book. He died in 1984 at the age of 71.

The rediscovery of Reynolds' is due in part to the passionate search for biographical information by former English corporate lawyer and university professor Andrew Hicks. After retiring to Thailand and writing two books about Thai bar girls, he became fascinated by the writer of the first acknowledged classic in the field. *Thai Girl* explores the problems of prostitution and cross-cultural relationships while *My Thai Girl and I: How I found a new life in Thailand* is a series of short anecdotes based on real life.

The most famous of all the books written about Thai bar girls is *My Private Dancer*.[209] Thriller writer Stephen Leather gleaned much of the material for the book sitting in a bar called Jools in Soi 4 just off Sukhumvit, nearby Bangkok's most infamous red light complex, Nana Plaza. It is 1996, The Year Of The Rat. Pete, a young travel writer, wanders into a Bangkok go-go bar and meets the love of his life. Joy is young, stunningly pretty, and one of the Zombie Bar's top-earning pole dancers. What follows is a roller-coaster ride of sex, drugs and deception, as Pete discovers that … far from being the girl of his dreams, Joy is his own personal nightmare.

Leather wrote: "I don't know if it was love at first sight, but it was pretty close. She had the longest hair I'd ever seen, jet black and almost down to her waist. She had soft brown eyes that made my heart melt, long legs that just wouldn't quit and a figure to die for. She was naked except for a pair of black leather ankle boots with small chrome chains on the side. I think it was the boots that did it for me."

My Private Dancer has become a cult classic. It continues to attract fans and is seen as a must read for anyone travelling to

---

[209] My Private Dancer, Stephen Leather, Monsoon Books, 2005.

Bangkok. One online reviewer, John Petrocelli, explains the books enduring appeal thus: "Imagine, picking up a novel where you were so absolutely riveted, so drawn into the characters that you could actually feel the drippy heat of a Bangkok night and the racing of your heart as a drop dead, brown-skinned Thai women in a go-go bar lets loose a smile that just locks up your heart.... Well, that's what happened to me. I was sucked right back into that vortex of illusion hidden between the pages of Stephen Leather's *Private Dancer*. If one has any questions to what was going on in the Bangkok bar scene, how middle aged white males go over there and fall completely, head-over-heels in love with these brown skinned Asian beauties ... or why men get hooked and live their 9 to 5's 11 months a year to fly clear across the world to this Asian Hotspot, this book answers it and more .... But it also destroys the illusions. It reveals the truth. The pathetic side. To impoverished Thai women, men are merely walking ATM cash dispensers. To the men, these are instant girlfriends, phenomenal actresses, whom within minutes, can elicit feelings of love no Western woman could compete with, all enveloped in a package of innocence ... of youthfulness, the male fantasy we were promised by Hollywood. If you're planning a trip to Bangkok and you're male and are tempted in any way to investigate the sex scene or just wondering about those beautiful smiling Thai women beckoning you on, with a knowing glint in their eyes, please read this book."

Caustic or compassionate, kind or creepy, amateur or professional, numerous texts explore the West's fascination with Thailand's approach to prostitution; and the sadness and damage left behind.

How To Take the Bar out of Your Girl[210] advises men to never make the mistake of thinking they are a prince in shining armour who is going to save a bar girl from prostitution and suggests that working in the bar scene, out each night with their friends competing for customers, is not a bad lifestyle for many girls.

Thailand Bar Girls: Angels and Devils, a collection of stories about aging, heavy drinking, heavily debauched expats purports to

---

[210] How To Take the Bar out of Your Girl, Bill Williams. Published by After the Rush.

be based on real characters: "It was another of those sultry, stifling hot evenings in April, when even a walk down to the nearest bar-strip was too much effort ..."

For every punter there is a sex worker. *My Name Lon: You Like Me?*, tells the story of a Pattaya prostitute: "From the age of 14, 'My Name: You Like Me?' was my greeting to over 1,000 sex tourists. My impoverished culture and my mother were the impetus for the sale of my dignity, but my actions saved my sister from the same fate."

Miss Bangkok: Memoirs of a Thai Prostitute tells the common story of a country girl lured to the city by tales of wild nights and easy money, both for herself and her family back in the village: "You can buy me for 2,000 baht a night. In return, I will do anything that is asked of me, but I won't kiss customers."

In *Travels in the Skin Trade: Tourism and the Sex Industry*[211] respected British journalist Jeremy Seabrook explores the peculiar impacts of Thailand's traditional tolerance and acceptance of prostitution and those who work in the industry. He attempts to put the numerous moral ambiguities surrounding Thailand's flesh trade into some sort of context: "The people in Thailand concerned with the sex industry offer some insight into why sex tourism has become both a problem and a challenge: the mismatch of perceptions between clients and sex workers; racism; dissatisfaction with Western constructs of sexuality and personhood; the socialisation of boys which turns them into aggressive, predatory men; the unequal status between clients and workers; and the uneven development between countries which confers such power on sex tourists. At the same time, the rapid industrialisation of Thailand, the mass migrations, scattering of traditional communities, the resistance of family support systems strained as never before, urbanisation and the degradation of the rural areas, drive people to the cities."

The renowned gender fluidity of the Thais, who are sometimes called the original gender benders, and the acceptance of what are

---

[211] Travels in the Skin Trade: Tourism and the Sex Industry, Jeremy Seabrook, Pluto Press, 2001.

essentially multiple sexualities, from masculine lesbians known as Toms to the country's world famous ladyboys, gays, heterosexuals, and a good deal in between, has long fascinated foreigners. Most Thai male prostitutes, for instance, go home to their girlfriends; and see no conflict between their work and their love lives.

English academic Richard Totman's famous book *The Third Gender*[212] records that kathoeys, the Thai expression for ladyboys, have long been a part of the cultural landscape of Thailand. While their performances in cabarets and the entertainment industry make them a leading tourist attraction, in fact ladyboys are integrated into the culture, working in offices, cafes and shops. Totman argues the men, now women, are the modern expression of an archaic tradition. Following the rites-of-passage to becoming a fully fledged kathoey through the lives of three individuals, the author asks: "If the existence of a 'third sex' is a universal property, is Western society so repressed by its cultural heritage that the Thais represent a norm in nature? Why are there so many kathoey in Thailand? Why are there so few in the Western world?"

Suburban tourists line up in droves to watch Thailand's glamorous ladyboy shows, to be entertained, titillated and amazed. Equally, on the seamier side of the equation, there are few males visiting Thailand who are not aware of the ladyboys' reputation for providing the best oral sex in the world. While some are well integrated into Thai society, and possess both status and wealth, tourists are less aware of the reputation of street walkers for violence and unpredictability, often brought on by heavy drug use, particularly of yaba. Ladyboy gangs, who rob tourists in packs, are a uniquely Thai phenomenon.

In the Forward for *Ladyboys: The Secret World of Thailand's Third Gender*, authors Susan Aldous and Pornchai Sereemongkonpol wrote of their journey from innocence to astonishment: "As we tentatively stepped into the world of Thailand's transgenders, weighed down as we were by our baggage of preconceptions and blatant misconceptions, we realised

---

[212] The Third Sex: Kathoey: Thailand's Ladyboys, Richard Totman, Souvenir Press, 2014.

we had entered a kind of parallel universe, full of shifting sands and shapeshifters. Nothing was quite what it seemed in this house of mirrors. But with every ladyboy we encountered, we discovered that our world's weren't so different after all. When we peeled away the make-up, the wigs and the breast implants, we found that these superficial physical modifications belie individuals governed by the same core emotions as anyone else. Eager to dispel the biases, and silence the jeers and snickering, we undertook to give a voice to the often marginalised Ladyboys. We tried not to baulk when we came face to face with tough-looking bouncers, conniving touts and some truly vile sex shows."

The famous beauty of Thai women extends to their lesbian sisters, much to the fascination of both male and female travellers. *Toms & Dees: Transgender identity and female same sex relationships in Thailand* is based on seven years of fieldwork. Toms are masculine woman, dees feminine. Academic Megan Sinnott, from Yale University, writes: "Masculine women have long been evident in the Thai system of sex and gender, but the linguistic and social marking of feminine women who are partners to masculine women creates a new and precarious field of identity."

Most tourists are more interested in sins of the flesh than the posturing performances of academic discourses. Just as heterosexual Western men see Thailand as some kind of paradise, so do many gays. The country's raunchy sex shows, numerous massage parlours, the world famous gay sauna Babylon in Bangkok, and of course its handsome men, "lowh puh-chai", attract visitors from all round the world. One of the most prominent foreign academics writing on Thai gay identity, Peter Jackson, also turned his hand to fiction in his book *The Intrinsic Quality of Skin*, which explores the romantic and sensual obsessions of a gay white man in Thailand. In amidst all the love and loss, other tales emerge. In the *Encyclopaedia of Gay Histories and Cultures* Jackson writes: "The popular culture of Thailand has a rich history of transgenderism and homoeroticism that has underpinned the emergence in contemporary Bangkok of the largest and most visible gay subculture in Asia outside Tokyo. Thailand presents a contrast to the histories of the gay and transgender communities in most Western societies. The emergence of large numbers of gay-identified men and of a significant commercial scene in Bangkok and other cities has occurred entirely as a cultural movement with no accompanying gay political movement, no institutional or legal support, and almost none of the community organisations or activist networks found in Western gay centres."[213]

In amidst all the stories of good fortune and common thievery, deception and deliverance, perhaps the most classic expat story of Thailand, certainly the best known, is that of Jim Thompson. It is a story of luxury, accomplishment and social status against the exotic backdrop of the East, a story many have tried to emulate, with varying degrees of success. Scion of a wealthy American family, raised alongside America's wealthiest families, Thompson was foremost a businessman. He co-founded the Thai Silk Company in 1948. The company never looked back after his silks were used in the musical *The King and I* and he was credited with revitalising the Thai silk industry during the 1950s and 60s. From newspaper articles, television newsreels and gossip, seemingly everyone knew of Jim Thompson. To this day his architecturally renowned house in Bangkok remains a major tourist destination, while upmarket outlets continue to sell high quality silk, attracting customers from around the world.

Thompson disappeared mysteriously while vacationing in the Cameron Highlands of Malaysia in 1967. Despite a massive manhunt his body was never found. Theories ranged from his being eaten by a tiger to being kidnapped by the CIA.

The Ideal Man: The Tragedy of Jim Thompson and the American Way of War, by journalist and Southeast Asian expert Joshua Kurlantzick, paints a lost world, when Bangkok, criss-crossed with canals, was known as the Venice of the East. Women washed themselves in modest sarongs and long-tailed boats carried crates of mangoes and red peppers.

---

[213] Encyclopaedia of Gay Histories and Cultures, Peter Jackson, Thailand, Floating Lotus Books, 1994.

The author records an evening at the Thompson house, when the man himself arrives home in the soupy, hundred-degree Bangkok heat from his silk shop in the Surawong business district, taking a seemingly endless parade of famous guests for tours of the house, including Eleanor Roosevelt, the du Ponts, Truman Capote, various counts and countesses, and marquises.

"As the dinner crowd sat down on the terrace—passing through rooms surrounded by bronze Buddha heads, Ming bowls, and Burmese tapestries inlaid with gold leaf—the out of town visitors, always overdressed for the Bangkok weather, oohed over Thompson's food and offered quick uncomfortable bows back to the retinue of servants who saluted Thompson and his guests with the hands-together Thai gesture known as the *wai* ... no one really came to Jim Thompson's house for the food. They came for Jim Thompson. By 1967, Jim Thompson did not just manage his extravagant house, he was the curator of another exhibit: his own legend. The best-known American in Asia, he lived the life that all these visitors to his house wished for."[214]

Sadly, in part due to the animosity between the host population and the Kingdom's influx of tourists, foreigners who do best in Thailand are often those who interact with the locals the least. Some expatriates, despite being resident for years, barely know any Thai words except "Kah-kuhn-kahb", thank you and "Sah-wah-dee-kahb", hello. And perhaps that common instruction to a restaurant waiter, "mai pet", not spicy; an instruction not much more than an insult to the nation's widely admired cuisine. Even common, traditional village greetings such as "Tinai Kuhn", where are you going, are beyond them. All their relationships with Thais are that of master servant buyer seller. These foreigners see the country as nothing but a quaintly chaotic, cheap and colourful backdrop for their own lifestyles. Their friendships and relationships, except perhaps those of the sexual kind, are with other Westerners. They gather in Western style bars and restaurants, speak their own languages and marvel at how inexpensive everything is, all the while

---

[214] The Ideal Man: The Tragedy of Jim Thompson and the American Art of War, Joshua Kurlantzick, Wiley, 2011.

telling each other stories about the latest insanities of Thai drivers and untrustworthy locals.

Yet foreigners of all kinds be they writers, sex tourists, seekers after enlightenment or holiday makers, continue to be drawn to and fascinated by the Kingdom. No survey of the growing body of literature written by and about expatriates in Thailand can but touch on the variety of fascinations, compulsions and stories, risqué or otherwise, the depths of experiences and extraordinary tales of foreigners in Thailand, the tragedies, triumphs and multiple intrigues in a place renowned for its ravishing landscapes and distinctive culture; a perfect place for adventures and misadventures of the soul and the flesh.

By the Chao Phraya River, Picture courtesy of Fedra Studio.

HUMAN TRAFFIC

Through the windows of taxis and limousines, tourists see them all the time, and have no idea who they are looking at. If Westerners think about them at all, the assumption is they are just the working poor, yet another colourful part of the teeming street life of Asia.

In fact there are millions of illegal immigrants in Thailand who are often the subject of exploitation. They are just as foreign to Thailand as the tourists themselves; and act as a kind of counterpoint to the floods of Western, Indian and Middle Eastern visitors flooding the country. Primarily from impoverished rural areas of Laos, Cambodia and Myanmar, they have a very different experience of Thailand to that of privileged Western tourists. Porous borders, with considerable stretches of unpatrolled land and river, allow for easy crossings. Driven by poverty and a desire for a better life for themselves and their families, they arrive in their hundreds of thousands.

British labour rights activist Andy Hall fronted a Thai court in September of 2014, facing a $US13 million fine and eight years in prison. His passport has been confiscated. His sin was to write a report alleging labour abuses within the Natural Fruit Company, a large Thai pineapple wholesaler which sells into the European Union. He wrote that the passports of Burmese migrant workers were confiscated and they were subjected to violence and slave-like conditions. He is a personal friend of Aung San Suu Kyi and helped organise her 2012 visit to Thailand. She addressed Burmese migrant workers at the fishing hub of Mahachai, 20 miles south of Bangkok, which is known as Little Burma.[215]

Human rights groups claim the Thai government is complicit in an attempt to cover up working conditions and abuses. Supporters around the world signed petitions calling on Natural Fruit to drop the charges. Hall's interest in the plight of Burmese migrant workers began in 2004 while on a back packing trip through Thailand. Hall, who speaks both Thai and Burmese, met

---

[215] Labour-rights activist Andy Hall on trial in Thailand: 'I've done nothing wrong, *The Guardian*, 8 September, 2014.

construction workers who had been disabled on the job and left without financial support. He says he was motivated by a strong desire to empower immigrants who comprise as much as 10 percent of the Thai workforce, primarily in the fishing, construction, canning and agricultural sectors.

Hall says he has been threatened by senior industry and political figures for attempting to expose the plight of the half a million people thought to be living in slavery in Thailand: "My work is not negative, it's not bad, it's not vicious – it's intended to make things better. If they're not willing to drop the cases, I am certain they, the pineapple industry, the Thai export industry and the Thai economy will suffer more."

Thailand's illegal migrants can be seen each morning, sometimes looking like traditional coolies, walking to the many construction sites across Bangkok. They are lucky if they get paid ten dollars a day. Foreigners might also spot them on the fishing boats just off the tourist drenched beaches in the south. Or perhaps more likely observe them only in a refracted sense, in the media stories reflecting international outrage over the human trafficking.

In a country where social status means everything, Thailand's increasing prosperity and low unemployment rates have led many Thai citizens to turn away from work in labour intensive industries.

More than a quarter of a million Cambodians, most of them undocumented workers, fled Thailand in the weeks following the 2014 coup, fearing a crackdown. In one of the country's largest ever repatriation efforts, the migrants were placed on crowded trucks or forced to shelter in makeshift tents along the border.

Cambodian Prime Minister Hun Sen accused the Thai Army of beating and abusing them.

The Cambodian Human Rights Action Committee, a coalition of 21 non-government organisations, claimed many workers were left stranded without enough money to get them home: "Due to inadequate preparation and coordination between the Thai and Cambodian authorities, the migrant workers have been forced to shelter in makeshift tents at the border, and hundreds more workers continue to arrive every day. Water, food, healthcare and shelter are severely limited."[216]

Thailand authorities denied the accusations of unreasonable treatment, claiming they were simply systemising migrant labour.

US President Barak Obama wanted an end to human trafficking as a major legacy of his administration. Via its funding of numerous research projects, the US government was the principal driver behind an accumulation of documentary evidence on slavery, forced labour and exploitation across a range of sectors in Thailand, particularly in the seafood industry. The resultant media coverage highlighted the issue and increased calls from activists for the elimination of exploitation and slavery in the supply chains to Western consumers.

The question of exactly who are victims of human trafficking and who are just migrants seeking a better life can be a vexed one. The concerns of intellectuals in the international community are very different to those of the rural poor seeking a better life on the Thai-Burmese, Cambodian and Laotian borders. A significant proportion of the Thai economy relies on irregular migrants. The United Nations suggests that it is clear from the available literature that the facilitating of irregular migration significantly contributes to making people vulnerable to human trafficking.[217]

The US Central Intelligence Agency's World Factbook records Thailand as a source, transit, and destination country for men, women, and children subjected to forced labour and sex trafficking. People from neighbouring countries, especially Burma, and also China, Vietnam, Russia, Uzbekistan, and Fiji, migrate to Thailand in search of economic opportunities. Forced labourers are exploited in fishing, low-end garment production and domestic service. Sex trafficking of Thai and migrant children and sex tourism remain significant problems. Widespread corruption among law enforcement personnel creates an enabling

---

[216] Statement Calling for Thai Government to Humanely Treat Cambodian Migrant Workers with Respect for their Rights and Dignity, Cambodian Human Rights Action Committee, 12 June, 2014.

[217] Migrant Smuggling in Asia: A Thematic Review of Literature, United Nations Office on Drugs and Crime, August, 2012.

environment for human trafficking and local authorities lack an awareness of the elements of trafficking and were deficient at identifying and protecting victims. Weak law enforcement, inadequate human and financial resources, and fragmented coordination among regulatory agencies in the fishing industry contributes to overall impunity for exploitive labour practices in this sector; no labour recruitment companies have been punished for forced labour or trafficking.[218]

In mid-2014 the US State Department determined that the Thai government did not comply with the minimum requirements for the elimination of human trafficking, and downgraded its international ranking on the issue to the lowest level possible. Faced with an indifferent government response, mounting evidence of the brazenly corrupt relationships between Thai officials and human traffickers, the tone of US and international condemnation hardened.[219]

There were fears that a downgrading associated with poor labour practices could hurt Thailand's reputation, with an impact on trade, particularly if consumers began to associate the country's seafood products with slavery.[220]

Lobby groups involved in the issue, some of which had received substantial funds from the US State Department for research projects, included Human Rights Watch, the American Federation of Labor and Congress of Industrial Organisations, The American Federation of Teachers, Free the Slaves, The Child Labor Coalition, the Environmental Justice Foundation, the National Consumers League and the Uniting Church of Australia. They claimed the Thai government had perpetuated policies that fostered trafficking of migrant workers within its borders.[221]

---

[218] CIA Library Publications, The World Factbook, Thailand, 2013.

[219] Trafficking in Persons Report, US State Department, June, 2014.

[220] Thai Union: US Downgrading could hurt reputation, trade, *Undercurrent*, 18 March, 2014.

[221] Joint Letter to Hon John Kerry Re Human Trafficking in Thailand, Human Rights Watch, May 9, 2014.

Coinciding with the State Department's downgrading, the groups issued a joint statement claiming the number of victims of severe forms of trafficking in Thailand to be significant and its government was at best complacent, at worst complicit: "Instances of gross abuse by government officials against migrant workers continue to be common. Owners of factories or boats frequently bribe police to allow human trafficking to continue, migrant workers are frequently victims of shakedowns and deportation threats by police, and some trafficking victims have even reported being forced to work for Thai officials while being held in custody after being identified as victims of human trafficking. There is no state mechanism through which to apply for asylum outside the camps on the Thai-Burma border."

The majority of Thai victims identified by the US State Department in the previous 12 months were found in sex trafficking; many of them from ethnic minorities or poor villages. "Women and girls from Thailand, Laos, Vietnam and Burma including some who initially intentionally seek work in Thailand's extensive sex trade, are subjected to sex trafficking. Child sex trafficking, once known to occur in highly visible establishments, has become increasingly clandestine, occurring in massage parlours, bars, karaoke lounges, hotels and private residences. Children who have false identity documents are exploited in the sex trade in karaoke or massage parlours. Local NGOs report an increasing use of social media to recruit women and children into sex trafficking. Victims are subjected to sex trafficking in venues that cater to local demand and in business establishments in Bangkok and Chiang Mai that cater to foreign tourists' demand for commercial sex."

The State Department's Trafficking in Persons 2014 assessment stated: "In one case, the government reported investigating and disciplining 33 local police officers on suspicion of protecting a brothel where child sex trafficking victims were found. However, trafficking-related corruption remained widespread among Thai law enforcement personnel. Credible reports indicated some corrupt officials protected brothels, other commercial sex venues, and food processing facilities from raids and inspections; colluded with traffickers; used information from victim interviews to weaken cases; and engaged in commercial sex acts with child trafficking victims.

"Local and national-level police officers established protective relationships with traffickers in trafficking hot-spot regions to which they were assigned. Thai police officers and immigration officials reportedly extorted money or sex from Burmese migrants detained in Thailand for immigration violations and sold Burmese migrants unable to pay labour brokers and sex traffickers."

The State Department alleged corruption by officials on both sides of the borders between Laos, Burma and Cambodia.

The United Nations Office on Drugs and Crime alleges that migrant smuggling could not occur on the large scale that it does without collusion between corrupt officials and criminals in Thailand. Recruiters established personal relationships with the authorities at border checkpoints in order to facilitate the passage of migrants. Police received payments for migrants and in return assisted them in finding employment. Smugglers and recruiters can make the journey to work in Thailand easier, cheaper and faster than through official channels, which are administratively complex, expensive and time consuming: "Law enforcement, border protection and immigration control activities can be circumvented or sabotaged with the complicity of corrupt public officials."[222]

One of the worst cases of people smuggling in Thailand involved the death of 54 Myanmar migrants in the back of a sweltering seafood transport truck after the air conditioning failed. The migrants were bound for the tourist island of Phuket, where many of their countrymen already worked. Among the survivors were 14 children. Forty six of the adult survivors were charged and jailed for illegally entering Thailand.

Human rights advocates criticised the police for processing the migrants as criminals when they had been victims of serious crimes. The Police argued that the migrants had voluntarily come

---

[222] Corruption and the Smuggling of Migrants, United Nations Office on Drugs and Crime, 2013.

to Thailand, were not destined for the sex trade, and were therefore not victims of human trafficking. A senior member of Thailand's National Security Council argued that with millions of migrants crossing the Thai/Myanmar border annually, classifying the 46 migrants as victims of human trafficking would undermine the enforcement of Thai's immigration laws.[223]

The US downgrading of Thailand to rank it as one of the world's worst countries for human trafficking met with a hostile reaction from within the country.

Chantawipa Apisuk of the *Bangkok Post* argued that the American government might enjoy playing the role of the world's headmaster, but the Trafficking in Persons report and the processes behind it were harming rather than helping some of the world's poorest workers. The International Labour Organisation was, he believed, a far more appropriate body to be dealing with questions of working conditions.

The hundreds of millions of dollars spent on attempting to eliminate human trafficking around the world had been largely wasted: "Migrant workers need to work to support themselves and their families. The implementation of anti-trafficking laws through crackdowns has, in effect, made providing for their family a criminal activity under the law and bilateral agreements with the USA. It must be pointed out that labour standards and quality of life for migrant workers have not been improved by the American anti-trafficking policy; instead, it is an obstacle. Workers should be able to address issues of unfair wages, dangerous work practices and working conditions. The anti–trafficking law hinders this process.

"Many migrant workers refuse to demand their rights due to the threat of 'rescue and deportation' as trafficking victims. The experience of migrants under current anti-trafficking practices is not one of protection and assistance according to the law. Under the anti-trafficking framework, migrants have been frequently kept

---

[223] Suffocation inside a Cold Storage Truck and Other Problems with Trafficking as "Exploitation" and Smuggling as "Choice" Along the Thai-Burmese Border, Erick Gjerdingen, *Arizona Journal of Comparative and International Law*, Vol. 26, No. 3, 2009.

in custody longer than any law prescribes. All people need is to be able to work in safe and fair conditions. What we should aim for is the improvement of workplaces and labour rights for all workers, including sex workers, rather than following the American anti-trafficking agenda, which has failed the very people it sets out to help." [224]

Throughout 2013 and 2014 there were reports and accompanying media exposes of slave-like conditions in the Thai fishing fleet. Accounts emerged of Burmese, Cambodian and Thai men remaining at sea for years, paid next to nothing and expected to work up to 20 hours a day seven days a week while being physically abused.

Thailand is the third largest seafood exporter in the world, with seafood exports valued at more than $US7 billion. Trade to the U.S. and Europe is estimated at around $US3 billion. Activists called for "net to plate" traceability to ensure consumers in the West were not benefiting from exploitative practices in the East. [225]

Much of the tuna, sardines, shrimp and squid Thailand exports is caught by the victims of human trafficking, with consumers in the West benefiting, *Time* claimed in an expose of the industry. Around one fifth of the catch ended up on American tables. The news magazine warned that countless Burmese migrants, many of them children, were forced to endure slave-like conditions: "And shockingly, the fruits of their anguish continue to be unwittingly enjoyed by families across the U.S., Europe and elsewhere... The industry heavily relies on trafficked and forced labour on unlicensed vessels. Victims typically hail from Cambodia, Laos and, most commonly, Burma. Beatings and starvation are commonplace. Many would-be migrants, not possessing valid documentation, pay brokers several hundred dollars to arrange their passage over the border, with the promise of well-paying jobs upon arrival. In reality, vulnerable individuals are sold to fishing boat captains for a huge profit, and then must work off several

---

[224] TIP report harms, not helps, sex workers, Chantawipa Apisuk, *Bangkok Post*, 30 July, 2014.

[225] Slavery at Sea: The Continued Plight of Trafficked Migrants in Thailand's Fishing Industry, Environmental Justice Foundation, 2014.

thousand dollars of 'debt'. Thai immigration and law enforcement officers are often complicit in these deals. Prosecution of perpetrators is rare. Many migrants get sold from boat to boat and don't see land for years." [226]

The trafficking of men to the Thai fishing industry began in earnest after Typhoon Gay in 1984, which resulted in the sinking of more than 200 boats and at least 1,000 deaths. Fearful Thai workers abandoned the sector, leaving a chronic labour shortage. Informal migrant and Thai labour brokers sprung up to facilitate the employment of migrants from Burma, Cambodia and Laos.

The 2011 Trafficking of Fishermen in Thailand by the International Organisation for Migration was one of the foundation reports on which other researchers built. It described as common practice operators holding trafficked fishermen on boats indefinitely, transferring the crew members between boats. When one boat was obliged to return to shore, the fishermen were forced to board another while still at sea. Both Myanmar and Cambodian fishermen reported seeing fellow fishermen attacked and, in some cases, killed by captains in instances where they were too weak or sick to work. Illegal migrants captured by the police could find themselves being sold directly to the industry. The report declared: "Fishermen who do not perform according to the expectations of the boat captain may face severe beatings or other forms of physical maltreatment, denial of medical care and, in the worst cases, maiming or killing."[227]

International media coverage of the Thai fishing industry relied heavily on two reports by the privately and publicly funded group the Environmental Justice Foundation. The reports, *Slavery at Sea: The Continued Plight of Trafficked Migrants in Thailand's Fishing Industry* and *Sold to the Sea: Human Trafficking in Thailand's Fishing Industry*[228] concluded that Thai authorities were complicit

---

[226] Child Slaves May Have Caught the Fish in your Freezer, Charlie Campbell,

[227] Trafficking of Fishermen in Thailand, International Organisation for Migration, 14 January, 2014.

[228] Sold to the Sea: Human Trafficking in Thailand's Fishing Industry. Environmental Justice Foundation.

in large scale trafficking operations and the mistreatment of workers. Thailand's fishing industry, and the seafood sector more widely, remained heavily reliant on forced labour as an integral part of their business model. Unscrupulous business owners, criminal trafficking networks and corrupt officials, all of whom had close connections with each other, continued to profit from the exploitation of migrant workers, while the Thai Government's activities to tackle the issue had been little more than window dressing. The substantially resourced reports provided evidence that the exploitation of migrant workers extended to child and forced labour, forced detention and extreme violence.

The reports provided testimony of the murder of crew members, supporting 2009 findings by the United Nations Inter-Agency Project on Human Trafficking that 59 per cent of interviewed migrants trafficked aboard Thai fishing boats reported witnessing the murder of a fellow worker. A high level of interconnectedness between the public and private sectors resulted in close personal relationships between business owners, politicians and civil servants from the local government level upwards. Convictions against public officials on corruption-related charges were rare, and the legal system offered inadequate deterrence against corruption. The Thais themselves perceived local government as corrupt. One Sub-District Chief, himself a fisheries magnate, was able to successfully mobilise enough support amongst local business owners in order to blockade a port area and bar entry to Government labour inspectors. Well connected brokers were seldom arrested.

Enforced slavery and dubious employment practices are only one aspect of Thailand's involvement in human trafficking. The country's geographical location at the heart of Southeast Asia, with its permeable borders, modern transport systems and lax law enforcement makes it an ideal transit zone for smuggling illegal immigrants to the West. Many but not all such operations go unreported. One of the best documented cases involved the smuggling of Sri Lankan migrants to Canada.[229]

---

[229] On the Smugglers Trail: The Series, *National Post*, 27 March, 2011.

The Canadian public first became aware that their country was the target of Southeast Asian smuggling rings with the arrival of the ship MV Ocean Lady in 2009. It was carrying 76 refugees. A number were Tamil Tigers who claimed they could not return to their home country for fear of arrest and torture.

The following year saw the arrival of a retired freighter, painted with the colours of the Thai flag, the MV Sun Sea. It arrived off the coast of British Columbia in August, 2010, carrying 492 Sri Lankan refugees and crew. Two of the would-be migrants were subsequently found to have been guilty of war crimes committed during the long-running Sri Lankan civil war.

Human smuggling is not just expensive for the migrants themselves, but for the targeted country. The case of the MV Sun Sea became a cause célèbre for refugee advocates across Canada who claimed the illegal immigrants were welcome and their detention constituted an abuse of human rights. The last of the MV Sun Sea refugees to be processed in Canada, a former Tamil rebel formally known only as B-189, was held at the Fraser Regional Detention Centre in British Columbia until 2014, more than three and a half years after the boats arrival.

Tharmaradman Arumaithurai aka B-189 had paid $20,000 for what he hoped would be passage to a new life. As always, one man's freedom fighter was another man's terrorist. Thanks to his past as a Tamil rebel he faced more than 50 detention hearings in Canada without being released. As for so many others, Thailand had been an integral part of his journey to the West. Arumaithurai revealed that he bribed a Thai immigration official to procure a Thai visa, then bribed his way through Colombo airport and flew to Bangkok. There he was housed in an apartment building with other Sri Lankans. Ultimately he boarded a small boat which took him to the MV Sun Sea, which was anchored off shore. His journey would not have been possible without the assistance of easily bribed Thai authorities.[230]

---

[230] Known until now as B-189, the last of the 492 MV Sun Sea migrants in custody faces an uncertain fate: this is his story, Stewart Bell, *National Post*, 14 February, 2014.

Immigration Minister Chris Alexander said: "Canadians welcome genuine visitors, immigrants, and refugees but have no tolerance for fraudsters, bogus asylum claimants, and criminals, including war criminals, abusing our generosity and risking the safety and security of the Canadian public."

The dangerously overcrowded MV Sun Sea led to a series of diplomatic notifications about the perils of people smuggling. The Sri Lankan Ministry of Defence warned that the runs were dangerous while Canadian officials cautioned that the trade carried a high potential tragedy and was already causing major disruption to orderly migration programs. The well intentioned but to their critics misguided advocacy of refugee lobbyists was also causing the government major political headaches. Activists had the ability to whip up public sentiment, while smugglers had the capacity to send several large, steel-hulled migrant vessels to Canada each year. Used ships were easy to find in Southeast Asian waters, and there was an ample supply of would-be refugees waiting in Thailand, Malaysia, India and Sri Lanka.

"Without getting into operational specifics, there are a lot of Tamils in Bangkok," head of the multi-country Anti-Human Smuggling Team based in Thailand, Inspector George Pemberton of the Royal Canadian Mounted Police said. The country formed a crossroads for Asia geographically, had very well developed transportation infrastructure and good support networks in Bangkok for migrants and refugees. The United Nations Refugee Agency was located in Bangkok, where there was a sizeable community of Sri Lankans. "There are a lot of Tamils in Malaysia who are here seeking refugee status," Pemberton said. "It would be naive to think that some of them wouldn't jump at the opportunity to find a faster way to get to a better life."

In the months following the scandal of the MV Sun Sea an international effort to destroy the supply chain of illegal immigrants to the West began. Thai, Canadian and Australian police cooperated in the operation, which resulted in 130 arrests of primarily Sri Lankans in Bangkok on 11 October, 2010, a further 61 arrests in the southern port city of Songkhla and Hat Yai near the Malaysian border later in the month, 23 arrests in Bangkok just before Christmas of the same year, and a further eight arrests in Bangkok in early 2011.

Australia's interest grew out of the fact that it had been particularly impacted by the arrival of "boat people", as they were known, asylum seekers often without any identification papers, many of them Sri Lankans. Refugee advocates, campaigning on what they saw as a human rights issue, ensured it was a live political issue. On the other side of the ideological dispute, much of the general public saw the uncontrolled arrival of illegal immigrants as a threat to Australia's sovereignty. More than 1200 asylum seekers died at sea during the period of the Rudd/Gillard Labor government from 2007 to 2013. The election promise to "Stop The Boats" was a key factor in the success of the incoming conservative government.

The crackdown on people smuggling resulted in the arrest of hundreds of would-be Sri Lankan immigrants. They had been bound for Canada and other Western destinations. Instead spent months, sometimes years, in Thailand's immigration detention system. Those detained reported that they had to sleep in shifts because of the lack of space and said they lacked clean drinking water, healthy food and proper medical facilities, and complained of the heat.

"We don't have any more power to bear this situation," one detainee said.[231]

The arrests were criticised by the United Nations refugee agency UNHCR for being arbitrary, indefinite, inappropriate for children and not aimed at the real criminals smuggling Sri Lankans to other countries. "While we understand the need to crack down on illegal human trafficking and smuggling, we are concerned that care should be taken to keep victims from being caught in the same dragnet," Asian spokeswoman for the UNHCR Kitty McKinsey said. "Our chief concern about the waves of arrests is that they do not appear to make a distinction between the organisers of human trafficking or smuggling — people who are willing to put tiny

---

[231] On the Smugglers Trail: The unlucky ones, Stewart Bell, *National Post*, 29 March, 2011.

babies and pregnant women at risk on the high seas — and their victims."

A Thai Immigration spokesman Major General Manoo Mekmok said the volume of illegal migrants was causing a strain on facilities: "Our detention facility is limited. And the sheer numbers of them that come in has caused us a lot of difficulty. We try to do our best to keep their living conditions decent, up to the United Nations standard, but some are very hard to provide, like shower and nice toilet."

Years after the MV Sun Sea scandal, another very public disgrace exposed the fact the Thai authorities had not just incompetently enabled trafficking networks to flourish, but had been actively involved.

The Rohingya are a Muslim ethnic minority in Buddhist Burma with historical links to the Bengali culture of neighbouring Bangladesh. Forbidden from owning land, they are essentially an indentured caste and are sometimes claimed as the most disadvantaged and persecuted of all the world's minorities. Some live as stateless people along the Indian Burmese border.

Thousands of Rohingya fled state persecution and ethnic cleansing in Burma in one of the biggest movements of boat people since the Vietnam War. They were then bought and sold by Thai navy, immigration and police officials either after they had landed in Thailand, or after being apprehended at sea.

Journalists with the Reuters News Agency Jason Szep and Andrew Marshall won a Pulitzer Prize for international reporting in 2014 after a multi-country investigation. Reuters alleged that hundreds of the Rohingya were taken from Thailand's immigration detention centres and delivered to human traffickers waiting at sea.[232]

The story recorded: "The Rohingya are then transported across southern Thailand and held hostage in a series of camps hidden near the border with Malaysia until relatives pay thousands of dollars to release them. Reporters located three such camps - two

---

[232] Special Report: Thailand secretly supplies Myanmar refugees to trafficking rings, Reuters, 4 December, 2014.

based on the testimony of Rohingya held there, and a third by trekking to the site, heavily guarded, near a village called Baan Klong Tor. Thousands of Rohingya have passed through this tropical gulag. An untold number have died there. Some have been murdered by camp guards or have perished from dehydration or disease, survivors said in interviews.

"Thailand portrays itself as an accidental destination for Malaysia-bound Rohingya: They wash ashore and then flee or get detained. In truth, Thailand is a smuggler's paradise, and the stateless Rohingya are big business."

Those whose families could not afford to pay for their freedom ended up being sold as slaves to Thai fishing boat captains, or forced labour on farms, some for as little as $US150. Reuters estimates that at least 800 people have died fleeing Mynamar, most of them Rohingya.

Little action was taken by the Thai government against officials involved in trafficking the Rohingya, although one senior police sergeant was dismissed from his post as a result.[233]

Sergeant Veerayut Ferngfull's dismissal was believed to be the first formal admission by authorities of a connection between renegade officers in uniform and people traffickers on the Andaman coast between Phuket and Ranong, a port on the border with Burma. He was sacked for driving a getaway vehicle that gave three Rohingya women and two children the chance to abscond from a family shelter, only to then be abducted. The women left the shelter voluntarily in expectation that they would be reunited with their menfolk in Malaysia once cash changed hands. Veerayut was alleged to have repeatedly raped one of the women at knifepoint over several days.

His sacking was primarily the result of the singular determination of campaigning journalist Chutima Sidasasthian.

Chutima and her colleague Alan Morison originally broke the Rohingya story back in 2010, winning awards including from the Society of Publishers in Asia, the Hong Kong News Awards and

---

[233] Crooked Policeman Sacked as Officials Acknowledge His Link to Accused Trafficker, Chutima Sidasasthian and Alan Morrison, *Phuket Wan*, 13 July, 2013.

the Human Rights Press Awards. Their contacts provided key access to the vastly better resourced Reuters journalists, who won the Pulitzer Prize for essentially the same story.

Ironically the pair were arrested and charged with criminal defamation by the Thai Navy for a report on the Rohingya in the same week that the Reuters journalists were being awarded the Pulitzer Prize. The charge related to a single paragraph taken from the Reuters story. Morison's passport was seized. Morison's business visa was replaced with a "criminal" visa. Because of his inability to renew his work permit, the absence of his passport threatened the existence of the *Phuket Wan*, one of the single most cogent and fearless advocates for change in the whole of Thailand. The Australian government refused to assist.

Morison and Chutima's arrest provoked international condemnation. The Foreign Correspondents Club of Thailand said the prosecution served only to stifle media freedom on an issue of profound importance to the rights of persecuted people. The United Nations Office of the High Commissioner for Human Rights called on the Thai government to retract the charges. Asian Director of Human Rights Watch Brian Adams called the charges a "dark stain" on Thailand's respect for media freedom. Reporters Without Borders described the charges as absurd.[234]

Phuket Wan, with its bold journalism, persistent coverage of corruption, its socially responsible highlighting of the astonishingly high number of deaths of foreigners in Thailand, and ceaseless advocacy for reform of the many safety scandals plaguing the tourist industry, has been a significant force for good.

How long it will survive under the military junta is a moot point.

In September of 2014 Amnesty International released a report, *Thailand: Attitude Adjustment: 100 Days Under Martial Law*, which slammed the government's repression of free speech and called for an end to abusive laws stifling debate.

---

[234] Australian journalist Alan Morison spends Time in Thai prison in fight for media freedom, Lindsay Murdoch, *Sydney Morning Herald*, 17 April, 2014.

Hundreds of arbitrary detentions, reports of torture and other ill-treatment, sweeping restrictions on freedom of expression and peaceful assembly and unfair trials in military courts were creating a climate of fear in Thailand, and there were no signs of a let-up. Censorship of the media, already a problem prior to the coup, had been stepped up, hundreds of websites taken down or blocked, censorship panels set up and people threatened with arrest and imprisonment for posting online any material critical of the junta.

"Three months since the coup, a picture emerges from our investigations of widespread and far-reaching human rights violations perpetrated by the military government that are ongoing," said Richard Bennett, Amnesty International's Asia-Pacific Director. "The Thai authorities should end this disturbing pattern of repression, end human rights violations, respect its international human rights obligations and allow open debate and discussion - all of which are vital to the country's future.

"It has become part of the military government's modus operandi to crack down on the smallest forms of dissent. The Thai authorities must lift all charges against any individuals brought solely for peacefully exercising their rights to freedom of expression and assembly, and release those detained or imprisoned under such charges immediately and unconditionally."

Bangkok Skyline by Joan Campderross-i-Canas

THE DISSOLVING PRESENT

"The Land of Smiles" was one of the most successful advertising slogans in history. Its exact origins are lost in time, but it does offer an insight into why there is so much misapprehension and misunderstanding between Thais and foreigners.

Thais regard a smile as an appropriate response for almost any situation. A Thai almost never cries, regarding such behaviour as a weakness or mental defect, and it is equally rare to see a Thai grimace or look angry.

In the Land of Smiles there are 13 major sub categories of smiles.

The Thai word for smile is "Yim" and the main smiles are:

1. Yim tang namtah - used when very happy; e.g., I've-won-the-jackpot smile
2. Yim cheun chom - the smile used when impressed with or when one admires someone.
3. Yim sao - the smile used when one is sad
4. Yim cheut cheuan - the smile a winner gives to a losing opponent or rival
5. Yim tak tan - the I'm right-and-you're-wrong smile
6. Yim mee lai nai - the smile that blankets bad intentions
7. Feun yim - the forced smile
8. Yim tak tai- the polite smile used for strangers or people that you barely know
9. Yim yor - the mocking smile; used to taunt or laugh at someone
10. Yim soo - things-are-so-bad-I-better-smile smile
11. Yim mai ohk - when you want to smile but can't, or the smile won't come out
12. Yim haeng - the dry smile for situations like "Is it today? Sorry, I forgot, please don't be mad at me"
13. Yim ya-ya - the smile used to apologise or to diffuse an embarrassing, tense moment.

Unfortunately it is the mocking smile, the forced smile and the smile concealing ill intent which all too many foreigners witness.

Thailand may never have been colonised, but in the 21st Century it has been colonised by default, overrun by foreigners of all kinds; retired couples there because it is cheap, old soldiers reliving days of women and song, backpackers more interested in each other than the beauties that surround them, craven thugs partying it up in some of the most disgusting ways imaginable. The Thais don't like and don't understand what they see; the disparity of wealth between themselves and visitors; the bland contempt with which they are so often treated in their roles as bar tenders and hotel staff; the lack of respect displayed in everything from tone of voice to overly casual modes of dress.

Thais prey on tourists partly because the development of the tourist industry itself has been so badly managed; their country flooded with people who treat them with disrespect just because they are working, be it in restaurants or brothels; the price of property has escalated beyond their reach, they live in tiny rooms while Westerners paddle in the pools of their villas. The culturally and historically instilled dislike of foreigners and the xenophobic and racist instincts of the Thais are repeatedly compounded as they watch the hordes of foreigners throng their streets and spread-eagle their fat bodies on beaches. The Thai language is melodic. To them foreigners sound guttural and ugly. Everything is loud, everything graceless, deranged white elephants sweating in the sun. Drunk, obnoxious, groping, stupid, these are the people they don't like; and will never like.

The individuals involved in the crimes against tourists didn't ask for their country to be like this; to be filled with garish signs and drunken strangers. They didn't ask to be poor while the foreigners are rich; to be surrounded in their own country by ugly people who treat them like servants.

The strip at Patong Beach
Picture courtesy of My Phuket Rent.

They didn't ask to be in a world where the easiest way to get ahead, to feed their families and themselves, is to rob someone or sleep with someone they don't know, don't like and will probably never see again. They feel no guilt because there is no guilt; there are only gulfs of misunderstanding, contempt for the gullibility of fat cat foreigners; and a longing to be with their own kind. With no understanding of the individualistic nature of the West, brought up from birth in a communal culture, with its own elaborately polite language and equally elaborate social courtesies, Thais rarely feel comfortable in the company of Westerners; and the gulf between Thais and tourists has intensified with each passing year; with every passing announcement of an increase in visitor numbers; with every desecration and excess.

A significant number of the murders and attacks on tourists in recent times have been perpetrated by teenagers who feel both emboldened and justified by the dislike their elders express towards the millions of foreigners trampling across their country.

A Thailand Safety and Security Forum, held in late 2013, attracted a number of heavy hitters in the industry. Organisers called on Thai officialdom to provide accurate pre-arrival tourism safety and security advice.

Thailand's tourism industry leaders pressed for new, effective measures to improve outcomes for business and leisure travellers. Thailand had always been critical of countries providing cautionary advice to their citizens, claiming it was damaging their country's reputation. Instead, the organisers argued, by providing accurate pre-arrival information, and warning tourists of the dangers they could face, and by confronting the high level of criminality perpetrated against foreigners, they would be enhancing their authority and the reputation of their country.

The conference built on earlier workshops which looked at ways of combating well-established "scams" that target tourists and how to better inform and educate visitors before they arrived in Thailand.

Keynote speaker Dr David Beirman, a senior lecturer in Tourism at the University of Technology Sydney, said a number of other popular tourist destinations with high crime rates, and particularly with large numbers of crimes perpetuated against tourists, including the crime capitals of South Africa and the Caribbean, issued safety warnings to tourists; and had seen their reputations enhanced and tourist associated industries grow.

He cited South Africa, which had some 28,000 murders and 100,000 assaults annually when it began issuing travel warnings to tourists. Tourism continued to expand despite the warnings. "It builds trust," Beirman said. "In their own best interests Thailand should be doing the same."

But no such warnings have been issued in Thailand, both out of a false perception of financial self-interest and because of the Asian cultural habit of preserving reputation above all else. Tourists are lulled into a sense of safety and security by the false advertising of Thailand as a warm and welcoming country; and ridiculed by locals for their naivety when, as they frequently do, they come into harm's way. One of the main problems the Thai government and the Thai Tourism Authority has is the failure to address safety and security for fear of the impact on their reputation as a destination.[235]

Dr Beirman said many ASEAN governments believed they risked losing "face" by admitting potential dangers and for more than a decade ASEAN heads of government and tourism ministers condemned cautionary western government travel advisories as hostile. "If you were upfront you would be enhancing your reputation," he said. "Tourists often blunder into places they shouldn't. Most crimes are about opportunity. If you have the opportunity some people are going to take that opportunity. Tourism is unintentionally contributing to crime. People are coming with a lot of money to spend."

He said for a foreigner to lose $100 was not such a setback, but for a Thai it was a healthy 3,000 baht, enough to feed their families or buy half a dozen bottles of the local whiskey. "Instead of someone who can enhance the reputation of Thailand, tourists become an object to make easy money."

Beirman said the Thai Tourism Authority was under no legal obligation to issue warnings to tourists, but needed to be persuaded it was both ethical and in their own best interests to do so.

"One of the problems the Thai government and the Thai Tourism Authority have had was that they were very reluctant to address safety and security, fearing that they would be losing face," he said. "The concept of face or reputation arouses extreme sensitivity. Most Southeast Asian tourist destinations seek to present a bright and trouble-free face to prospective travellers and stakeholders. Generally, government destination marketing organisations promote only the virtues of their destination and either ignore or airbrush negatives. If you were upfront, you would be enhancing your reputation. You would be open about letting people know what to look out for, and places to avoid."

The question becomes how to provide the service of offering cautionary advice to tourists without losing face. Beirman said Thailand had provided excellent information on the dangers of

[235] Saving face and promoting tourist safety in south east Asia, David Beirman, *The Conversation*, 22 January, 2014.

natural disasters, such as the 2011 floods. But on issues that could be seen as casting aspersions on the Thai national character no such warnings existed.

"Thais are sensitive to criticism from foreigners and spokesmen from the Thai Tourism Authority, including its governor Surpahon Svetasreni, pointed out the admission of safety and security concerns in official government tourism promotion literature could be misread as an official admission that Thailand is dangerous," Beirman said. "The mood may be changing, however. The Thai Tourism Authority's January advice, issued to tourists about avoiding demonstrations in Bangkok, suggests the authority is at least implementing the advice from the conference. The Thai Tourism Authority has finally recognised that proactive safety warnings will gain it credibility as opposed to losing face. ASEAN countries have become increasingly sophisticated in managing tourism risk and security in recent years. However, it appears that many Southeast Asian government tourism authorities will only refer to security and safety risks in their destination marketing when their reputational backs are against the wall."

President of major tourism organisation Skal International Bangkok, Dale Lawrence, said it was time to stop brushing unsavoury issues under the carpet, to better protect the interests of travellers while enhancing the reputation of Thailand. "Now we must act in unison to ensure that all business and leisure travellers leave Thailand with enjoyable and memorable experiences."

Chairman of the Joint Foreign Chambers of Commerce in Thailand Stanley Kang said, "Amongst the membership of the 30 JFCCT chambers there are many tourism operators, individual owners, managers and employees that are tourists in Thailand on a regular basis. It is in all of Thailand's interests that tourists are well taken care of whilst holidaying in this wonderful land. Tourism is a massive source of income for Thailand and its people. With modern communications tools, every small bad story is highlighted many times around the world within minutes of it occurring.

"This news not only affects the single location or operator where the event takes place but, in effect, brands Thailand and all its people and tourism operators as a whole. We cannot, and should not, stop these stories from spreading but we should take great care that these actual events are very few and far between."

In fact many negative stories about outcomes have and continue to be suppressed; making it difficult for travellers to make informed choices. Thailand has never been a great example of freedom of the press. The monarchy is kept in power not just by tradition and social manipulation but the use of brute force and the imprisonment of hundreds of people for even the most minor of criticisms. Tens of thousands of websites are blocked for political reasons. Newspaper editors are under strict instructions to tow the government line. Self-censorship and a deceptive will to conceal their own involvement, along with fears that negative stories damage the country's reputation, means authorities hide, ignore or mislabel many of the accidents and misfortunes befalling tourists. The suppression of negative stories concerning foreigners has escalated with the arrival of the military junta in 2014. The once daily, sometimes comical, often sad stories on the deaths and mishaps occurring to foreigners have almost disappeared from the English language press. Tourists are still being frequently robbed; they are still dying in violent and unjustifiable circumstances. Thailand is still the most dangerous tourist destination on Earth. But from reading the newspapers, no one would have been any the wiser.

None of the bodies funnelling tourists to Thailand or raking money off them take any responsibility for their safety or issue any appropriate warnings. Not the airlines dumping tourists by the millions through the airports of Thailand. Not the hotels with their ever smiling concierges and professionally polite reception staff.

Not the governments of the tourist's origin countries, who, while issuing a few little read cautions about Thailand make no genuine concerted effort to alert the young, restless, adventures and fun loving travellers now roaming the globe in hordes. These same governments could convince an entire generation to give up smoking cigarettes, but they can't issue appropriate safety warnings in the simple and graphic terms necessary to make an impact on the public.

Nor do the travel agents and tour companies, happily raking in their millions, warn that far from sending their customers off to a paradise on Earth, a great place to relax and party, surrounded by a warm and welcoming people, they are dispatching them to the single most deadly tourist destination on Earth, where safety equipment and procedures are entirely inadequate, where the locals hate them with a passion and where their deaths, injuries, disappearances, and robberies will be treated with indifference by the authorities.

The insurance industry, making hundreds of millions of dollars out of travellers to Thailand, provides no statistical analysis on the deaths and injuries of foreigners. Insurance companies do not release figures on claims and payouts; the claims high, the payouts low, as is the nature of the industry. There is no information available on overall spend, how many claims are made on what grounds and the percentage of those claims which are successful.

The insurance industry has very low levels of customer satisfaction, yet governments repeatedly advise their citizens to take out travel insurance. One common slogan is "if you can't afford insurance you can't afford to travel". In other words taxpayers are funding the promotion of an industry which is not transparent, gives no public account of its actions and policies, no proof customers are getting value for money and no account of their profitability.

Peculiarities of law in the countries of origin often means it is illegal for the travel operators selling the insurance to explain or give advice to the customer about what is actually in their insurance policies.

In reality many of the situations tourists find themselves in while travelling in Thailand, from hiring a motorbike to going to a bar to being inconvenienced by a military coup, are not covered by travel insurance. Most problematic situations in which tourists find themselves are not included. Many travellers are unaware, for example, that their insurance is invalidated if they have been drinking or are under the influence of other substances, precisely the circumstances in which so many get into trouble. Nor were travellers forced to change or cancel their arrangements as a result of the 2014 coup compensated. Claims arising from riots, wars, rebellions, civil disruptions and military insurrection are common exclusions in travel insurance policies.

Insurance companies are successfully selling policies to 80 per cent of the travelling public primarily because of government support; and thereby taking advantage of a high level of ignorance. A survey undertaken by research company Quantum for the Insurance Council of Australia found that 23 per cent of Australian travellers did not know what was covered in their travel insurance, one in three admitted to not reading their insurance policy in detail and 44 per cent did not consider what their travel insurance policy excluded.

In effect governments are promoting the insurance companies' exploitation of public ignorance. By doing their advertising for them they are helping to instil the illusion that as long as tourists have travel insurance they are covered for any mishaps which occur overseas. Travel insurance lulls travellers into a false sense of security and helps to create the impression that Thailand operates under much the same laws and in much the same way as their own country.

Government advocacy for travel insurance also has the unintended consequence of allowing tour operators, airlines and hotel chains to ignore their responsibilities towards the welfare of their customers.

As previously established, the UK Foreign Office is the only international body which collects and publishes appropriate statistical data on the behaviour of its citizens overseas.

Otherwise none of the taxpayer funded groups which observers could be forgiven for thinking had a legally obligated duty of care to their citizens even keep a record of the number of deaths of foreigners in Thailand per year, or any breakdown by nationality or cause of death.

Certainly not the Thais themselves. The Tourist Authority of Thailand, the Thai Ministry of Tourism and the Thai Tourist Police all ignore requests for such information, thereby attempting to avoid any negative publicity which could besmirch an in fact already badly besmirched reputation. Year after year the TAT has rushed to boastfully announce its visitation rates. The Thai government can spend tens of millions of dollars promoting its desecrated beaches and tawdry bars but it cannot provide a simple statistical breakdown on the welfare of tourists while in their country. In other words, Amazing Thailand can count, to the very last man, woman and child, the arrival of tourists in their country. But it cannot count the body bags going home.

The United Nations World Tourist Authority has a mandate to monitor tourism in the economic, policy and development context. Despite the issue having been a subject of major controversy for years, the UNWTO does not collect statistics on the deaths and injuries of tourists in Thailand. Critics could be forgiven for wondering what could be more fundamental to the economic development policies of tourism than the welfare of travellers in a destination notorious for its lack of adherence to basic safety protocols and high death rates of tourists. One of the UNWTO's basic concerns is that the collation and publication of such data might attract adverse media coverage.

Ultimately it is the world's taxpayers, many employed in difficult, boring and demeaning jobs, who pay for the UNWTO's 110 staff and six regional offices; members of the working class who are enticed to Thailand by the promise of cheap holidays and good times. With many hundreds of them meeting calamitous ends, it is no exaggeration to say unsophisticated tourists thus tempted are being lured into a death trap.

The US State Department, which manages to collect and publish a vast amount of information about every country on Earth, does not bother to keep a record of the deaths of its own citizens on Thai soil. Counting the number of bodies being repatriated to America should be a simple accounting matter.

While it has in recent years provided a headline figure on the number of deaths coming to consular attention, which clearly demonstrates that Thailand is the most dangerous destination on Earth for Australians, the Australian government does not produce any statistical analysis on causes of death and no trend data. A spokeswoman for the Australian Department of Foreign Affairs, which has a budget of $7.1 billion per year, claimed it would be too great a strain on their resources to provide the annual death toll for the last 10 years.

But then Australia is not alone in failing to protect its citizens by withholding or not collecting even the most basic of data on the welfare of its citizens while in Thailand. Most countries providing human fodder for the Thai tourism industry do not publish the number of deaths of their citizens.

The rare exception is the UK Foreign Office, which annually provides excellent statistical data on the conduct of British citizens overseas. And that data amply illustrates that many of its citizens meet a sticky end as a result of the unregulated mayhem of the Thai tourist industry. As previously stated, the number of British dying in Thailand is second only to Spain, a popular retirement destination with 17 times the level of visitation.

While the British government provides by far the best analysis of the fate of its citizens abroad, proving that Thailand is an extremely dangerous destination for its citizens; serious questions are being asked about why it does not issue sterner warnings before they get on a plane.

The paucity of information, the lack of available data to enable travellers to make informed decisions on how best to spend their holiday funds, the failure of governments and tourist bodies worldwide to make public data on the deaths and injuries of foreigners in Thailand, amounts, at the very least, to a breach of duty of care.

Since its formation in the 1960s the Tourist Authority of Thailand has had only one barometer of success, visitor numbers. It is a policy which has caused enormous damage to the country's environment, social cohesion and international reputation. Being thought of as the world's largest brothel and most laissez faire of all the world's tropical theme parks was not the aim of the original founders of the Thai tourist industry. While numbers have soared, there has been no corresponding care given to the safety of facilities, reform of the nation's mafia run entertainment industry, its unpatrolled beaches, or even elementary actions like cracking down on rampant drink spiking.

Thailand has paid a very high price for the unparalleled and uncontrolled greed which has led to it relying almost solely on tourism as its major source of foreign revenue. At the same time, while everyone from corrupt police to street touts have gorged themselves on "walking ATMs" or "fruit for the picking", as tourists are called, locals, too, have paid a very high price.

There are no explanations or warnings to potential customers of the numerous dangers the disease riddled sex industry of Thailand presents; that there are no mandatory health checks of sex workers, as is often the case in the West; and safe sex education campaigns are virtually non-existent. The few bars that do participate in sporadic publicity campaigns on World AIDS Day often fail to enforce condom use throughout the rest of the year, for the same reason that drives the rest of the criminality in Thailand, money.

Thailand has more than four times the rate of HIV infection of any other country in Southeast Asia, with 1.4% of the population testing positive. The disease is particularly severe in provinces that receive large numbers of tourists. The dominant mode of spread is through sexual transmission. More than 1.1 million Thais tested positive for HIV between 1984 and 2008. According to the World Health Organisation more than 610,000 were living with the disease in 2011, the last year for which figures are available. Characterised by hysterical antidrug campaigns and without harm reduction programmes, Thailand has by far the highest level of HIV infection amongst injecting drug users of any country in the region, at almost 50%. There is also an alarming and increasing rate of HIV infection amongst men who have sex with men. The overall rate in Thailand for this group is 11.1 percent, but with pockets of much higher prevalence. Studies have shown 31 percent of men who have sex with men in Bangkok are HIV positive, a rate which has increased rapidly from 17 percent in 2003. In Thailand more broadly male sex workers, many of whom come into contact with tourists, have an infection rate of 16.3 percent, ranging up to 21 percent in high tourist areas. While rates of infection are increasing across all age groups, the age bracket from 23-28 in the large tourist cities of Bangkok and Chiang Mai is showing the highest rate of increase. There are also high rates of infection in the younger cohort from 15-22, indicating a worsening epidemic. Awareness of HIV/AIDS is poor, with one study indicating 80 percent of men who had sex with men and subsequently tested positive had never had a test before and thought they were HIV negative.

Male sex workers across Thailand demonstrate very low levels of condom use and escalating rates of infection. Female sex workers report only erratic condom use, with instances where only half of all commercial sex encounters involve a condom.[236]

In Thailand, despite the overt nature of the industry, prostitution remains illegal. It is an offence for sex workers to carry condoms because their possession would indicate they were working as prostitutes. Archaic laws also make it illegal for health workers to provide syringes to drug users.

The number of Thai nationals who have died of AIDS has already exceeded 600,000 and is heading rapidly upwards. Thailand has the highest number of deaths of any country in the world outside of Africa. Higher than its' neighbour China, which has a population almost 15 times the size. A social tragedy which would have galvanised any other nation on Earth into drastic action is largely shrugged off or ignored

In a class conscious society there has been no outcry, few outreach programs and only spasmodic public health campaigns for one simple reason: many of those who are dying are sex workers from poor rural families. Driven into the sex trade by poverty and the noble desire to help their extended families, sleeping with foreigners solely for money, they pay the ultimate price, returning to their beloved villages only to die.

As Elizabeth Becker observed in her ground breaking work *Overbooked*, most travel writing is entirely uncritical of the tourist industry itself, with a higher level of patronage and symbiosis in the form of sponsored travel than any other branch of journalism. Few travel writers venture beyond the cosseted confines of their five star hotels; and tell exactly the story the industry want told.

---

[236] HIV Aids in the South-East Asia Region, World Health Organisation, 2012.

Many, caught in a bubble of genuflecting travel operators and subservient hotel staff, write what is little more than advertising copy. Newspapers and other media outlets publish the material because it is cheap; and because the travel industry is one of their major sponsors. Industry operators use travel writers because full page features extolling the glories of a destination is less expensive and superficially more credible than buying advertising space. Thailand has long been a beneficiary of this style of consumer-oriented journalism, with most puff pieces concerning the quality of hotels and resorts; and not the dangers, tragedies and misadventures that real-life tourists experience firsthand.

In 2014 Thai tour operators reported a sharp 35 percent drop in sales. In an effort to help the industry recover from the sustained political problems which had paralysed the country and discouraged millions of tourists, the Tourism Authority of Thailand and the Thai Ministry of Tourism were granted an extra budget of $US35 million. The TAT announced it would adjust its marketing strategy in order to meet the 2015's revenue target of 2.2 trillion baht.

Promotional packages, roadshows and product briefings were aimed at Europe and South Africa, as well as North and South America. The TAT coordinated with consulates in many countries to stage Thai festivals, events aimed at attracting half a million visitors in 40 European and American cities.

A key part of the strategy was flying 1,000 journalists and travel writers, including bloggers, to the country for "familiarisation" tours. The TAT declared it would prioritise journalists from countries that had large numbers of potential visitors, particularly China. [237]

The gushing copy began to flow within weeks, with uncritical pieces appearing in travel sections around the world. The dangers of the destination itself were entirely ignored. Most of the travel writers were not even cognisant, or failed to mention, the high death rates amongst tourists, the concerns of the diplomatic corps

---

[237] TAT To Invite Foreign Journalists To Boost Tourism, KhaoSod English, 16 June, 2014.

or the efforts by the military junta to clean up the most obvious disgraces within the industry.

Despite the stories extolling the virtues of Thailand's five-star hotels and the country's many wonders, the reality on the ground remains problematic and will take years to fix, if it is ever fixed at all.

On the streets, beaches, bars and nightclubs of Thailand, tourist mayhem continues.

Navy chief Admiral Narong Pipattanasai, who supervised the Tourism Ministry, said restoring the confidence of tourists was the first priority among all revival measures. "We will quickly communicate with international travellers that Thailand is safe for them to visit," he said.[238]

That statement, as the deaths, injuries and robberies of so many tourists amply and unfortunately demonstrates, is simply untrue.

But the Thai Ministry of Tourism was hardly alone in peddling patent falsehoods about the safety of Thailand. Some of the richest men in Asia did exactly that.

Two months after the coup, American born Thai resident and billionaire businessman William Heinecke, owner of more than 1,500 restaurants, 100 hotels and 250 retail outlets, wrote an open letter to the international ambassadors serving in Thailand: "I am distressed by the interpretation by a number of Western governments and the international media of both the coup that recently took place in Thailand and the situation that led to the coup. Put succinctly, many of you have gotten it wrong. I cannot think of one Western country that has in recent memory experienced the social and political gridlock that Thailand suffered through for the past six months, resulting in government and political paralysis against a backdrop of increasing violence and needless loss of life. The military showed great restraint."

Heinecke claimed Thailand was not only facing political challenges, but also the compounding effects of exaggerated media reports which paint a distorted and unrealistic picture of the situation

---

[238] Thailand Puts Tourism as Top Priority, Gives Over $30 Million for Efforts, Latitude Travel Services.

in the Kingdom. While such reporting may sell newspapers and draw TV audiences, it is fear-mongering which promotes a misunderstanding of the situation—this in turn influences government travel warnings worldwide and has a disastrous effect on tourism. He said there are no concerns whatsoever for personal safety within Bangkok's large expatriate community or the millions of tourists still enjoying their holidays in Thailand, yet this was not mentioned in the international media reports or travel advisories.

"Hospitality has a huge impact on the Thai economy, generating millions of jobs and billions of dollars in revenue for a country that is known throughout the world for its charm, safety and hospitality. However, 62 countries have issued travel advisories for Thailand, 18 of which contain a "red alert" advising citizens to defer all travel to Thailand.

"These travel warnings are baffling to those of us who understand Thailand and fly in the face of the fact that Thailand continues to peacefully welcome millions of travellers from all over the world. It is the responsibility of all parties, and the media in particular, to present the situation accurately and in proper context to promote understanding, rather than misunderstanding, of the situation. All parties involved need to think hard about the detrimental effect that their words and actions are having on the people of Thailand.

"Thailand remains a peaceful and welcoming country, with unique natural and cultural attractions for travellers to experience and is very much open for business - this is the reality and this is the message that is not being sent by most major international media outlets and embassies. We all agree that the tourism industry is critical to the Thai economy and the growth of Thailand, and it should not become a casualty of misunderstanding, misrepresentation and hyperbole. Thailand very much remains open for business and is as safe, friendly and welcoming a destination for tourists as it has always been."[239]

Tell that to the bereaved families.

---

[239] An open letter to the ambassadors represented in Thailand and the international media, William Heinecke, Thai-Canadian Chamber of Commerce, 13 June, 2014.

Bangkok Sunset by Jackson Cam

Thailand's terrain of tourist incident throws up everything from the sad to the macabre, bodies washing up on the shore, bodies plummeting from the balconies of condominiums, drowned, knifed, slashed, drugged.

In January, 2014, Australian expat Adin Medzic, 47, died during the early hours of the morning after falling down the stairs of his apartment building in Patong. In the same month popular Phuket radio announcer Paul "the Doris" Norris, 45, was killed when his motorcycle was struck by a taxi. The driver was charged with reckless driving. Originally from Britain, he had been a founding partner and shareholder in 91.5FM since 2008. His voice was familiar to virtually all expat listeners. His last message on Facebook read: "Keeping all you lovely #Phuket people happy."

Also in the same month 11 suspects, most of them minors, were arrested and charged for seriously injuring a tourist in the seaside resort town of Hua Hin. Simonivet Pou, 26, was attacked after he tried to help another foreigner in a street brawl. Nine of the suspects were between 15 and 17. The victim required brain surgery.

In February French national Julie Humbert was killed in a car accident in Phuket. She had ten years experience with luxury/

charter yachting and had most recently been working with Galileo Yachting training staff for super yachts. In the same month a 62-year-old Norwegian man was found dead on his bed in a Patong apartment by a maid. He reportedly had an oxygen mask on his face and investigators concluded he probably died of a pre-existing condition. Also in the same month a 70-year-old German man died naked in a short-time motel room in Phuket City. Police concluded he may have overdosed on generic sex drugs then suffered a heart attack during or soon after a love-making session. Another German, Georg Erwin Bach, 64, crashed an ultralight and authorities concluded he either died from a heart attack, the impact of the plunge or from drowning.

The next day, Russian world swimming champion Vladimir Karmazin died at home in southern Phuket.

In March, 2014, a Finnish man, Kalevi Kantsila, 59, was killed after deliberately lying down in front of a tour bus.

In April the naked body of a Caucasian man was found floating in the sea off the luxurious Amanpuri Resort near the popular upscale beach district of Surin. Rescuers estimated he had been in the water for as long as five days. He was originally reported as having a cupid's arrow and heart tattooed on one arm and an ineligible tattoo on the other. Once the sand was swept from the man's arm, it became clear the "cupid sign" was actually a heart shape with a sword behind it. [240]

In the same month police and medics were called to a house in East Pattaya. Neighbours discovered the body of the British owner inside with his five-year-old son.[241] The boy was thought to have been trapped inside the house with his dead father for at least seven days. Nearby residents were finally alerted to the tragedy by a foul odour coming from the house and the sound of the boy crying. Inside the bedroom was the body of Mr. Robert Sorensen aged 36, a former teacher in Pattaya. The boy was taken into care by Welfare Officers. Officials attempted to locate the boy's Thai

---

[240] Mystery Body with Cupid Tattoo Found in Sea off Phuket Resort, *Phuket Wan*, 21 April, 2014.

[241] 5 Year Old Son Locked in house with dead British Father in East Pattaya, *Pattaya One*, 28 April, 2014.

mother and the British Embassy in Bangkok offered consular assistance.

The next month an Irish teacher from Dublin who had been working at Baan Maireab School in Phuket, Denis Bates, 30, died after being injured in a motorbike accident.

In June 2014 a story headlined "Italian Body Washes up on Pattaya Beach" recorded that Antonio Lardo, 66, had sustained a three centimetre wound to his forehead. A witness said that three days before he had seen the man lying down in front of a grocery store looking stressed.

The same month police found the naked body of a 27-year-old American woman on the island of Koh Samui. The death allegedly involved drugs and sexual bondage. Her body was found beside a private cliff top swimming pool overlooking the Gulf of Thailand. An empty vodka bottle was found floating in the private swimming pool while inside the villa detectives found handcuffs, a whip, morphine and packs of Viagra. Her British boyfriend was helping police with their inquiries.[242]

Again in the same month a 19-year-old Chinese tourist, Guo Jiachang, drowned off the island of Koh Chang in exactly the same location that had claimed the lives of numerous tourists over the years, including five in the previous 12 months. The announcement by authorities that more lifeguards would be stationed in the area was met with scepticism.

Owning a bar in Thailand, a dream for many Westerners, does not preclude them from being killed by locals, with a number of business operators meeting untimely ends. In August of 2014 a German bar owner was stabbed to death in Koh Samui after an altercation with local teenagers he found drinking alcohol and sitting on his motorbike. The man, who owned the 99 Beer Bar on Chaweng Beach, one of the island's entertainment districts, was with his Thai girlfriend in the parking lot of the club when he became angry with the Thai youths. Witnesses said the three Thais

---

[242] Bondage, Drugs Riddle: Naked Body of Young American Woman Found at Exclusive Samui Resort, Chutima Sidasathian, Phuket Wan, 26 June, 2014.

punched the German in the face, beat him with beer bottles and stabbed his neck with shards of glass.

In September of 2014 authorities claimed that a 21-year-old Welshman Jack Davies "suicided" after a night out in a bar on Phi Phi island. Davies came to Thailand inspired by the movie *The Beach* starring Leonardo DiCaprio, which was filmed nearby. He was affectionately described as a "little legend" by friends, with one tribute reading: "You've left footprints across everyone's heart." Police suggested the young man may have been disturbed by new visa arrangements making it more difficult to extend after 90-days, a move designed to stop foreigners working illegally, as Davies was doing. It was an unlikely cause of suicide and his parents claimed to have evidence that his death was suspicious.

Also in the same month Hungarian man Moshe David, 40, and another accused co-conspirator were sentenced to life imprisonment for the murder of a man Peter Reis, 47, in 2012. The argument was over an alleged 15 million baht property deal swindle. His compatriot, Lajos Kvalka, 50, admitted to helping clean up the blood and dumping the body near a pond, but claimed to have not been involved in the bludgeoning murder. After legal proceedings in Phuket were finalised, David was due to be sent back to Koh Samui, where he faced charges of murdering Hungarian billionaire Laszlo Csepai.

Again in the same month a 51-year-old American ran into the Nana Hotel in Bangkok in the early hours of the morning with blood streaming from his face. Staff said the man would not say who attacked him; and instead jumped from the fifth floor.

Thailand's military leaders vowed to clean up the Kingdom's tourist resorts after repeated complaints of scams, assaults and police extortion, but that didn't stop the violence. Also in September two young British backpackers were found murdered after their drinks were spiked at a beach party. Their naked bodies were discovered on the island of Koh Tao, a smaller, more intimate island than its neighbours Koh Phangan and Koh Samui, popular with backpackers and dive enthusiasts. The UK Foreign Office condemned "vicious, unprovoked attacks by gangs". The deceased were David Miller, 24, a university of Leeds engineering student from Jersey and Hannah Witheridge, 23, from Norfolk. The young woman, whose throat was cut, had been raped. The young man was chopped in the back and the side of his head with a hoe, while Witheridge had her face chopped from the front. Blood stained the beach. "It's very gruesome," a policeman said.[243]

The chaotic investigation led to hostile headlines including "Man says police beat him after he declines to be witness in Koh Tao murder cases" and "Terrified pal of murdered Brit pair flees Thai island following local mafia death threats" David Miller's friend Sean McAnna, 25, who was also on the island, claimed local gangsters tried to fit him up with the crime. He made a desperate 4am Facebook posting: "Thai mafia are trying to *kill me. Please help me.*"

The *Bangkok Post* was scathing in its assessment of the erratic police investigation, saying the island was not closed off, the rooms of the murdered pair were not taped and access to the crime scene not restricted.

Police claimed Thais would not commit such a crime and released two men had refused to provide DNA tests.

With international attention on the case, two Burmese men were charged with the crime; and police were then promptly forced to deny reports from the Labour Rights Network for Myanmar workers in Thailand that the men may have been tortured into a confession. Without trial, the two men, who subsequently withdrew their confessions, were paraded before the international media and forced to re-enact the crime. The re-enactment, which ended with a round of applause from the locals, included directors with loud-hailers and the two diminutive Burmese in crash helmets and flak jackets bowing in supplication and asking for forgiveness. Posts of anger and disbelief filled foreign internet forums in Thailand and the newspaper comment sections of British newspapers.

The UK's *Daily Telegraph* observed: "Thai authorities frequently accuse migrants from Myanmar and Cambodia of

---

[243] Also insert endnote: "Very gruesome": British tourists found dead on popular beach in Thailand, *CBS News*, 15 September, 2014.

committing crimes in the Kingdom, where they make up a vast, poorly paid and low-status workforce."

The nation's Prime Minister, coup leader General Prayuth, stoked outrage by suggesting the behaviour of the Europeans had to be looked at; and when forced to apologise made things worse by suggesting that foreigners felt that Thailand was beautiful and safe, and they could walk anywhere and do whatever they want, including wearing bikinis. The only women who should feel safe wearing bikinis were those who were not attractive.[244]

While General Prayuth was on an official visit to Myanmar President Thein Sein requested a "clean and fair" trial for the two men. There were a number of protests, including in Japan. Amnesty International called for an investigation into the allegations the men had been tortured.

In the wake of the murders Tourism Minister Kobkarn Wattanavrangkul said tourists may receive identification wristbands listing emergency contact information. "When tourists check in to a hotel, they will be given a wristband with a serial number that matches their I.D. and shows the contact details of the resort they are staying in so that if they're out partying late and, for example, get drunk or lost, they can be easily assisted," he said.

Throughout the 21st Century Thailand has remained uniquely blessed and uniquely blighted; a country, as many have observed, which is both beautiful and cruel. At times its landscapes resemble nothing more than a science fiction movie, with its ribboned expressways, sky trains, interlinking shopping malls, high rises superstitiously abandoned before completion, choking traffic, thronging streets, rotting canals and glistening up-scale hotels towering over chaotic street markets and wooden slums; a kaleidoscope of the modern and the medieval.

It is a country to which foreigners are forever drawn; not just because of its tawdry sex shows and glamorous cabarets, not just because of its no-limits reputation as party central gone delinquent, but because of its often charming, some say child-like, certainly

---

[244] What the Murder of Two British Tourists Tells Us About Thailand's Dark Side, Charlie Campbell, *TIME*, 23 September, 2014

fun-loving people, the beauty of its folk music, the excellence of its cuisine and its un-holds barred race to adopt all that is new. The old saying, "we are drawn to that which is most likely to destroy us", is forever true of Thailand.

The country's open, extremely dangerous criminality, its brazen mafias and corrupt police, late night bars and gambling dens, its charming courtesies amidst the most blatant thievery, the vicious carelessness and many international criminals who have made it their home, the flexible moralities, appreciation of all things sensual amidst Buddhist ritual and humbleness of purpose, the dismissal of Western concerns over probity and conscience, all mark the Land of Hungry Ghosts as a place for seekers and the sought.

But for too many tourists it is also a place of terrible tragedy, of pointless accident, bad roads, dilapidated ferries, neglected facilities, of knife attacks and drink spiking, threats, violence, murders, treacherous lovers and wanton displays, an appalling indifference to loss of life. All set against some of the most stunning landscapes in the whole of Asia.

Even in an environment of media suppression the scroll of headlines tell a savage story of social chaos, official mismanagement, uncontrolled development and unparalleled greed: "Suspected foreign drug dealer arrested in Pattaya", "Murdered man found washed up on Phuket Beach", "Seven Indian Tourists Hurt as Minivan comes off Highway in East Pattaya", "Prison Inmate-controlled drug network cracked by Pattaya Police", "Bad monks beware, Thailand launches behaviour hotline", "Farang on 14 year overstay scams 3 million Baht from Thai women", "Russian shot in Phuket beachfront drive-by", "Pattaya Ladyboy Gang Beats Three People And Chases Them On Motorbikes", "Threatened with murder, Italian stab victim now under Phuket police protection", "English Tourist stabbed in neck by drunken Thai man in South Pattaya", "Chinese women tourists beaten in Phuket robbery attempt"."Four men sought for vicious Phuket attack on Chinese tourist", "Iranian Plundered by Ladyboys", "3 Australian tourists fall from Phuket resort balcony",

"Drunken Stealing Spree Leads Phuket Ladyboys into Replay in Handcuffs".

And on: "Phuket bike gang knife and rob two tourists", "Children Mourn Father Who Couldn't Resist the Appeal of Phuket Surf", "Phuket Tourist Attacks Sure to Spark Crackdown on 'Very Bad Boys'", "Mob violently bounces Aussies from Kangaroo Bar", "Phuket stab-and rob man 'needed money for sister's education'", "Italian runs from Thai girlfriend, arrested in Phuket for two year overstay", "Two Frenchmen and Thai busted for stealing in Karon", "Foreign Husband Mysteriously Disappears in Srisaket Province", "Russian Man Shows His Penis to 7-11 Cashiers", "Pakistani's rented car stolen by two Ladyboys from East Pattaya Love Motel", "German expat mugged by Phuket teen gang", "Russian tourist attacked by robbers in Thailand", "Oman tourist found dead in South Pattaya Hotel", "Murder in Thailand: another tourist shot dead", "Increasing violence against tourists threatens Thailand tourism industry", "American tourist stabbed to death by Bangkok taxi driver", "Phuket Death of Man in Pool".

And on: "Naked American assaults Bar cashier inside South Pattaya convenience store", "Heartbroken farang man attempts to jump off hotel", "Oman tourist stabbed on Walking Street, South Pattaya, by bar worker", "Phuket police close in on shooter of Russian tourist", "Officials raid 'aphrodisiac', sex-toy vendors", "Maltese Tourist encounters thieving Ladyboys on Pattaya Beach", "Australian tourist dies in Patong motorcycle crash", "3 foreigners arrested for fraud", "Woman Loots 200,00 THB off 65 year-old German", "British Tourist drowns at South Pattaya Hotel", "Confused Russians fight with transsexuals at South Pattaya Hotel", "Kata jet-ski operator attacks Israeli tourists", "Two female tourists die mysteriously", "Fishermen find body of murdered British tourist", "Scotsman Brutally Assaulted By Thais, Police Say", "Thai man arrested, charged with murdering tourists", "Massive fall in foreign tourist arrivals in Thailand".

Into an eternally dissolving present. In a place like nowhere else; one of the most dangerous tourist destinations on Earth. And one of the most beautiful.

CPSIA information can be obtained at www.ICGtesting.com
Printed in the USA
LVOW07s0037130315

430113LV00005B/518/P

9 780992 548742